LOVE IS IN THE EARTH -

KALEIDOSCOPIC PICTORIAL
SUPPLEMENT Z

Copyright © 1998 by
EARTH-LOVE PUBLISHING HOUSE
3440 Youngfield Street, Suite 353
Wheat Ridge, Colorado 80033 USA

Published by
EARTH-LOVE PUBLISHING HOUSE
3440 Youngfield Street, Suite 353
Wheat Ridge, Colorado 80033 USA

First Printing 1999
Second Printing 2004

Library of Congress Catalogue Card Number: 98-93852

ISBN: 0-9628190-5-0

Printed in Korea

LOVE IS IN THE EARTH -

KALEIDOSCOPIC PICTORIAL SUPPLEMENT Z

By: ♪ ♫ ♪ **MELODY** ♫ ♪ ♫

Images by HP Scanjet
  Assisted by Bob Jackson & ♪ Melody ♫

Illustrated by Julianne Guilbault

Edited by Laodeciae Augustine

EARTH-LOVE PUBLISHING HOUSE

3440 Youngfield Street, Suite 353
Wheat Ridge, CO. 80033

Cover Art and illustrations created by Julianne Guilbault - I would like to thank Julianne Guilbault for her artistic and elegant creation of the cover art, which is entitled "Steppin' Out", and which she created for this **"Love Is In the Earth - Kaleidoscopic Pictorial Supplement Z"**. Julianne and I have been friends through many lifetimes and have worked together toward the furtherance of the "brotherhood" of "All That Is". She has been active in crystal awareness for years and is truly the personification of creativity, both living and being the essence of originality and ingenuity. She has been involved in graphics design and illustrating for over twenty years, utilizing the mediums of watercolour, pastels, charcoal, pen and ink, and acrylic. She has sculpted fantasy art which remains in private collections throughout the world. I thank her also for her encouragement and support in both the preparation of this Supplement and in the compilation and illustration of all "Love Is In The Earth" books. Julianne may be contacted c/o Earth-Love Publishing House LTD.

I am especially grateful and give my warmest thanks to Lynn Fielding, our attorney, through whom this book and the prior books in the "Love Is In The Earth..." series have become a reality. Lynn has also just released a book, " The 90% Reading Goal", which truly shows his dedication to all of our brothers and sisters. Lynn and I are very good friends and I sincerely appreciate his help, his guidance, his love, and his encouragement in pursuing my path. His expertise and his expediency has enabled us to continue to make this series of books available to you, my friends.

Watch for the "Love Is In The Earth Tarot Deck For The Millennium" - to be released also this year in preparation for 2000.

Scanned Images were used for this book instead of slides which were used for previous books. However, 39% of the scanned images were taken from slides which were created by Jim Hughes assisted by ♪ Melody ♫, and 5% of the scanned images were taken from slides which were created by Douglas Taylor. The images within this book cannot be considered as photographs/slides, since they are actually scanned images. I would like to thank Jim for the quality time we shared during the creation of the slides which were used for imaging; Jim and I have a lovely rapport and we both truly enjoyed the photography sessions. He always has a smile and a refreshing, gracious, and relaxing attitude. I would also like to thank Douglas for his lovely slides and his love of beauty. The new process of imaging is an exciting (state-of-the-art in scanning minerals) mechanism for providing a truly clear picture of the mineral - I am genuinely happy with the quality. True-life images of 56% of the mineral-reproductions within this book were obtained by scanning the actual true-life minerals.

I am extremely grateful to both Bob Jackson and Laodeciae Augustine who were both trainers and performers in scanning and in technical support.

I am also very thankful for Savage Garden; their music took me "to the moon and back" during the weeks of image scanning. They continue to remind all of us that each of us can "be anything" we "want to be" <u>and</u> that "all that you need will surely come."

Cover Colour Separations by Pacific Scanning.

The author may be contacted c/o Earth-Love Publishing House LTD.

DEDICATION

TO

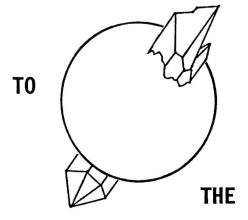

THE

EARTH

**"IF YOU JUDGE PEOPLE,
YOU HAVE NO TIME TO LOVE THEM"**

Mother Teresa

ACKNOWLEDGEMENTS

I truly thank the following people for their assistance in helping to make this book a reality.

José Orizon, Maria Ines, Ricardo, Daniel, and Julianna de Almeida, *and* Natalia and Renato - for their true friendship and true hospitality during the times we have shared, for their delightful ways, for their many gifts of minerals and of time, and for their love.

José Eduardo, Ligia, Marcello, Luciana, Mariana Barbosa - for their love and encouragement, for their friendship, their hospitality, their kindnesses, and for their many gifts of minerals.

Bob & Dan Beck - for their being, for their smiles, and for their love.

Bob & Micki Bleily - for their loving nature, their love and encouragement, their love and respect of the mineral kingdom, and their lovely fabrication of exotic cabochons.

José Roberto Bortoluzzi - and his family, for their love and their hospitality, for their smiles and good tidings, and for their love of the mineral kingdom.

Mike Brown - for his love and encouragement, for his sensitivity to the sanctity of the Native American ways, and for his awareness and practice within crystal-consciousness.

Pai Carumbé - in memory and for his being and for our connection of understanding and love between Brasil and America.

John Crowley - for his love, encouragement, his light which shines through his presence.

Edward Salisbury Dana - for teaching me, via his textbooks of mineralogy, about the multitude of crystalline structures which exist today.

Howard Dolph - for his love, for his being, and for the eternal light which glows from his being and shines through his eyes.

Jean Jacques Echlancher - my brother - for his love, for his being, for his ever-present radiance, for his gift of many minerals, for his patience, and for our many good times.

Jimmy, Kathy, & Bobby Fecho - for their love and encouragement, for teaching me about, and helping me during mining operations, and for helping to make my purchase of the "Melody Green Mine" in Mt. Ida, Arkansas, a reality.

Eliud Ferres (Salim) - for his love and encouragement, for his ever present smile and great stories, for his knowledge, for his kindnesses, and for his true friendship.

Lynn Fielding - for his loving assistance in making the "Love Is In The Earth" series a reality and for his continuing friendship and expertise applied to my life.

Bob Frie - for his love and encouragement in all areas of my life and for our wonderful repasts and effectual meetings.

♫

Bruce Geller - for his expert assistance in determining the mineralogy and chemistry of many minerals within this book.

Betty & Wayne Green - for lovely smiles and unconditional love.

Júlio, Solange, Júlio Jr., and Mauricio Grós - for their continued love and encouragement, their delightful presence, and their wonderful hospitality.

Lucy Gross [Mama] - for her being, her inner and outer radiance, her love, encouragement, understanding, assurance, motivation, patience, and support in all I attempt and all that I am, for stimulating my interest in all of the kingdoms of the Earth, and for further helping me to both recognize and understand my heritage.

W. R. Horning - for his love and encouragement, and for continually stimulating my interest in the mineral kingdom.

Robert Jackson - for his love and encouragement, for his patience, for his assistance in providing scientific and metaphysical information for this book, for making available [via Earth-Love Minerals, 3440 Youngfield Street, Suite 353, Wheat Ridge, CO 80033 USA, and via Earth-Love Gallery, 3266 Youngfield Street, Wheat Ridge, CO 80033 USA] the wonderful minerals of the world, for his creations as a silver/goldsmith, and for sharing in the great adventures of the mineral kingdom.

Herbert Kessler - for his continuing progression toward the understanding of the unknown.

José Villani, Teresa, Mariana, Barbara, and ♥ Vinicius♥ Mahkoes for their love and bright smiles, for their friendship, and for our many good times.

Anthony Malakou - for being a part of the beginning of this progression.

José Maria - for his being, for his love of the beautiful minerals of Brasil, for his radiant smile, and for his hospitality.

Marguerite Martin - in memory and for stimulating my interest in the greater realm of minerals and for her love and encouragement toward continuing interest in the mineral kingdom.

Mano - for his love, for his appreciation of the mineral kingdom, and for his hospitality.

Julie Murphy - for her unconditional love, confidence, reassurance, and for her "knowing".

Elenita, Natalino, Rackel, Gustavo, and Mariana Oliveira - for their true hospitality during the many good times we have shared, for their gifts of lovely minerals, and for their love.

Osho - in memory and for his being and for initiating consciousness.

Butch & Joy Parker - for their unconditional love, their true friendship, and their ever-present delightfulness.

Chris Pittario - for her love and encouragement and her delight in life.

♫

Antar Pushkara & Jude Painton - for their love and encouragement in my life, for being my kinsmen, and for sharing their radiance and manifestation of inner calm, peace, and understanding with all who touch their lives.

Gregory Sluszka - for his love and encouragement and never-ending and astute insights into all worlds and all realms.

Rob Smith - for his love and encouragement, for his friendship and his ever-present smile, and for his love of the mineral kingdom.

Jerzy Stasiulewicz (Yurek) - for his love and encouragement, for his friendship, his constant smile, his lovely Baltic Amber and buffalo grass, and for all of our good times.

Milt Szulinski - in his memory, for his being, for his love, and for his encouragement.

Layton Talbott - for his love and encouragement and for his sweetness and light.

Tião do Cristal - for his lovely smiles, his bright eyes, and our good times together ♥

Angel Torrecillas - for his love, encouragement, absolute honesty, sharing celebrations, and his lovely smile, lasting friendship, radiant glow, and many gifts of lovely mineral specimens.

Don Toth - for his love, encouragement, for his research and development of many elixirs.

Roger Trontz - for his love, for his wonderful light nature, and for our many good times together.

Josef Vajdak - for his love and encouragement and for his love of the mineral kingdom.

Liza Van De Linde - for her love and encouragement, for her openness and care, and for her friendship.

Antonio Viana - for his being, for his love of the beautiful minerals of Brasil, and for his hospitality.

Zee Haag - because he's the only "Z" I know and this book is named for him - and because, as we all know, "the first shall be last, and the last shall be first".

I sincerely thank those people who introduced to me and/or gifted me with "new" minerals: José Orizon de Almeida (GreenObsidian with Perlite, Tubed-Quartz, "Ouro Verde" Quartz); Daniel Foscarini de Almeida (Rockbridgeite/Frondelite, "Metamorphosis" Quartz, Quartz with "Lodalite"); Mac & Marie Anderson-Whitehurst (Blizzard Stone, Blackened-Electric-Blue Moonstone); Glenn Archer (Radiolarite-sedimentary); Ligia Barbosa (Purple Herderite); Richard Two-Bears ("Greenstone", Drusy Botryoidal Quartz); Sammy Benatar (Orange Quartz With Stars); Leslie & Dale Bowen (Mozarkite, Growth-Interference Calcite, and Quartz with Chert); Bob and Micki Bleily (Lime Opal); Mário L.S.C. Chaves ("Lightning" Quartz); Jim Cowan (Botryoidal Jade, Copper Schiller Sunstone); John Crowley (Blizzard Stone); Earth-Love Gallery (Septarian Nodule Carved Bear); Bobby Fecho (Arkimer Diamond); Jimmy Fecho (Novaculite); Eliud Ferres - Salim (Lavender Tourmaline); Michael Flaherty (Shiva Lingham, CSD); Peter Giangrande (Fossil Algae); Bill Hagestein (Nunderite, "Greenstone", Brucite); Ken Harsh (Dalmation Stone, Chinese Red Phantoms); Andrew Hodge (Bowenite - True New Zealand Greenstone, and Kyanite with Fuchsite); Bob Jackson (Franklinore, Kimzeyite); Joachim

♫

Karfunkel ("Lightning" Quartz); Walter Levine (Kyanite w/Fuchsite); Bruce & Barbara MacDougall (Striated Picture Zeolite/Clinoptilolite, Printstone); Ron & Karen Nurnberg (Nebula Stone); Dan Ryder (Fossil-Seeded Selenite); Susan Slayton & Joel Haslam (Cosmic Egg); Pierre Stéphane Salerno (FlowerStone, Perthite, Dallasite); Steve Goins (Calcite Schmoos, Ginger Quartz, Chalcopyrite Geodes); Bob Rolen (Petrified Palm); Martin Rosser (Mt. Hay Thunderegg); Kim Sang (Cat's-Eye Emerald); Bonnie and Marv Seeman & Annette Blansett (Yellow Mica); Bob Simmons (Bediasite); Campbellite (Buz Stringer); Angel Torrecillas (Enhydro Selenite); Don Toth (Murmanite); Gary Wallace (Hollow Stalactite); Craig M. Williams {(Bowenite - ("True" NZ Greenstone) and Kyanite with Fuchsite}.

In addition, I want to thank the following people who provided scientific data, information about techniques, and/or for research about properties (further verified) of specific minerals: Leslie "Wild Child" Bowen (Electric Green Obsidian); Bob Jackson ("Keystone", "Franklinore", technical support, and chemistry); Mac Anderson-Whitehurst (Nuummit); Roberto Kip Davidson (Carrying Angels); Melody and Valodya, Canada (Banded Red/White/Brown Agate), TAOMCHI (Labradorite), and Steve Ulatowski (simulated and synthetic minerals).

I also want to recognize the delightful "words of wisdom", shown and credited throughout this book, which were provided by the loving and astute minds of others: Orizon de Almeida, Daniel Foscarini de Almeida, The Bible, Dick Bonsignore, Perry Davis, Leif Dragseth, Paul Ellerman, Fern Eyre, Eliud Ferres (Salim), Lynn Fielding, Wayne Green, Bill Hagestein, Kari Hagstrom, Hannibal, Jim Hilton, Bob Jackson, Hal Jessen, Lane Johnston, José Luis, Tia Maia, Julie Murphy, Kelly Ram, River Starr, Mother Teresa, Gary Wallace, and John Wittman.

I also thank Alexandra Freeborn, Raul do Teofilo Otoni, John & Pat Holm, Pedro Barreto, Luiz Lobo, Pat & Jim Dover, Dr. and Mrs Harry Butler, Tony Gemas, Fernando Torrecillas, Adolfo Torrecillas, Edvaldo Pereira dos Santos, Rian Patric dos Santos, Nevaldo, Valmir Ferreira Caires, José Estrada, Si and Ann Frazier, Geruza Helena Borges, Larry Garnello (in memory), Kay Schabilion, David Pearl (Kenya), Gary Moore, Richard Wegner, Marlee Scopa, Ronnie Davis, Carlos do Teofilo Otoni (quem faz cabachon de obsidiana azul-elétrica), Michael A. Siegel, Helmut Hoffmann, Linda Olson, Amanda Olson, David Schulz, Barry and Lesley Leech, Barbara and George Manojlovich, Mario and Aurora Vizcarra, David and Colleen Shannon, Connie and John Gold & Daniel & Tammy & Nicole & Steven (and Justis, Maggie, Jillian, and Lila), Guilhermi Costa, Marcilio Chaves, Henri Vandormael, Ron Coleman, Jimmy Coleman, Julie & Alfonso Portillo, Osorió Mendes Q. Neto, Vicente do Cristal, Josafá do Cristal, Túlio Lanis Zambelli, Pedrinho do Corinto, Marissa and Ely F. de Souza, Clo and Paulo Freire, Reinaldo do Belo Horizonte, Naoki Ninomiya, Fernando Mascarenhas, Newton Keleh, Luiz and Luisa Menezes, Jeff Goodman, Clive Queit, Paul Botha, John Wittman, Ryo Yoshida, Mr. Yasuda, "Eagle" Eguchi, Jerry Fraley, "Granny", Towanna Kinsch, Frank Hollingsworth, Robb McFall, Donna Hart, Bobbie & John Akers, Consuelo Piccarella, Michael Leybov, Mark Regan, Jeff Pranchak, George Stevens, George Zraket, Mahria Jordan, Jean Grover & Gladys Chase & Victor, Stuart Hall, Susan & Fred Sullivan, Janelle and Larry Ford, Sue Neill, Ed Maslovicz, Jean Schroeder, Bob Isaacs, Jim Arndt, Des Greaves, Jacquie Seipp, Bruce Caminiti, Shavanti, Gil Nelson, Mario Cezar, Alexandre Peixoto, Max Grós, "Seattle John", the Brasilian players: Romario, Edmundo, Dunga, Bebeto, Tefarel, de Nilson, Cafu, 'se Carlos; and all members of TAOMCHI for their assistance and their kindnesses. I truly am thankful to all of those people who have touched my life and have assisted in the furtherance of my being. Thanks to my many friends on this wonderful Earth ♥

♫

TABLE OF CONTENTS

♪ **DO SOMETHING,
JUST FOR YOURSELF.
TODAY!** ♫

INTRODUCTION

♪ **WHEN YOU SEE YOUR OWN BEAUTY,
YOU ARE NEVER UNACCOMPANIED** ♫

AUTHOR'S NOTE

After many years of research and of making the information from the research available through the "Love Is In The Earth" series, I want to personally thank each of you for your support and your blessings, and for actually "working" toward the perfection inherent in all and continuing on the path of healing of the self and our brothers and sisters.

You have most likely noticed the title of this book - "... Supplement Z". This indicates that I have completed a cycle and that I, most likely (as you know - never say "never"), am finished writing books about minerals - at least books with the same structure as this series has displayed.

There are many possibilities in my life, some of which I have no idea, and others of which I have some idea.

My next book will be entitled "Love Is In The Earth - Reality Check" - a book of humour reflecting a multitude of amusing vignettes which speak to the time period from my initial research and recording through the publishing of this supplement. This is projected to be released in January, 2000.

In addition, a project, which is currently in progress and which has been requested by tens of thousands of my sisters and brothers throughout the world, is the finalization of "Love Is In The Earth - Crystal Tarot" - The Tarot For The Millennium. This should be released during the autumn of year 1999, and a CD ROM version will also be available for those who wish to use the Crystal Tarot in the computer environment.

I will continue teaching both Level I and Level II workshops for awhile, but only outside of the United States and Canada. There is now a group of Level III graduates (from the United States and Canada) who were hand-selected throughout an eight-year period, and who are endorsed, certified, and accredited to teach the "Melody Level I and Level II" classes, and to provide certification for same. TAOMCHI is the organization representing these Level III graduates. There will be additional Level III graduates from other countries.

PUBLISHER'S NOTE

That which began as a promise for a "trinity" of books has become a magnificent collection of "THE Reference Books Describing The Metaphysical Properties Of The Mineral Kingdom". Currently available and/or projected to be available are the following "Love Is In The Earth" series of books:

"Love Is In The Earth - A Kaleidoscope Of Crystals Update" retail price $18.95); having been updated, this book now contains 728 pages, a new cover, and is definitely the most comprehensive book addressing the metaphysical properties of over 800 minerals and over 45 configurations of the quartz crystal.

"Love Is In The Earth - Laying-On-Of-Stones" (retail price of $12.95); A guidebook for laying-on-of-stones, including arrays for bodywork, self-help, other-help, and including a mineralogical update, master number information, and a cross-reference index of astrological signs and associated minerals.

"Love Is In The Earth - Mineralogical Pictorial" (retail price of $27.95); 984 full colour photographs of the minerals discussed in "Love Is In The Earth - A Kaleidoscope Of Crystals Update" and "Love Is In The Earth - Laying-On-Of-Stones".

"Love Is In The Earth - Kaleidoscopic Pictorial - Supplement A" (retail price of $18.95); This book describes the metaphysical properties and provides photographs for over 100 "new" minerals. The book contains geologic, scientific, and metaphysical information, and includes chemical compositions, Mohs scale, and locality. It is a great companion book to the series.

"Love Is In The Earth - Kaleidoscopic Pictorial - Supplement Z" (retail price of $18.95); This book describes the metaphysical properties and provides colour reproductions for over 120 "new" minerals. The book contains geologic, scientific, and metaphysical information, and includes chemical compositions, Mohs scale, and locality. Another great companion book to the series.

"Love Is In The Earth - Reality Check" (to be released in 2000) - a book of humour describing laughable events which occurred in the life of the author during this "crystal" clear time-period of her life.

"Love Is In The Earth - Crystal Tarot" - The Tarot For The Millennium" (to be released 9/99) - Also a CD ROM version!

TO THE READER

This last Supplement to "Love Is In The Earth - A Kaleidoscope Of Crystals Update" and "Love Is In The Earth - Mineralogical Pictorial" has been prepared to serve as another companion for these two books. In addition to the Table of Contents, Acknowledgements, Introduction, and the Index, the following information can be found within:

 1) Descriptions of the properties of over 120 "new" minerals;
 2) Colour reproductions of typical specimens of these "new" minerals;
 3) Descriptions of the properties of minerals and configurations which were reported in "Love Is In The Earth - A Kaleidoscope Of Crystals Update", and for which information from further research has become available;
 4) A Cross-Reference Index relating the Zodiacal Designations and the Mineralogical Associations;
 5) A Cross-Reference Index relating the Numerical Vibrations with the Mineralogical Associations; and,
 6) A Table of the 105 Chemical Elements which have been established to date. This will assist the reader in determining the chemical constituents of a mineral. Additional information identifies the category for each element, and identifies which elements are "Rare Earth", "Native", and "Transuranic".

The mineralogical information accompanying the images and the description of the mineralogical properties have been obtained from "Dana's Textbook Of Mineralogy"; Nickel & Nichols "Mineral Reference Manual"; "Hey's Mineral Index - Third Edition"; "Glossary of Geology - Third Edition"; the Arkansas Geological Commission's "Mineral, Fossil-Fuel, And Water Resources of Arkansas"; "Dana's New Mineralogy"; Bruce Geller (mineralogist); Nassau & Prescott White Paper; and from additional mineralogists throughout the world. Where there was disagreement between the references or the chemical composition, either all sets of information were given or the most recent set of information (Dana) was given. Please note that there are almost 4000 minerals which are known today, and which truly derive from the ancient past.

This supplement brings continuity of research to assist one to travel within the subtle realms of energies of the mineral kingdom, providing for additional adventures into the avantgarde and assisting one in maintaining a loving affinity and a true appreciation of minerals. Information has been derived from "hands-on" experience, geological research, experimentation, and channeled information; prior to inclusion herein, all channeled information and experiences have been validated via further experimentation and in a controlled environment. The information presented is based upon the combination of the physical principles of interaction and the scientific principles of molecular bonding.

Although each of us has the infinite power of the universe within the self, we tend to find it easier and are predisposed to accept support from that which is from outside of the self. Each crystalline structure/form has its own individual energy and its own "personality". Mineralogical structures which contain more than one mineral possess a melding of the energies of the minerals contained. Each can be used in unique ways to assist one in understanding the multi-faceted nature of existence on the Earth plane. The consciousness of the planet is leading humanity to the re-discovery of an ancient and forgotten healing art in which the utilization of minerals/crystals is prominent. Dis-ease/disorder in ones life usually entail lessons which will allow the release the burdens of unconsciousness. Although one must ultimately heal oneself, the healing process may be facilitated by the catalytic presence of many things. To experience dis-ease is to experience a disconnection from wholeness, a loss of awareness of the innate and universal source of perfection. From antiquity, the members of the mineral kingdom have been appreciated and valued for their utility and their beauty; they have been used for centuries to act as catalysts and to assist one in becoming re-united with the source of perfection. Right intention during use of the mineral advances the melding of ones personal energy with that of the mineral kingdom, furthering the propagation of the light, the love, and "the good of all".

May you continue to your state of fulfillment, always knowing that you are the wonder of the world. I wish you peace within yourself, love to guide you, and the understanding leading to bliss. May you know and experience love - from within, from upon, and from surrounding the Earth   The Reader is encouraged to read the remainder of this section prior to continuing to the information given within the text.

SIMULATED AND SYNTHETIC MINERALS

The following provides a list of some of the simulated and synthetic minerals which are currently being manufactured, and sometimes, sold as natural minerals; it is included to emphasize the need for one to purchase minerals from those who are familiar with the mineral business and have expertise in same.

A "Synthetic" is a man-made stone which duplicates the exact chemical composition and crystalline structure of a precious/semi-precious stone. A "Simulant" is a man-made material which resembles a natural precious stone, but differs in composition.

Alexandrite	Diamonds	Sapphire
Aquamarine	Emerald	Spinel (all)
Amethyst	Garnet, Green	Tanzanite
Ametrine	Morganite	Topaz, Blue
Beryls (all)	Quartz	Tsavorite
Citrine	Ruby	Polish Zincite

MINERALS WHICH NEVER NEED CLEANSING

Within this Supplement there are five additional minerals which never need cleansing and never hold negativity; Borax, Frondelite, Green Obsidian with Perlite, "Metamorphosis" Quartz, "Ouro Verde" Quartz. As a continuing update, the entire list of minerals which never need cleansing and never hold negativity are:

Borax	"Metamorphosis" Quartz
Citrine	"Ouro Verde" Quartz
Citrine/Smokey Combination	Rhodizite
Frondelite	"Super Seven"
Green Obsidia with Perlite	Tektite(Guangdong)
Halite (Electrified Translucent Massive)	Tektite (Philippine)
Kyanite	Yoderite

Please note that, due to the discovery of the properties of "new" minerals, there are now fourteen minerals which comprise this category.

ASTROLOGICAL SIGNS

In order to assure that the reader of the "Love Is In The Earth" series has gained information and definitive knowledge with respect to the utilization of the Astrological Signs which are related to each mineral, the following information is again emphasized.

If one selects a mineral with a specific Astrological Sign, that means that attributes of that sign are reflected by that mineral.

Hence, for example, if one is a Virgo by birth sign, and if one were to select a mineral with respect to the qualities of an Astrological Sign, one would most likely choose a sign different from ones birth sign in order to bring in other attributes which one does not currently have. Where the Astrological Sign designation is "All", the positive attributes of each sign, dependent upon intent, are brought to play.

ELIXIRS - REVIEW

In order to assure that the reader has gained information and procedural knowledge with respect to the preparation of "Elixirs", the following information is again reiterated.

CONSERVATISM

The sections within this book which provide information with respect to the properties of the "new" minerals, provide also for more conservatism with respect to recommendations for the preparation of elixirs via the "normal" and "non-normal" methods. This will be a continuing practice. These varying methods are discussed in "Love Is In The Earth - A Kaleidoscope Of Crystals Update".

If there is a question concerning the toxic nature of a mineral, always research the chemical composition prior to utilization of that mineral, and - to be safe - prepare the elixir via the "Alternative Method" (as reported in "Love Is In The Earth - A Kaleidoscope Of Crystals Update".

PREPARATION

The preparation of an elixir is based upon the concept of energy transfer. Our world is comprised of atoms; atoms are the smallest unitary constituent of any chemical element and are comprised of a complex aggregate of protons, neutrons, and electrons.

The number and arrangement of the protons, neutrons, and electrons determine the element. When an element is stimulated (e.g., via heat or pressure), electrons are emitted. In our world today, virtually nothing exists in a vacuum; hence, there is a somewhat constant, if erratic, stimulation occurring continuously, and a subsequent egress and ingress of the electrons from the minerals.

When a mineral is placed into water, for example, for the preparation of an elixir, the electrons of that element are stimulated and tend to mix with the water; hence, bringing the essence of the mineral to the water. Although the change is not seen by the physical eye, it has been felt over and over again by those experiencing the essence of elixirs.

For the alternate methods of elixir preparation, there remains the emergence of the electrons and the permeation of the water by the electrons.

CHEMICAL ELEMENTS

A Table of the 105 Chemical Elements which have been established to date is provided (see Pages 352-356). This will assist the reader in determining the chemical constituents of a mineral. The table has been prepared with the chemical designation given first, the chemical name given second, and comments (e.g., identifying the accepted category for each element and identifying which elements are "Native Elements", "Rare Earths" and "Transuranics") shown last.

"WE MINERS OF THE HEART"

Kari Hagstrom
Minnesota, USA

"NEW MINERALS"

**"I HAVE ALL THESE PLANS...
THEY ARE GRAND - DON'T YOU SEE?
BUT MY MIND HAS MORE HANDS
THAN MY BODY AND ME!"**

Fern Eyre
Miamisburg, Ohio, USA

CONDOR AGATE - A fortification agate comprised of SiO$_2$ with additional polymorphs of silica; Hardness 7; Locality: Condor Mine, Argentina, South America. Imaging by HP Scanjet, Assisted by Bob Jackson and ♪ Melody ♫; In the Collection of ♪ Melody ♫, Applewood, CO, USA.

Condor Agate is a fortification agate and in the chalcedony class, exhibiting a range of red colours. The mineral was first discovered in the Condor Mine and was named after same. Agate was first described by Pliny in 77 A.D. and was named for the River Achates in Sicily, a location where it is found.

The following properties are in addition to those listed in the AGATE and CHALCEDONY sections of "Love Is In The Earth - A Kaleidoscope Of Crystals Update".

This mineral has been used to further the study of mathematics and philosophy. It acts to stimulate both the left-brain and the right-brain when one is involved in problem-solving. It also serves to bring insights into "new" ways of theoretical thinking and to assist one in penetrating mental blockage.

Condor Agate has been beneficial to alleviating the accountability related to responsibility, to assail sensations of melancholy and inferiority, to allow one to both understand and to dispense with self-criticism, and to smooth the state of anger.

The mineral has been used in the development, purification, and balancing of the base chakra and for the amplification of the energy field. It can further cleanse negativity from the base chakra and from the energy fields of the physical, emotional, intellectual, and spiritual bodies, while transferring the vitality of any companion mineral to the affected area.

It has been said to encourage honors, wealth, and happiness, to provide composure, to stabilize the emotional system, to alleviate tension and stress, and to amplify positive feelings. It has also been used to eliminate greed.

It also assists one in attuning to the animal kingdom and in recognizing the healing forces within same. It has been especially useful in attunement with avian (especially the falcon) community, and has expedited "absent-healing" while producing an energy which is both cooperative and receptive.

When in proximity to another mineral, provides a stabilizing influence to the energies of that mineral.

It has been used to enhance mental faculties and motor skills for metal-working, and to bring a protective force when one is working with molten materials. It can also be used to "clear" a "foggy" mind and to assist one in attentiveness.

Condor Agate has also been used to protect one from exploitation and victimization.

It has been used to enhance physical strength and coordination, in the treatment of digestive disorders, brittleness of fingernails (as an elixir), muscular problems in the arms, carpel tunnel syndrome, paralysis, and to assist in the rejuvenation of tissue.

Vibrates to the number 4.

AGATE - GRAVEYARD PLUME   [Astrological Sign of Pisces]

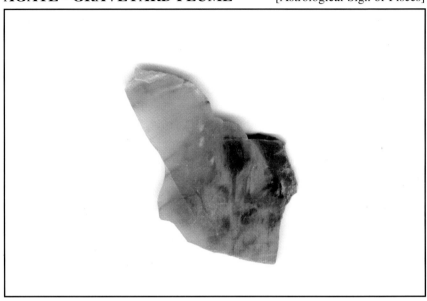

GRAVEYARD PLUME AGATE - SiO_2 with other polymorphs of silica; Hardness 7; Locality: Oregon, USA. Imaging by HP Scanjet, Assisted by Bob Jackson and ♪ Melody ♫; Collection of ♪ Melody ♫, Applewood, CO, USA.

Graveyard Plume Agate crystallizes as masses of variegated chalcedony; the structure/colouring is shown in the image above. Agate was first described by Pliny in 77 A.D.; it was named for an occurrence on the River Achates in Sicily. None of the experts known to the author have been able to determine the origin or the first description of the name, Graveyard Plume.

The following properties are in addition to those listed in the AGATE and CHALCEDONY sections of "Love Is In The Earth - A Kaleidoscope Of Crystals Update".

This mineral has been known as the "Stone of Adaptation", bringing one the abilities to accommodate the varying situations which occur and which are out of ones realm of experience <u>and</u> assisting one to modify the structure of ones perception and to adjust ones personal response in order to harmonize that response with the situations which could, otherwise, be uncomfortable.

Graveyard Plume Agate has been used to stimulate vividness in dreams, and to expand one memory capabilities.

It encourages one to take the initiative and furthers autonomy and confidence in thought and action.

It has been used to assist one in both understanding and releasing the memories of unpleasant situations, and in understanding lessons; it is a mineral which actually assists one in "putting matters to rest".

The mineral can be used to support one in surmounting emotional ordeals, to bring the heart and the intellect into synchronicity, and to help one to look within and to find the esteem that is inherent.

It further awakens the actualization of the Conscious Self, allowing for percipient recall of judicious action, while furthering a continuous alignment with the spiritual realm and assisting one obtaining answers from that level of wisdom; the transfer of these answers to the physical intellect is also facilitated.

Graveyard Plume can be used to both strengthen and support one during changes, helping one to prepare for transformation and allowing one to consciously recognize the hidden layers of "cause" which support states of anxiety, distress, and dis-ease. It further assists one in releasing the cause; hence, decreasing or eliminating the effect. It helps one to understand that any control is personal control and that in order to actualize ones full potential, the state of personal action is required.

It has been used in medicine wheel ceremonies in the Pacific Northwest in order to reach the ancestral spirits and to provide the channel for the integral knowledge with respect to the questions of the participants. It provides for both acquisition and distribution of information, dependent upon the consciousness of the participant.

Graveyard Plume Agate has been used in the treatment of skeletal degeneration, circulation disorders, and insomnia. It can assist in the restoration of emotional and intellectual stability.

Vibrates to the number 4.

ALLANITE

ALLANITE - Ca(Ce,La)(Al,Fe)$_2$(SiO$_4$)$_3$(OH) or (Ce,Ce,Y)$_2$(Al,Fe)$_3$(SiO)$_4$(OH); Hardness 5.5 - 6; Locality: Queensland, Australia. Imaging by HP Scanjet, Assisted by Bob Jackson and ♪ Melody ♫; Collection of ♪ Melody ♫, Applewood, CO, USA.

Allanite crystallizes in the monoclinic system as masses, embedded grains, and tabular and acicular prismatic crystals. The colour ranges from resinous brown to black and it, sometimes, exhibits pleochroism (brownish-yellow/reddish-brown/greenish-brown). The mineral was first described by T. Thomson in 1810; it was named for T. Allan and modified following Levinson's rule for nomenclature of rare-earth minerals.

This mineral can be used to initiate the state of self-fulfillment, bringing to fruition the self-actualizing characteristics and the properties of manifestation. It is an excellent stone for assisting in service-oriented activities.

Allanite has been used to promote a blending and magnification of one with another through the merging of talents; it acts to bring the proficiencies of groups together to produce new forms which are created without the loss of personal identities. It furthers an interconnected development of new talents, bringing resolution, equilibrium, and a creative flow with universal energies·

Allanite can provide for increase in that to which one attunes it. This short but clear statement shows that Allanite is truly a stone to experience in all aspects of one life.

It further has been used to enhance discriminating judgment, to heighten perception, to stimulate participation and interaction, and to supplement personal power. It acts to dispel the aspects of dissension and opposition which occur in ones life and to alleviate fluctuation between states, purposes, and opinions; allowing for insight into each situation.

Allanite has provided for contact with the ancient builders of Greenland and can be used to initiate insight into the ancient methods and associated wisdom which are stored within that continent. It should be noted that any locality of occurrence of the Allanite mineral specimen will promote access to this information.

This mineral exhibits a protecting quality and is an excellent preventive which can be used to shield one from many forms of negative energy. Simply having a piece of Allanite on ones person brings in this protective, shielding aspect of the stone which works on the physical, etheric, and emotional levels.

Allanite has been used to enhance courage and to ameliorate pain. It has been carried by those who face uncomfortable situations to encourage both bravery and determination in completion of any task for which one holds fear.

It can also help to protect against the negative vibrations of pollutants, at the physical level, via the creation of an energy field which it builds within the aura. Allanite has been used to provide remedial action for behavioral disorders. It has also been used in the treatment of cancer of the intestines, disorders of the intestines/intestinal upsets, and in amelioration of bone and teeth disorders.

Vibrates to the number 2.

AMETHYST - HONEYCOMB [Astrological Sign of Gemini]

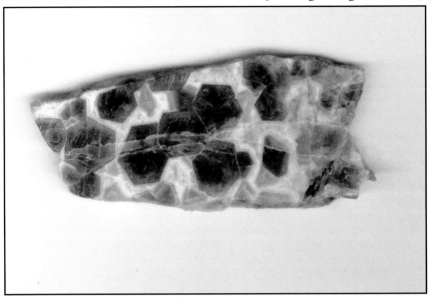

HONEYCOMB AMETHYST - SiO_2 with ferric iron structured with a quartz to citrined-quartz honeycomb effect; Hardness 7; Locality: Brasil; Imaging by HP Scanjet, Assisted by Bob Jackson and ♪ Melody ♫; Collection of ♪ Melody ♫, Applewood, CO, USA.

Honeycomb Amethyst crystallizes as masses, exhibiting the colours shown in the image. Amethyst has been described as early as 315 B.C. (by Theophrastus) and was named for the Greek word "not drunken", since it was thought to prevent intoxication. Citrine was first described by E.S. Dana in 1892; it was named from the Greek word for "citron", referring to its colour.

The following properties are in addition to those listed in the AMETHYST and CITRINE sections of "Love Is In The Earth - A Kaleidoscope Of Crystals Update".

Honeycomb Amethyst assists one in realizing that any career is similar to the design on patterned floors, actually "a thing" made incomprehensible by proximity and by the layers of meaningless activity that cover it. It assists one to recognize that a career, as such, is only a step in the pathway which leads to the furtherance of ones development, serving one only in physical sustenance and in lessons to be learned in order to advance. It helps one to appreciate that changes are necessary for growth, and to remind one to not get "caught-up" in the day-to-day intricacies of the games. Hence, the mineral truly acts to further ones development via understanding of the adventures (albeit perceived as negative) and to maintain a positive outlook in all situations. It actually acts to assist one in contemplating situations by removing the self from same, furthering the removal of any cause of distress and assisting one in recognizing the structure of the "game".

In the search for lost things, people (including the self), and answers, the energy of the mineral tends to assist one to move in an instinctive manner, with the instinct being both self-preservation and attendant success.

Holding Honeycomb Amethyst, the user may focus on that which is lost; insight to, and pathways open for, the direction to proceed, have been received via an influx of thoughts and actions which would be beneficial to the furtherance of "finding".

It is an excellent stone for guided-imagery and has been used in same to raise the level of health by putting one more in tune with the Inner Self and the physical body. It further assists one in recalling images that are highly meaningful and then serving one to allow the imagination to spontaneously produce variations and inventions of its own. This creates inner dialogue between the consciousness and the Inner Self. Using relaxing, calming images as the basis for the dialogue, one may recall these same images and dialogue throughout the day (even when waiting in queues in supermarkets, traffic lanes, etc.). As one performs this exercise, he/she will, most definitely, integrate the "honeycomb-relaxation" into everyday life (especially during contact with the "worker bees" buzzing in and out of ones life).

Honeycomb Amethyst has been used in the treatment of cellular disorders, leukemia, anaphylactic shock, allergies, muscle and tissue reparation, and to promote the rapid healing of cuts and abrasions.

Vibrates to the number 4.

ANAPAITE [Astrological Sign of Gemini]

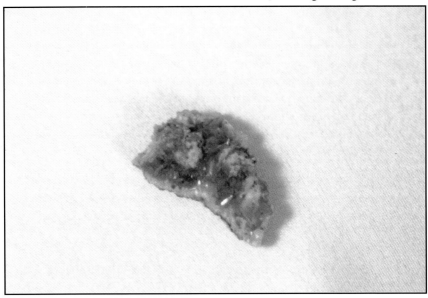

ANAPAITE - $Ca_2Fe(PO_4)_2$♥$4H_2O$; Hardness 3.5; Locality: Kris Mountains, Ukraine, Russia. Imaging by HP Scanjet, Assisted by Bob Jackson and ♪ Melody ♫; Collection of ♪ Melody ♫, Applewood, CO, USA.

Anapaite crystallizes crystals in the triclinic system in the colour ranging from green to greenish-white. The mineral was first described by A. Sachs in 1902, and was named for the locality of first discovery, Anapa, in the Black Sea region.

This mineral can stimulate automatic-writing and psycho-kinetic abilities.

It increases the strength of ones essence and can facilitate both the sending and receipt of telepathic messages; it has been used to expedite the receipt of special assignments from the spirit world - these assignments being suited to the growth of the recipient and being quite beneficial to same.

Anapaite has also been used as a "merchants stone", bringing efficiency to the activities of business while advancing advantageous results in business ventures.

The mineral has been used to assist one in gaining information about that which is being hidden from one (specifically, initiating the transfer of information in the physical realm which is of concern to the user); it further promotes acceptance of this information in the physical realm such that the recipient of the information, from the messenger who brings the information, does not feel distress with the messenger (i.e., the recipient feels no animosity with the messenger, even if the message will bring the requirement for change to the recipient).

It has been used when swimming with the dolphins to bring enhanced communication, and to allow for clearer understanding of messages which are transmitted.

Anapaite is truly a "stone of message", bringing facts, details, and intelligence, so that one may act (and not re-act) to situations and circumstances which surface. It further dispels vulnerability to the unknown, assisting one in being both prepared and strengthened in response. The mineral further assists one in "tuning-in" to "somatic indications" (intuitive feelings), and in accepting and acting upon the guidance and/or literal data which is gleaned.

Anapaite enhances emotional self-awareness and provides the building block for the underlying emotional intelligence such that one can elude and dispense with negative feelings. It has been used in the management of ones feelings and moods to balance emotions and to promote mastery over situations when one may be emotionally "out-of-control". It works especially well with "rage", promoting the re-structuring of, and the conscious reinterpreting of a situation in a positive framework (instead of producing the unrewarding act of venting the anger in a negative manner). The mineral acts to bring one to a meditative state such that negative emotions are distracted, diverted, and transformed to positive emotions.

Anapaite has been used to bring both strength and stamina when fasting, can assist one in weight-control, and has been used to ameliorate dehydration. It is an excellent mineral to be used for diagnosis and for insight into amelioration techniques.

Vibrates to the number 4.

ATACAMITE

ATACAMITE - $Cu_2Cl(OH)_3$; Hardness 3 - 3.5; Locality: Atacama, Chile, South America. Imaging by HP Scanjet, Assisted by Bob Jackson and ♪ Melody ♫; Collection of ♪ Melody ♫, Applewood, CO, USA.

Atacamite crystallizes in slender prismatic crystals which are vertically striated, crystalline aggregates, and fibrous or granular to compact masses. The colour is ranges from bright green of various shades and dark emerald-green to blackish-green with an adamantine to vitreous luster. The mineral was first described by D. De Gallitzin in 1802 and was named for the original locality of Atacama, Chile.

This mineral has been used to prevent assault and to remove one from situations which are potentially dangerous. It brings an energy of "warning" which is noticeable when one has the potential to encounter danger, and furthers an easily accessible escape.

It is a stone of "self-motivation", bringing the energy of positive motivation with the marshalling of feelings of enthusiasm, zeal, and confidence which are paramount for achievement. The energy furthers optimistic attitude such that one realizes that if "it looks like a failure or if it looks negative, it could be that something better and more fulfilling is coming". Atacamite promotes the application of effort and practice, such that one can learn to think more hopefully, and such that one can recognize negative self-defeating thoughts as they occur so that one can reframe the situation in less catastrophic terms.

Atacamite also brings the energy of equity, creativity, and benevolence for all and is excellent for altruistic pursuits. It allows one to recognize the harmony of the universe and to understand that each segment of the universe perpetuates an intrinsic model of perfection in order to allow the unfolding of irreproachability.

It possesses an energy which can remove energy blockages and can totally open the crown chakra and the heart chakra, cleansing and activating at the same time. It is excellent for use in meditation [no-mind] and assists one in attaining and in maintaining the state.

The mineral has been used to increase the bio-magnetic forces in the body and to align the body with the magnetic fields of the Earth. It has been used extensively in magnetic healing and to provide receptivity to radionic treatment. During radionic analysis [where one holds a sample specimen and places a sample on the witness], or when used as a pendulum, the energy of the stone permeates the energy of the user and points to the problem[s] involved and/or to the answers required.

Atacamite is a healer of the spirit, providing for a soothing energy and bringing peace of mind.

It has also been known to guide one through the unknown, protecting while promoting ones independence in action, and has further assisted in transformation of dis-ease in the physical realm and in transition from the physical realm to the spiritual realm.

The mineral has been used in acupressure/acupuncture treatments to incite the movement of the Chi. It can also be used in the treatment of arthritis, disorders of the eyes, convulsions, and seizures, and to promote the flexibility in muscular structure.

Vibrates to the number 1.

**"THE BEST OF LIFE
IS ALWAYS THE FIRST TIME
OF AN ADVENTURE"**

Dick Bonsignore
California , USA

BEDIASITE **-** Meteoritic glass from outer space; Hardness 5 - 5.5; Locality: Bedias, Texas, USA. Imaging by HP Scanjet, Assisted by Bob Jackson and ♪ Melody ♫; Collection of ♪ Melody ♫, Applewood, CO, USA. Gift of Bob Simmons, Vermont, USA.

The Bediasite Tektite is a natural glass of meteoritic origin. The name Tektite was first described by F.E. Suess in 1900. The name "Bediasite" is from the locality of origin. The following properties are in addition to those listed in the TEKTITE section of "Love Is In The Earth - A Kaleidoscope Of Crystals Update".

This mineral can be used extremely well for dowsing and for cloud-busting. Placed within a wand, it has acted to enhance the other attendant minerals.

It has been used to assist one in "discernment through the fog", encouraging the acknowledgment of the patterns of that which encompass ones reality, and advancing the sensitivity to the interpretation suggested by those deficient in specificity. It is a grounding stone which also produces an alignment of the meridians of the body and an alignment of the subtle bodies.

Bediasite has been used for uninterrupted interdimensional accessing of preeminent dimensional galactic energies, to attract to the Earth plane those ideals and resonances which are optimal to ones foundations for expansion and furtherance on the Earth plane.

It facilitates concentrated and focused interdimensional interconnectedness between ones consciousness and the higher planes. It expands access to the vibrational energies which one can access, while allowing for a more encompassing passageway to those energies.

The mineral works quite well at the base chakra and has also stimulated the capability to feel the "pattern" of the communication and sometimes the pattern and structure of the communicator from whence the communication is being broadcasted.

Bediasite has been used to promote somnambulistic pursuits and to enhance dreaming. It acts to bring purpose in these activities and to eliminate judgment while providing a "guiding hand".

The mineral can bring strength and fortitude to endeavors and has acted to facilitate the swift and complete understanding of situations which one encounters.

It further assists in the elimination of archaic distress, allowing for awareness of the consequences of anger so that one may advance through the "halls of karma". It has been used to promote the elimination of mental, physical, emotional, and spiritual chaos.

Bediasite has been used to advance balance and lapses during the attainment of conscious ambitions, such that when one attains the result, the energy necessary to enjoy the result is concomitant.

It further produces a feeling of well-being and energetic control in ones life.

Bediasite has been used in the treatment of afflictions of the head, physical and mental instability, and exterior growths.

Vibrates to the number 2.

BLIZZARD STONE

BLIZZARD STONE - A combination of primarily Forsterite (Mg_2SiO_4), Anorthite ($CaAl_2Si_2O_8$), Orthopyroxene and Clinopyroxene (orthorhombic and monoclinic pyroxenes) = $(Ca,Mg,Fe,Mn,Na,Li)(Al,Mg,Fe,Mn,Cr,Sc,Ti)(Si,Al)_2O_6)$, Hercynite ($FeAl_2O_4$), and Magnetite ($Fe_3O_4$); Hardness 5.5 - 8; Locality: Alaskan Wilderness, proximate Homer, Alaska, USA; Although not of meteoritic composition, the composition was determined by Gary Huss, PhD, American Meteorite Laboratory. Imaging by HP Scanjet, Assisted by Bob Jackson and ♪ Melody ♫; Collection of ♪ Melody ♫, Applewood, CO, USA. Gift of Mac and Marie Anderson-Whitehurst, North Carolina, USA.

Blizzard Stone crystallizes as silica-deficient ultramaphic masses and falls in the category of gabbro (an igneous rock that cooled slowly deep in the earth, allowing the crystals to grow several millimeters across. It also contains small amounts of olivine, serpentine, chrome garnet, magnetite, actinolite, and biotite. The colour is represented by a black, serpentine-rich matrix with white calcium-rich feldspar crystals (anorthite). The mineral was first discovered by Steve Monroe ago and the name was chosen to represent the contrast of the crystals dark background.

This mineral promotes "dominion" - the increase of dominion and jurisdiction with respect to ones reality and the release of the domination of others; it actually supports one who has been dominating and assists the person in allowing another to have both autonomy and freedom and it further sustains the other in the recognition and comprehension of consequences which can occur due to decision-making without outside dominion.

Blizzard stone can promote unanticipated developments which can assist the user in realizing the importance of individuals and events which have been disregarded or neglected. It is an energy to further ones depth of self, to bring appreciation to availing energies, and to reveal any familial, indigenous, or individual situations which have been concealed and which need attention in order for one to grow and to progress with peace and harmony.

The energy does not enable the continuance of repression of emotions; it acts to bring these emotions, and the substructure sustaining them, to the consciousness so that the negative can be released and faithfulness to the self is fortified. The energy allows for this confrontation with the self or with external forces to be executed without the normal trauma.

It has been used to relieve discordance and violence in temper and expression. It is a lovely mineral to give to the proverbial gloomy and unsociable acquaintance.

It also prompts correctness in judgment and thought, heightening the balance of the frequency of brain-wave transmissions.

It can provide for a connection to the Higher Self, awakening the energy of the third-eye and expediting the clarification/verbalization of events.

Blizzard Stone has been used to locate energy blockages within the body and has been used extensively in dynamic healing and to provide receptivity to radionic treatment.

Blizzard Stone has been used in the treatment of "hot flashes", cellular swelling and infections, disorders of the immune system, bruising and sprains, to provide purification within the body, to alleviate the effects of fevers, and to balance the alkalinity of the body.

Vibrates to the number 9.

BORAX

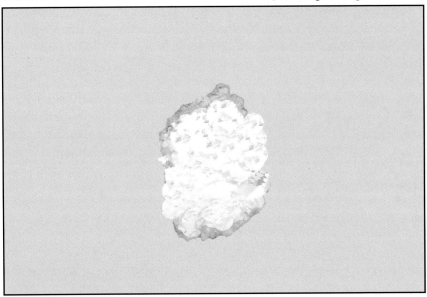

BORAX - $Na_2B_4O_5(OH)_4$♥$8H_2O$; Hardness 2 - 2.5; locality: Boron, California, USA. Imaging by HP Scanjet, Assisted by Bob Jackson and ♪ Melody ♫; In the Collection of ♪Melody ♫, Applewood, CO, USA.

Borax crystallizes in the formation of prismatic crystals in the monoclinic system. The colour range includes white, greyish-white, bluish-white, and greenish-white. The mineral was first described by G. Agricola in 1546 and was named for the Arabic word (bauraq, buraq) for "white".

This mineral advances the concept of "function" via the utilization of the concept of "content". It further assists one in the realization of the significance of "function" with respect to the living and operational structure of the physical form. It promotes the movement of structure (physical, emotional, and spiritual) such that manipulation of discrete elements within the structure is accelerated.

It has been used to facilitate the meditate state which is required for psycho-kinetic pursuits. It has further acted to assist one in the removal of obstacles in ones emotional and spiritual lives and to encounter the pathways of development which are most beneficial to ones lessons.

Borax has been used by the Native American Indians in ancient ceremonies to dispel negativity, to provide protection (with gridding), and to assist in the entry to the ancient and sacred grounds of power, and facilitating a bright spiritual enclosure within which communication with the spirit world is provided.

Gridding areas with the mineral has produced a protective energy and a positive environment.

This is another stone which does not hold and accumulate negative energy, but dissipates and transmutes it, working-out problems on both the physical and subtle levels. It, hence, never needs clearing or cleansing.

Borax can be used to increase stamina and to further the energetic pursuits related to exploration and investigation. It provides an excellent energy for research, bringing forth an influx of information and historic knowledge to the user; the energy actually acts to guide the researcher to the locations (within resource people, libraries, newspapers, encyclopediaes, etc) which contain the information.

This mineral can be used to stimulate the crown chakra, to cleanse the chakras and the aura, to access past-lives as well as future lives; it further assists one in the realization that all eventualities are a part of ones present path.

It has also been used to assist one in understanding and in regulating situations which repeat within ones life, such that lessons are learned and the situations are easily managed.

Borax has been used in the treatment of stomach upsets, swelling, bloating, and obesity. It has also been used to remove toxins from the body, to remove infections from inflammations and wounds, and to alleviate water retention.

Due to the solubility/fragility of Borax, do not prepare an elixir of this mineral via the normal method.

Vibrates to the number 6.

BOWENITE

BOWENITE - $(MgFe)_3Si_2O_5(OH)_4$; Hardness 5.5 - 6; Locality: New Zealand. Imaging by HP Scanjet, Assisted by Bob Jackson and ♪ Melody ♫; In Collection of ♪ Melody ♫, Applewood, CO, USA. Gifts of Craig M. Williams and Andrew Hodge, New Zealand (left); Bill Hagestein, New Zealand (top-right, bottom-right); and, Richard Two-Bears, New Zealand (middle-right).

Bowenite crystallizes as very fine granular masses. The colour ranges from apple-green to greenish-white. It is also known as Tangiwaite and Tangawaite. The mineral was first described by G.T. Bowen in 1822 and was named for same by J.D. Dana in 1850. Bowenite is also known as "Greenstone".

This mineral is the most sacred stone to the Maori tribes of New Zealand. It has been esteemed as a great talisman and is worn as amulets; it was known to protect one from enemies and from destructive forces which may come to ones life. It has been known to cause enemies to withdraw, inciting a feel of danger within the enemy and providing the message, to the enemy, that he/she "gave no thought to this world" (hence, furthering the intellectual and spiritual development of the enemy at the same time as providing protection to the holder). Protection from destructive forces tends to be facilitated by a protective energy field which radiates in all directions from wherever it is placed. In addition, currently, a gift of "Greenstone" is truly a symbol of love, friendship, and thankfulness.

If a pendant, carving, or piece of the mineral is conveyed through generations, it is said to bring a continued association with those who also held it, promoting contact with the spiritual world of ones ancestors.

It has been used to change weather patterns; gridding the area of intended weather-change, the focus is upon a center stone (of the mineral), with intent for "the good of all".

Bowenite has been used to enhance the ease of relocation, to assist one in making a "clean-break" from past traumas and environments, and to rid one of abrasive adversaries and opponents. It has been used in the realm of athletic endeavors, to provide "the edge" and to promote indestructibility.

It is the "stone of the warrior", bringing success in business pursuits, personal pursuits, and intellectual pursuits.

It has been used to increase abundance in trade and in merchanting, and has facilitated advancement in achievement in the physical realm. It is truly a stone to bring elevation and distinguished eminence to the holder.

The energy of Bowenite can be used to dispel tears and sorry, to assist one in finding ones counterpart (soul mate), and to facilitate the adventure of change and unpredictability of ones life. It promotes the energy of freedom and lightness as we travel through this world.

It assists one to eliminate speculation, via providing insight to answers.

Bowenite has been used to assist in the assimilation of Vitamin A and Vitamin D, in the treatment of disorders of the heart and the patterns of the veins, to balance cholesterol, and to encourage the correct RNA/DNA structures. It has also been used to combat depression, to stimulate fertility (both in plants and humans), and to ameliorate acrophobia.

Vibrates to the numbers 1 (Tangiwaite), 2 (Tangawaite), 3 (Bowenite) and 5 (Greenstone).

BREWSTERITE

BREWSTERITE - $(Sr,Ba,Ca)(Al_2Si_6)O_{16}$ ♥$5H_2O$; Hardness 5; Locality: Strontian, Scotland. Imaging by HP Scanjet, Assisted by Bob Jackson and ♪ Melody ♫; In the Collection of ♪ Melody ♫, Applewood, CO, USA.

Brewsterite crystallizes as masses and prismatic crystals. The colour ranges from white to grey and from white to yellow. The mineral was observed at Strontian in argyll, Scotland, was first described by H.J. Brook in 1822, and was named for D. Brewster.

This mineral has been used to assist in the time continuum such that the time one expends actually seems to expand to accommodate the activity in which one is engaged. It assists one in accomplishing tasks expediently, with the advantage of "having time" to "do the things you want to do".

Brewsterite can be used to assist in telecommunications productivity, advancing ones abilities (and tending toward the advancement of the proficiency of mechanical systems) in competency, reliability, and dependability. It has also been used when "surfing the Web", to assist the user to locate, with rapidity, specific pre-defined sites, to access same with alacrity, and to peruse with freedom from time schedules.

The mineral has been used to increase memory storage, to facilitate ease of retrieval of information from the memory, and to strengthen the accuracy of the memory.

It further can assist one in the removal of addictive attributes, promoting the recognition of the addiction, the attribute, and the manner in which one can detach from same (both within the self and from outside of the self).

It has been used to enhance abilities in chemistry, physics, and the culinary arts. It provides for an innate wisdom concerning methodology and techniques which will assist in these endeavors, and which will provide for innovation in development of a "fresh look" at old processes.

Brewsterite provides for a connection between the grounding energy of the Earth and the facets of individual control which are revealed via the instinct. It facilitates reflection via revelation. It promotes protection of the self from intense conditions which could bring discord and/or rejection to the self.

The mineral has been used to suspend alienation in relationships, withholding degeneration due to aging or lack of enthusiasm, while providing for resolution and for assiduity in associations, and assisting in charismatic appeal where one determines exactly what is to be attracted. It also acts to stimulate ones ability to lessen the gravity of any situation.

Brewsterite can be used to further ones sense of humour and to show one that which is internal to the self and to others with respect to emotional, physical, and intellectual circumstances. It can draw forth negativity from these centers while transferring the positive forces of another mineral to same; hence, performing as a expediting courier.

It has been used to provide freedom from addiction to earthly substances, to ameliorate disorders of the liver and pancreas, and in the assimilation of carbohydrates.

Do not prepare an elixir of this mineral via the normal method.

Vibrates to the number 9.

BRUCITE

BRUCITE - Mg(OH)$_2$; Hardness 2.5; Locality: Persberg, Sweden. Imaging by HP Scanjet, Assisted by Bob Jackson and ♪ Melody ♫; In the Collection of ♪ Melody ♫, Applewood, CO, USA. ♫

Brucite crystallizes as masses, plate-aggregates, folias, fibres, fine grains, and tabular crystals. The colour range includes white, colourless, pale green, grey, blue (and yellow, pink-red, and red in manganese-bearing varieties). It has occasionally been found to contain Zinc. The mineral was first officially described by F.S. Beaudant in 1824; it was named for Archibald Bruce who unofficially first described the mineral.

This mineral has been used to facilitate the "perfect break" from that which one wishes to break-away. It provides a supporting energy to separate and to detach oneself from unwanted conditions, circumstances, and persons.

It has been used to provide mental flexibility and to assist one in "looking at all options", supporting insight into solutions which will be both beneficial and uncomplicated. It has further assisted in bringing one to resolution via the recognition of advantageous alternatives.

Brucite has been used to eliminate the "heat" from heated-discussions, providing for a balanced and stable discussion of ideas and ideals; it is an excellent energy for group interactions.

During the initiation of a new project or relationship, the mineral has been used to introduce an energy of "pure energy", a flame which is eternal, such that one can proceed with acceleration and strength. It has worked well to assist one in determining that which needs to be addressed in order to further ones goals. It has also assisted one in determining whether a relationship or a project is one which will be ultimately useful to the fulfillment of ones path.

The mineral can be used to collect the darkness which occurs in the presence of depressing and negative atmospheres. Frequent cleansing (via "beaming" the mineral with white light), is recommended.

Brucite can bring one to optimal states of communication on the physical plane, providing for stimulating insight into connections between the self and others, and into the karmic conditions which have brought one and another together. It can bring one the recognition of the "brotherhood" which is on the Earth-plane.

The mineral can be used to produce an energy which is predisposed to encourage reckless-abandon (when consciously directed), such that inferiority complexes are dispelled and one becomes more balanced in the "middle-way". It also provides for the purification, the cleansing, and the elimination of that which is the basis for the inferiority.

It can be used to dispel infectious disorders after the symptoms appear, and has been used to provide the energy to endure any indelicacy during recovery periods from dis-ease.

It can also be used to ameliorate alkalinity of the body, to clear arteries and veins, to provide sheen to the hair (via elixir), and to promote muscular flexibility, temperature regulation (body), bone-mending, and form enhancement (via elixir). It has been used in the treatment of intestinal disorders, bruises, multiple-personality disorders, and chills.

Vibrates to the number master number 33.

BRUNCKITE

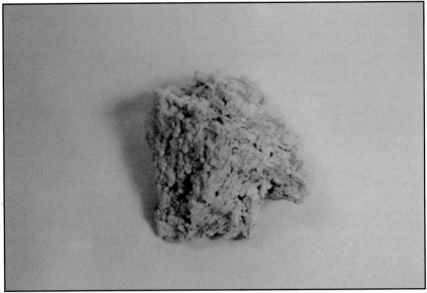

BRUNCKITE - ZnS; Hardness 3.5; Locality: New South Wales, Australia. Imaging by HP Scanjet, Assisted by Bob Jackson and ♪ Melody ♫; Collection of ♪ Melody ♫, Applewood, CO, USA.

Brunckite is a cryptocrystalline variety of sphalerite. The colour ranges from white to blue to tan. The mineral was first described by R. Herzenberg in 1938, and was named for B.O. Brunck.

This mineral is negatively electrified, assisting one in the removal of negative willful-ness and in the elimination of distracting intellectual thoughts and emotions which could affect the emotional and intellectual bodies.

It further serves to induce non-caustic qualities and perspectives, providing assistance during exercises of the intellectual processes and producing grounding of the inductive and deductive reasoning skills.

Brunckite tends to boost energy levels, to promote flashes of insight, and to stimulate the dissipation of barriers which could block ones process or the execution of ones responsibilities.

The mineral has been used by the Peruvian shamen in ceremonial healings; it has evoked and awakened the powers of creativity and intuition with respect to healing. It is said to bring together the synthesis of healing on the physical plane with healing on the etheric plane.

Brunckite can also provide for the development of ones psychic expertise and can encourage one to "be ones own psychic", promoting the insights to allow one to remove the blockages in the intellect which could preclude the receipt of information from the psychic realm.

It has been used as a fumigant and to discourage infestations of insects and negativity within ones environment.

It provides a protective field around the environment in which it is placed and a shelter of protection around the physical body. Applied to agricultural pursuits, it has been used in gridding arrangements to suppress infestations of insects. It is also of assistance in discouraging insects from remaining in ones environment; being quite helpful with gardens and houseplants.

The mineral can also provide for protection from negative forces which may be present when dealing with the public.

Brunckite has been used to stimulate the throat chakra such that one may speak in any situation with ease. It can also assist one in singing and in the original creation of music.

It can also be used to activate the outer chakras in order to facilitate the alignment of the ethereal meridians and to promote connectiveness with the physical body. It is useful in massage techniques (placed beneath the massage table) to produce an energy flow through energy blockages.

Brunckite can be used to assist in the amelioration of broken bones, motion sickness, skin eruptions, bacterial infections, and intestinal parasites. It has also been used in the treatment of disorders related to infections within the body and to promote balance for the intake of nutrients, and to increase the sense of smell.

Vibrates to the number 4.

"CRUSH THOSE 'BUTS' "

Lane Johnston
Fayetteville, Ohio, USA

CALCITE - GOLDEN RAY
[Astrological Sign of Leo]

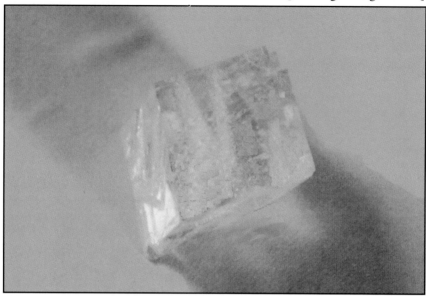

GOLDEN RAY CALCITE - $CaCO_2$; Hardness 3; Locality: Mexico. Imaging by HP Scanjet, Assisted by Bob Jackson and ♪ Melody ♫; Collection of ♪ Melody ♫, Applewood, CO, USA.

Golden Ray Calcite crystallizes as masses, grains, stalactites, scalenohedrons [twelve-faced crystals, each face exhibiting three unequal sides], and rhombohedrons [six-faced crystals, each face the shape of a rhombus]. It is, however, characterized by the rhombohedron crystallization. The colour is represented by a beautiful sunshine-golden hue. Calcite was first described as "Kalkspat" by A.F. Cronstedt in 1758, as "Calc-Spar" by R. Jameson in 1804, and translated to "Calcite" by J.K. Freiesleben in 1836; it was named for its Calcium content. "Golden Ray" was added to the name to represent the golden sunshine-colour. The following properties are in addition to those listed in the CALCITE section of "Love Is In The Earth - A Kaleidoscope Of Crystals Update".

This mineral is a stimulus to the advancement of growth and to the re-awakening <u>and</u> recognizing of those with whom one has been closely associated in other distinctive lives. It can help one to ascent past the outer dimensions, and to resonate in oneness with the self and with

♪ 62 ♫

others. It assists one in unifying with the brothers and sisters of this dimension, with those from the realms of the spiritual and astral spaces, and with those from the stars; during these activities, the dominant loving energies are constructed to create the dazzling golden/white radiance of the enlightened state and the undivided essence of the heart of the life force.

It acts as a repository stone which accumulates knowledge, as well as energy, ideas, and love. If one needs infused with energy, the Golden Ray Calcite can be used like a battery. It can also be used to attract people toward one for friendship or business.

This mineral stimulates the intellectual powers, and provides for stability and grounding during both physical and mental activities. It has been used to assist one in defining and refining those attitudes and "beliefs" which are self-limiting.

Golden Ray Calcite assists one during the process of divination, providing wisdom in the response to prophetic questions. It can be used to activate the crown chakra and to provide for the alignment of the chakras with the ethereal plane. It assists in the removal of negativity from the chakras and further stimulates the base, navel, and solar plexus energy centers.

Golden Ray Calcite is an excellent stone for communal cohesion, with realistic stimulation for lifework and in life-pursuits. It is an mineral which brings the energy to support one in not saying another is "wrong", in "keeping ones own counsel", in not complaining, in speaking softly and not arguing, and in not criticizing.

This mineral can be used to remove blockages within both the nervous system and the circulatory system. The energy is excellent for clearing-away infection and disorder at the onset of the symptom. It can also be used to provide insight to the attitudes which have caused these problems. It has also been used in the treatment of disorders of the liver, gall bladder, and endocrine glands. Dis-ease has been treated via elixirs and via holding the stone while transfixing the image of the stone to the area of the body which is in disorder.

Vibrates to the number 1.

CALCITE - Growth Interference [Astrological Sign of Libra]

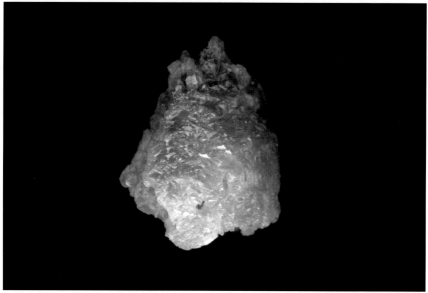

CALCITE - Growth Interference - Calcite ($CaCO_2$) which exhibits growth interference; Hardness 3; Locality: South-Eastern USA. Imaging by HP Scanjet, Assisted by Bob Jackson and ♪ Melody ♫ ; Collection of ♪ Melody ♫, Applewood, CO, USA.

Growth-Interference Calcite is configured such that the structural interference of another mineral is quite obvious during the growth of the Quartz. These Calcites exhibit interpenetrations and perforations within their structures, where the interfering mineral was once located. Calcite was first described as "Kalkspat" by A.F. Cronstedt in 1758, as "Calc-Spar" by R. Jameson in 1804, and translated to "Calcite" by J.K. Freiesleben in 1836; it was named for its Calcium content. The following properties are in addition to those listed in the CALCITE and section of "Love Is In The Earth - A Kaleidoscope Of Crystals Update".

This mineral can be used to ensure that the cycle which embraces the fields of experience needed by individuals in order to reach their birth potentials, achieves the same recognition as the more widely acknowledged cycles of the signs which emphasize social, cultural, and collective factors.

Growth-Interference Calcite can be used to assist one in maintaining the appearance and in maintaining ones speech to appear completely at ease when one is in a state of anxiety (e.g., when ones heart seems like it is pounding against ones rib-cage).

It has been used to calm emotions of grief and contrition, bringing a clarity to the reasons behind the feelings and assisting one in releasing same. The mineral also promotes the appreciation of friends and friendships. It assists one in "listening hard", and in being attentive in conversations, such that one does not "space-off" and such that one may glean information from the conversation.

It can be used to stimulate the freedom to speak from the heart, further acting to bring an energy to "one-on-one" conversations, such that "the other" can "see" the necessity, and will have both the time and the inclination, to respond from the heart.

The mineral can also assist in cleansing and, hence, rectifying disoriented, trapped energy which leads to atrophy. It helps in the resolution of opposites, promoting the communication of the will as a love-based force.

It is an excellent stone for re-birthing and for releasing blockages which restrain one from the spiritual path.

It has been used as a wand-like director of atmospheric electricity, providing a pathway, to the Earth and to the user, for electrical and magnetic forces; it assists in the transfer of the magnetic electricity to the ethereal bodies of the user to assist in the alignment and polarization of these bodies with the physical body.

It further assists one in the conscious access of ethereal consciousness, via the third-eye, providing an instrument through which an understanding and an actualization of the healing process can be manifested.

It has been used in the treatment of leukemia, bone breaks, disorders of the auto-immune system, stomach distention, and PMS. It can also serve as a stimulant for the thymus and can be used for self-healing.

Vibrates to the number 2.

CALCITE - With "SCHMOOS"   [Astrological Sign of Libra]

CALCITE With "SCHMOOS" - A combination of Calcite ($CaCO_2$) which is a pseudomorph after Akaite, and finely-grained sandstone (SiO_2 grains); Hardness 3 (Calcite) - 7 (SiO_2 grains compacted); Locality: Baltic Sea coast in Russia. Imaging by HP Scanjet, Assisted by Bob Jackson and ♪ Melody ♫; Collection of ♪ Melody ♫, Applewood, CO, USA. Gift of Steve Goins, Oklahoma, USA.

Calcite with "Schmoos" crystallizes as a combination of pseudomorphed Akaite and finely-grained compact masses of sand which exhibit varying rounded "schmoo" (or pear-like) shapes. The calcite colour varies in the calcite range from brown to rust, and the sand is a tan to grey colour. The mineral was first made available in 1998 by Steve Goins. The following properties are in addition to those listed in the CALCITE and SANDSTONE sections of "Love Is In The Earth - A Kaleidoscope Of Crystals Update".

This mineral provides the insight that "now" is always a time for change and for alignment with ones life-purpose. It further a multitude of insights with respect to relationships such that one can realize that although two people may take the same path to reach the same destiny, they may take it at differing time (i.e.,in each his own time) or they may take a different path altogether to reach the same goal or destiny. This knowledge promotes the understanding in relationships to allow growth via uniqueness and to yield to the non-control of another. The development of "people" skills and emotional intelligence (e.g., the capacity to know how another feels) is further enhanced by Calcite with "Schmoos".

The mineral brings the energy to incite impulse control, furthering the knowledge that the nature of emotional self-regulation is the ability to delay impulse in the service of a goal, hence, instilling the wonderful concept of "patience". The mineral tends further to produce a patience which is required in order to function in a utilitarian manner.

The Calcite with "Schmoos" have been used for centuries by the ancient tribes which inhabited the area of the Baltic Sea to bringing knowledge to the user of both the ancient ways and the future ways.

The "Schmoos" are optimistic and delightful stones and, when held, tend to eradicate worries and to heighten ones state of well-being. They help with transitions and progressions, with variations in ones life, and to relieve states of depression and anger.

This mineral is for both the young and old; for those who have not yet lost the wisdom which they brought to Earth during this lifetime and for those who have regained and supplemented the wisdom which they brought to the Earth during this lifetime. They also provide a grounding force, allowing for an increase in mental faculties, while stimulating amiability toward others.

In addition, the "Schmoos" promote receptivity to frequencies which are usually inaudible. They can also be used to enhance the abilities of clairaudience.

Calcite with "Schmoos" have been used to ameliorate physical instability, bone loss, restrictions in the muscular system, depression, deficiencies in Vitamin C and Calcium, disorders of the pancreas, and RNA/DNA balancing.

Vibrates to the number 1.

CALCITE - SAND

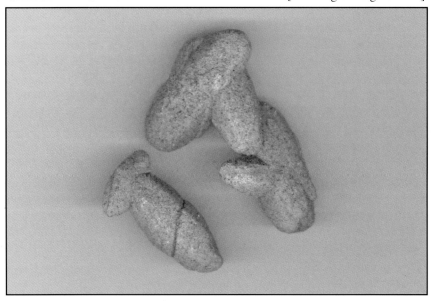

SAND CALCITE - A configuration of finely-grained compacted grains of SiO_2 and is a pseudomorph after Calcite; Hardness 7 (SiO_2 grains compacted); Locality: Rattlesnake Butte, South Dakota, USA. Imaging by HP Scanjet, Assisted by Bob Jackson and ♪ Melody ♫; Collection of ♪ Melody ♫, Applewood, CO, USA.

Sand Calcite crystallizes as masses, in the Calcite configuration, of compact grains of sand and exhibits a tanish-brown colour. The mineral was named for the composition and the pseudomorphic qualities of the mineral. The following properties are in addition to those listed in the CALCITE section of "Love Is In The Earth - A Kaleidoscope Of Crystals Update".

Sand Calcite promotes the knowledge that he/she "who wills the goal, can will the mode". The energy brings the ideal that we create our world by the way we think and by the way live, and that we always choose the path that will teach us what we need to learn, and we do, indeed, make our paths through the lives we live.

This mineral "stone of originality" and is conducive to both the building and the strengthening of ingenuity and solidarity within relationships and/or groups.

Sand Calcite assists one to sustain strength against confusion which may surface within the mind, providing for stability within ones reality, and facilitating action and reformation with ease. It assists in dispersing the illusions of ones reality, providing insight into deceptions and further inviting truth in all situations.

It can help in revealing that which is concealed, and in promoting clarity in thought and sight.

It can also be used to allay harshness of personality and to promote the feeling and understanding of loving acceptance of humanity, while bringing the more refined and gracious aspects to ones behavior. It has been used to discourage temper tantrums and general grouchiness.

Sand Calcite is a stone which can be used to assist one in change, providing one with adaptability to a variety of atmospheres and situations. It furthers ones expertise in flowing with irregularities in ones activities, surroundings, and ventures.

It is said to have originated from the changes occurring during a cleansing period of our Earth, and to have been "made" in order to instill stability within the realm. It has been used for gridding unstable areas of the Earth (where there is instability in either the Earth, itself, or the inhabitants).

Sand Calcite assists us in remembering to ask ourselves the question, "Did whatever you do help you to be a better be-ing, than ever you were before?" It stimulates the thought processes which are necessary for one to reason compassionately and with a thorough understanding of ones actions and deeds.

It has further been used to promote lucid dreaming and recall of same.

Sand Calcite can be used in the treatment of wounds and broken bones. It has been used in the treatment of Alzheimer's dis-ease and the Hantavirus, and to ameliorate water retention and to assist in the restoration of degenerative eyesight, weak fingernails, and thinning hair.

Vibrates to the number 1.

CAMPBELLITE

CAMPBELLITE - A combination of Copper, Calcite, Cuprite, Chalcotrichite, Chrysocolla, Turquoise, Malachite, Tenorite, and additional copper minerals; It is a secondary ore of copper from weathering ore veins; Hardness variable; Locality: Campbell Shaft, Bisbee, Arizona, USA. Imaging by HP Scanjet, Assisted by Bob Jackson and ♪ Melody ♫; Collection of ♪ Melody ♫, Applewood, CO, USA. Gift of Buz Stringer, Bisbee, Arizona, USA.

Campbellite crystallizes as masses and is not yet recognized by the mineralogical community. The following properties are in addition to the properties listed in the COPPER, CALCITE, CUPRITE, CHRYSOCOLLA, TURQUOISE, MALACHITE, AND TENORITE sections of "Love Is In The Earth - A Kaleidoscope Of Crystals Update".

This mineral has been used extensively in dynamic healing and to provide receptivity to radionic treatment. In addition, it provides for amplification of the entire energy field of the body and has also been used by healers in the United States for both diagnostic healing and for communicating with the spirits for diagnostic communications. It is a very fulfilling exercise when one uses this mineral as a control energy when determining diagnosis and amelioration information which is received during healing situations; it has been used via the normal dowsing method and via "dowsing" through the utilization of the third-eye.

Campbellite brings an energy of metamorphosis and continued change, which throughout all times is concentrated with determination of both the acceleration and the ease of reformation of the self. The concepts of impetus and catalytic motion are reflected in one who holds this stone.

It is a stone which brings the transfer of electrical impulses; it provides for an electrical stimulus, facilitated through the subtle bodies, which produces a dielectric charge due to the alignment of the subtle bodies with the physical body.

It also provides for an electrical connection to the ethereal body during period of danger, and transmits the message of possible personal jeopardy; the ethereal body, subsequently, acts to send a message to the ethereal body from whence the threat is coming, and the peril is released to the ethers and transformed into the white light of healing.

Campbellite also assists in communication, bringing the love of the heart to the actualization of the spoken word. It facilitates relationships of physical love, as well as spiritual love. It can bring a loved-one close in heart and in mind, and can enhance the telepathic and electrical connections between each two emotional, physical, intellectual, and spiritual bodies.

This mineral has also been used to provide for a release of electrical impulses when placed under pressure, and is an energy amplifier. It is said to help the mind and body to remember - the mind, to remember information brought to bear during astral travel and channeling experiences; the body, to remember the state of perfection during disease in order to return to the natural state of flawless-ness.

Campbellite has been used in the treatment of disorders of the nervous system and to dissipate energy blockages which could propagate the improper flow of neural impulses. It has been used to facilitate balancing of the metabolic processes, and in the treatment of fevers and flus.

Vibrates to the master number 44.

CARBON - C60

CARBON - C60 - A non-metallic native element with 60 carbon atoms atomically arranged sphericoidally; Hardness 1 - 2; Locality: Karelia, Russia. Imaging by HP Scanjet, Assisted by Bob Jackson and ♪ Melody ♫; Collection of ♪ Melody ♫, Applewood, CO, USA.

Carbon - C60 is one of three non-metallic native elements. It is the first natural occurrence of carbon which displays 60 carbon atoms in a sphericoidal configuration. The mineral was first discovered in the late 1980's and has not yet been officially named by the mineralogical community.

This mineral is one for the "mid-life crisis" (Dante's "selva oscura"), bringing light and happiness to "the dark wood where one may find himself/herself lost at mid-life". The energy acts to promote both reflection to ones past and to mirror ones future so that one may become charmed by what is known as "the best is yet to come".

Carbon - C60 is a stone for future-seeing, bringing all of the options for the future into view and assisting one in selecting the "best of the best", and assisting in the origination of the restructuring of ones life in order to bring the highest choices for the future.

It is a stone which facilitates stability in monetary matters, assisting in the balancing of input/output and in equilibration of financial status, relationship status, aging status, etc.

It was used during ancient times as a talisman against fearfulness and deceit and was recognized as an energy to dispel susceptibility to unwanted conditions. It promotes the gathering of strength with age and enhances the energy to incite both unity and love of oneself and of others.

Carbon - C60 is a reminder of ones goals towards spiritual awareness; as ones maturation and development becomes revealed within the heart, one can transfer the feeling and the being to others, via the energies of the mineral.

It can instill the aspect of trust to relationships and situations, bringing confidence to ones emotional and intellectual characteristics, and bringing fidelity to interpersonal associations.

It is an excellent stone for meditation, bringing the state of "no-mind" to the state of reflection, and can activate the forces of accumulation; helping one to manifest abundance in selected areas of ones life.

Carbon - C60 has been used to the remove voids from ones aura and to fill the emptiness with purity. It inspires imagination and ingenuity, in the environment of the pristine areas of ones life.

It can activate the crown chakra and can produce a connected force between the base intelligence of "feeling" and the realm of higher knowledge. It assists in removal of the darkness from ones mind such that one can identify the impediments to be avoided on ones path.

It has been used in the treatment to counteract poisoning, to clarify and stimulate the sight, and as a metabolic balancing agent, to dissipate cataracts, stomach upsets, intestinal parasites, and to cleanse the blood.

Do not prepare an elixir of this mineral via the normal method.

Vibrates to the number 8.

CARPHOLITE

CARPHOLITE - MgAl$_2$(Si$_2$O$_6$)(OH)$_4$; Hardness 5 - 5.5; Locality: Krásno, Czechoslovakia. Imaging by HP Scanjet, Assisted by Bob Jackson and ♪ Melody ♫; Collection of ♪ Melody ♫, Applewood, CO, USA.

Carpholite crystallizes in the orthorhombic system in radiated and stellated tufts, sometimes occurring on quartz. The colour ranges from straw-yellow to wax-yellow to tan-yellow. The mineral was first described by A.G. Werner in 1817; it was named for the Greek words meaning "straw" and "yellow".

This mineral can assist one to enhance the activities of sharing, to discourage selfishness, and to provide for the regulation of ones life through both motivation and rationality. When one is in need of some "common sense", this is an excellent source.

Carpholite has been used to strengthen channeling activities, to remove spiritual blockages which impede channeling, and to provide for conscious awareness during these activities. It is also an energy which can be very useful to "past-life ascension", providing for a view of experiences with a non-re-living of same.

This mineral has been used to assist in the maintenance of relationships, bringing conscious realization of the virtues of the other and compartmentalizing obstacles such that each can be addressed independent of the other. It can calm stressful situations and instill energy when needed.

It has been used to protect against theft and to preclude the "running away" of ones money.

Carpholite brings an energy to facilitate a "pioneering" spirit and can further produce an inquisitiveness into the unknown avenues of the creative forces. It can guide one to the "effortless road" in ones endeavors.

It is a stone for the crown chakra and for the intellect, bringing the energies together in synchronicity, and providing a balancing between ones thoughts and ones aspirations.

Carpholite has also been used to multiply energy and to enhance ones protective fields.

It is quite effective during use as one of the stones in gridding operations; use of Carpholite in a grid which is designed to produce composure, brings a structure of harmony and consistency to the environment; use of the stone to complement a grid and to encourage visitation by those of extra-terrestrial origin, provides for a structure of protection and strengthens the invitation.

It has been used to further the actions related to practicality in ones lifework, bringing the qualities of precision, analytical capabilities, and stability to employment situations. It can also be used to augment ones scientific, and mystical and magical abilities, enhancing personal alignment with the n-dimensional realms of being.

Carpholite has been used in the treatment of deficiency in Magnesium, to promote oxygenation of the blood, to ameliorate brittleness of hair, and to stimulate the production of estrogen.

Vibrates to the number 8.

CHONDRODITE

CHONDRODITE - $(Mg,Fe)_5(SiO_4)_2(F,OH)_2$ or $2Mg_2SiO_4 \heartsuit Mg(F,OH)_2$; Hardness 6.5; Locality: Newton, New Jersey, USA. Imaging by HP Scanjet, Assisted by Bob Jackson and ♪ Melody ♫; Collection of ♪ Melody ♫, Applewood, CO, USA.

Chondrodite crystallizes in the form of monoclinic crystals as twins, trillings and lamellae. The colour range includes yellow, brown, red, greyish-green, and orange-brown. The specimen in the image shows Chondrodite with black graphite. The mineral was first described by C. d'Ohsson in 1817; it was named from the Greek word for "grain" which represented the crystalline structure in appearance.

This mineral increases the area of penetration of energy to the chakras during the "laying-on-of-stones", hence, allowing for the supplementation and the increase in intensity of the energies which are normally available during the exercise.

Placement, in this case, would be via suspension of one stone in the space above the subject, at the area of the navel; or, two stones can be utilized via placing one stone approximately six inches from the crown chakra and the other stone approximately six inches from the feet.

Chondrodite can also be used dispel irritation and uneasiness, helping one to accept and to rejoice in life and to understand that all actions and circumstances are instruments in the fulfillment of ones personal destiny.

It provides a wonderful energy for supplementation of strength and stamina.

In addition, the mineral can be used to produce an infusibility with that which is not "right" for ones path, actually "blocking" the influx of that which will not further one in his/her path.

Chondrodite has been used to stimulate travel [physical plane] and adventures. It can facilitate a connective force between those of the stars and those of this plane, bringing intellectual information which both supplements and relates to that which is already a part of ones intelligence; this stone does not provide for the transmission of random information or information with respect to questions one has not recognized.

The mineral has been used in ceremonies related to the four directional energy forces. In medicine wheel ceremonies, is usually placed at the location of magnetic north. In healing ceremonies, where the directional aspects are utilized and when the intent is to bring in additional forces from the universe, the stone is placed at the head.

It is an excellent third-eye stone, stimulating visionary experiences and assisting one in traveling deeply within the inner being; it assists the energy from the third-eye to be transported throughout the body, producing an intuitive understanding of the complete cellular structure.

Chondrodite has been used to assist one in becoming a vegetarian and/ or in maintaining vegetarianism, promoting the knowledge of correct food combining and correct food intake.

The mineral has also been used to assist in the assimilation or Iron, and to ameliorate deficient immune systems and dysfunctional cellular structures.

Vibrates to the number 7.

"COSMIC EGG"   [Astrological Sign of Virgo]

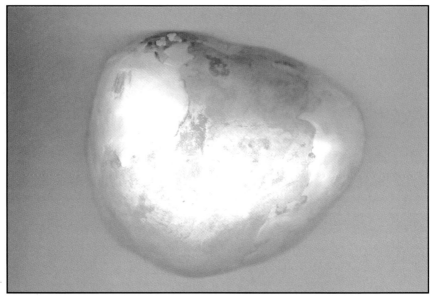

"COSMIC EGG" - B(OH)$_3$ [Sassolite outer coating] with Hydrous Borate interior; Hardness 1 (thin outer coating) and 5 (interior); Locality: In proximity to a Boron deposit in California, USA. Imaging by HP Scanjet, Assisted by Bob Jackson and ♪ Melody ♫; Collection of ♪ Melody ♫, Applewood, CO, USA. Gift of Susan Slayton and Joel Haslam, California, USA.

The "Cosmic Egg" crystallizes as an egg-type structure with a translucent Sassolite coating over a transparent hydrous borate (possibly Shabynite) composition. The mineral was first made available by Susan Slayton and Joel Haslam; it was named by same to reflect the structure/configuration.

This mineral has been used to facilitate the transcendence of the creation of advancement, combining the energies of non-restriction with the application of a devoted stamina. The synthesis of the vibratory messages of the energy coupled with Mother Earth/Father Sky, brings the correspondence to wholeness in entirety of all who experience the stone.

The "Cosmic Egg" has been used to access the "underworld" of cosmic energies where one may draw upon the energies of the highest reality as the source of all life and the manifested world. Used in tantric meditations, the mineral truly facilitates the flow of the inner state of meditation to the outer actualization of spirituality. One who receives a vision from either the visible world or from the nourishing invisible world, can sustain and preserve the visions, and can employ the energies of the mineral to assist in realizing those thoughts. It actually assists one in appreciating ones desires, and facilitates the building of ones dreams in this physical reality.

It can also assist one in obtaining bargains and in retaining monies. The energy equips one to understand that the acceptance of responsibility to the self leads to virtue in ones enterprises and in the regulation of money.

The "Cosmic Egg" tends to release ones limitations to the ethers, such that permission is granted which allows one to actualize aspirations and to attain limitless achievements. It inspires, motivates, and induces ambition toward the accomplishment of objectives.

It is a cosmic mineral, bringing the knowledge of universal truths. It has been used to assist one in the study of the arts and sciences and in the realm of mathematics, physics, and metaphysics.

The mineral has been used as a "seer stone", to access information from the past, present, and future. It has been used with Quartz Crystal elixirs to enhance the qualities of same and to provide increased "second-sight".

The "Cosmic Egg" can be used for "gazing" to provide access to the sacred texts of the ancient ones. By directing the mental focus to a period of time and/or appropriate location, one may access varying texts from varying ancient civilizations.

It further enhances memories of that which occurred prior to birth and refreshes ones knowledge concerning the realm of "after" life.

The "Cosmic Egg" has been used in the treatment of hypertension and to balance the acid/alkaline states of the body. It can help one to achieve a bodily construction which resists physical disorders, is said to enable one to consume alcohol without exhibiting the effects, and has been used in the treatment of chromosome dysfunction.

Vibrates to the number 9.

***CRASH-SITE DEBRIS (CSD)* -** A combination of tetragonal SiO_2 (Cristobalite), hexagonal SiO_2 (Quartz), Fe with minor Si and Mn, SiO_2 with Ca-Al-Fe-Mn impurities, an unknown mineral, a Pyroxene which falls in composition between Hedenbergite and Johannsenite, Mg isotopes, enrichment in Mn, Sb, Ag, Sn, Cr, Hf, Zr, Mo, W, Ta, and Ca, and 15 Rare Earth elements; Hardness is variable within the structure, ranging from 4 - 7; Locality: United States (further locality information is considered proprietary). Imaging by HP Scanjet, Assisted by Bob Jackson and ♪ Melody ♫; Collection of ♪ Melody ♫, Applewood, CO, USA. Gift of Michael Flaherty, Minnesota, USA.

Crash-Site Debris (CSD) crystallizes as masses with: a chilled-oxidized-porous black/brown rim/crust (Cristobalite and a brown/orange (Fe) component within the crust, and anhedral Quartz grain inclusions); light-to-dark green component (Cristobalite); tan/grey spherules (Cristobalite with a Pyroxene which has a chemical composition between $CaFeSi_2O_6$ [Hedenbergite] and $CaMnSi_2O_6$ [Johannsenite]); a grey component (unknown, and currently labeled Gellerite); with spherules of Fe metal with minor Fe oxide coatings and possible $5Fe_2O_3 \cdot 9H_2O$ (Ferrihydrite) in the coating; and, with spherical voids. The masses are enriched in Mn, Sb, Ag, Sn, Cr, Hf, Zr, Mo, W, Ta, and Ca; they also contain 15 Rare Earth elements. The Cristobalite is of an exceptional purity; A non-natural origin is inferred. Cristobalite was first described by G. vom Rath in 1887; it was named from the locality of first discovery, Cerro San Cristobal, Mexico. Pyroxene was first described by R.J. Haüy in 1796; it was named from the Greek words meaning "fire" and "stranger". Iron was first described in 1677 by the Oxford English Dictionary; it is synonymous with "Mars" of the Alchemists. Gellerite is the name elected by those who are making the CSD available; the name was selected to provide recognition for Bruce Geller, the mineralogist who analyzed the mixture and provided analytical reporting for same. The following properties are in addition to the properties listed in the PYROXENE, CRISTOBALITE, and IRON sections of "Love Is In The Earth - A Kaleidoscope Of Crystals Update".

CSD has provided contact with n-dimensional beings of extra-terrestrial origin, bringing information with respect to technological advances, innovative metal-working techniques, advanced healing methodology, music and art development, and elevated alchemy. The contact has always been one of harmony, accord, and scientific communication.

It has further enhanced "highs" associated with both physical and mental pursuits. It has also been used in games of levitation to assist in the initial elevation.

The material is thought to be "expulsion material from the gravity amplifier" of a galactic ship. It has facilitated both non-physical time-travel and universal-travel, assisting the user to gain entrance through the dimensional doorway and to proceed to the pre-determined (and/or the non-pre-determined) site.

It is also a "stone of survival", bringing knowledge of emergency actions and endurance, and supporting sustaining energies. It has been used to dissolve negativity, to raise consciousness and conscious understanding of that which is not apparent within this physical reality, and to act as the promotor/the expeditor for physical and n-dimensional pursuits.

CSD has been used in the treatment of leukemia, tumors, fevers, and obesity, to assist in brain-wave regulation, and to enhance the functioning of the immune system.

Vibrates to the numbers 6 (Crash-Site Debris) and 8 (CSD).

CREASEYITE [Astrological Sign of Capricorn]

CREASEYITE - $Cu_2Pb_2(Fe,Al)_2Si_5O_{17}$ ♥$6H_2O$; Hardness 2.5; Locality: Mammoth-St. Anthony Mine, Pinal County, Arizona, USA. Imaging by HP Scanjet, Assisted by Bob Jackson and ♪ Melody ♫; Collection of ♪ Melody ♫, Applewood, CO, USA.

Creaseyite crystallizes in the orthorhombic system and is configured as green acicular tufts. The mineral was first described by S.A. Williams and R.A. Bideaux in 1975; it was named for S.C. Creasey.

This mineral has been used to promote that free flow of concentration that actually seems to come from nowhere and actually points one in the right direction for solving the problem.

It further assists one in accessing the hundreds of "outer chakras" which impact the well-being of the physical form. These are the locations of where ones life energy comes into contact with ones physical being to create a vibration that is visible outside the body as light waves which emanate from an ethereal source.

Creaseyite additionally assists one in seeing the connections from the "outer chakras" to the chakras located in the physical form.

The energy of this green mineral actually strengthens the third-eye chakra, which can be weakened by fear and insecurity. Creaseyite provides a strong indigo colour to the area of the third-eye and facilitates the viewing of that colour in the aura, demonstrating the increase in intuitive and instinctive energies within the person and the augmentation of trust and security within that energy.

Creaseyite is also known to facilitate the acceptance of responsibility. It provides the message, and the understanding, that "you are your responsibility" and that "only you (not another person) can take responsibility for disappointing yourself". On the other hand, it acts to absolve one from responsibility and facilitates purging from ones life that which should be eliminated such that one can continue to both develop and to progress.

It truly promotes the acceptance of responsibility and the release of subjectivity to the "beliefs" or constraints of others, allowing allows for the creation of power, harmful to none, on all levels through accountability and guardianship of the self and the Earth.

It further assists one in observing ones programs, procedures, and approaches, and produces an energy to provide a reminder that although a plan may be attractive, one must occasionally examine the results, the consequences, and the conclusions, to assure that the attraction remains.

Creaseyite also acts to provide remediation to painful transformations, and can be used to enhance the understanding of evolution in ones life. With the experience of the state of constant change of form, structure, and substance, the mineral may be used to ameliorate the more exacting changes.

This mineral has been used in the treatment of Lymes Dis-ease, lupus, severe burns, and skin cancer, and to enhance the DHEA hormone. An elixir has been used for soothing and smoothing the skin and for the diminishment of wrinkles.

Do not prepare an elixir of this mineral via the normal method.

Vibrates to the number 2.

**"UNLESS YOU PUT IT IN THE "NOW",
IT WILL ALWAYS BE IN THE FUTURE"**
Leif Dragseth
Alaska, USA

DALLASITE

DALLASITE - Unspecified composition; Hardness 3.5 - 7; Locality: Vancouver Island, British Columbia, Canada. Imaging by HP Scanjet, Assisted by Bob Jackson and ♪ Melody ♫; Collection of ♪ Melody ♫, Applewood, CO, USA. Gift of Pierre Stéphane Salerno, Alberta, Canada.

Dallasite crystallizes as masses and was first described by R. Webster in 1962. The colour ranges from dark-green to black.

This mineral has been used to enhance expertise in the operation of graphic computer programs, instilling a "knowing" in the management of data and combinatory functions.

It can further assist in allowing one to release the emotions of petulance and sullenness, bringing honesty in all endeavors and integrity to ones interplay with others.

Dallasite has been used in gridding arrangements to reduce the ambient temperature, as well as the heat-index, on areas of our Earth, providing relief from "heat waves" and inclement increases in temperatures due to unusual weather patterns.

It is a mineral to produce "was" as an operative, having effectiveness in remedial processes. For example, when looking at the past, one is reminded of the "was", and is provided the impetus to view the "was" with an objective, detached, unbiased way methodology. The energy of Dallasite actually assists the user to release subjective judgments and feelings concerning the "was".

It brings the ability to recognize a feeling as it happens and furthers ones emotional intelligence such that greater certainty about ones life assures that one is a better navigator of same. It further has acted to bring self-confidence, levity of spirit, and faith, reliance, and trust in ones actions such that one may feel self-assured in the accomplishment of tasks which are presented. It poses the axiom that one's personal "way" is the "right way", and instills assertiveness within both the intellectual and the emotional realms. The mineral has been used to assure that one is not influenced to go in a direction which he/she does not wish to travel, and allows the user to dispense (kindly) with any interference in his/her path.

Dallasite assists one to focus on global spirituality and on positivity in all areas, such that one can promote much more healing in our world. It advances the recognition that even when one experiences that which is considered negative, one can certainly promote positivity by sending love - always. The energy assists in centering the self with kindness so that only kindness is projected; it furthers the sending of only positivity to those who need it most. It should be noted that it is relatively easy to send love and blessings to those who are of our same mind - the true test comes when we can send the same to those who are dissimilar to us and who may also project negativity.

Dallasite actually has an inherent programming which facilitates only the transmission blessings so that the recipient may realize and, if necessary, correcting his/her dissenting thoughts/ways and so that one may advance in spirituality.

Dallasite has been used in the treatment of disorders of the heart, to lower homocysteine and to prevent coronary artery disease. It can also be used in the treatment of fevers, Meniere's Dis-ease, and hypertension.

Vibrates to the number 2.

"DALMATIAN STONE"　　　　　[Astrological Sign of Gemini]

"DALMATIAN STONE" **-** A Quartz/Tourmaline Trachyte, which includes poikolitic Tourmaline $(Na,K,Ca)(Mg,Fe,Mn,Li,Al)_3(Al,Fe,Cr,V)_6 Si_6O_{18}(BO_3)_3 (O,OH,F)_4$, Quartz (SiO_2), Microcline $(KAlSi_3O_8)$, and Iron oxides (present due to clay-attack of the Microcline); Hardness 5 - 7.5; Locality: Mexico. Imaging by HP Scanjet, Assisted by Bob Jackson and ♪ Melody ♫ ; In the Collection of ♪ Melody ♫, Applewood, CO, USA. Gift of Ken Harsh, Ohio, USA.

"Dalmatian Stone" crystallizes as grey-white to tan Quartz-Microcline masses which contain poikolitic (non-typical structure which is scattered throughout the mass) Tourmaline of volcanic origin. This book provides the first reporting of the chemistry of the mineral; it was named by miners and merchants based upon its resemblance to the pattern of the coat of a Dalmatian.

The following properties are in addition to the properties listed in the TOURMALINE and MICROCLINE sections of "Love Is In The Earth - A Kaleidoscope Of Crystals Update".

The "Dalmatian Stone" provides the message that as we travel the highway toward the furtherance of our own spirituality, we shall always remember that each one of us can make a difference and that each lesson brings us more knowledge that we need - sometimes difficult, sometimes easy. As long as we are learning and growing, we are fulfilling our purposes.

This mineral supports one in disengaging from the outmoded, encouraging unique and exhilarating techniques to achieve ones goals. It provides for a foundation in issues of self-realization and self-love, for with the consciousness of love one can become united with all aspects of the world.

The "Dalmatian Stone" can be used to balance the yin-yang energy and to stabilize the physical, emotional, and intellectual bodies, bringing them into symmetry with the etheric energies.

It permeates the aura, providing for a cleansing effect to smooth dysfunctional energies and to dispel negativity. It helps one to unite the energy field of the physical with the ethereal in order to balance the form and to focus one toward a pre-determined goal.

Bringing a playfulness to the user, the "Dalmatian Stone" can be used to enhance ones "lighter-side". It further assists in sustaining allegiance, constancy, devotion, and fidelity. It is a lovely stone to share during all types of relationships.

It conveys a cautioning energy with respect to alerting one when danger is proximate. It further acts to bring composure with calm action during the period of danger.

The "Dalmatian Stone" assists one in being on the physical plane, and being in the corporeal body with gladness.

The mineral has been used by veterinarians in the calming of animals.

It has also been used in the amelioration of cartilage problems, to facilitate stamina and endurance in athletes, and to soothes the nerves. It can be carried by runners and athletes to assist in the elimination of sprains and spasms.

Vibrates to the number 9.

DEFERNITE

DEFERNITE - $Ca_3CO_3(OH,Cl)_4 \heartsuit H_2O$; Hardness 2 - 3; Locality: Otavi Mountains, Namibia, Africa. Imaging by HP Scanjet, Assisted by Bob Jackson and ♪ Melody ♫; Collection of ♪ Melody ♫, Applewood, CO, USA.

Defernite crystallizes in the orthorhombic system as blades. The colour range includes colourless, red, rose-brown, and red-brown. The mineral was first described by H. Sarp, M.F. Taner, J. Deferne, H. Bizouard, and B.W, Liebich in 1980; it was named for J. Deferne.

This mineral has been used as a purifier and is quite useful for cleansing the aura, the chakras, and the energy meridians.

It has also been used with Amethyst to remove unwanted energy implants; the presence of Defernite and Amethyst within ones energy field has also successfully protected against both energy implants and psychic attack.

A combination of the mineral, Carnelian, with Defernite has been used to eliminate psychic attack and to assist earth-bound spirits to leave an area, sending the spirits "to the light". Gridding with these two minerals can protect one and ones environment from the return of negative energies.

When consciously directed, Defernite has also been used to facilitate postponements in engagements, responses, and obligations. It assists one to have a time for preparation prior to the commitment, but does not eliminate same.

Assisting one to appreciate that which is growing spiritually, it acts to teach one the refinements of tenderness and care. It also provides one with a sense of harmony - harmony in ones life, harmony in the universe, and, even, the harmony of disarray - allowing one to understand that one need be neither defenseless nor desperate in the sphere of the creation or in the improvement of ones personal reality.

Defernite can combat lethargy, passivity, restlessness, excitability, and non-acceptance of oneself. It can stimulate initiative, optimism, diplomacy, and independence.

It further imparts the messages that there is no requirement for one to pursue love or to perpetually search for life, and that there definitely is a need to pursue and to emancipate all of the constraints which one has instated within the self.

It emits a philosophic energy, free of convention and partiality. It is excellent for use in policy-making and policing, providing wisdom with respect to the passageways available for right-achievement in all areas of ones life.

Defernite is especially supportive during periods of confinement, providing a comforting and calming energy and to assist in stabilizing ones condition.

It has been used in the elimination of toxins from the body and to enhance circulation, both of energy and of the blood. Used as an elixir it has relieved "chills" and has also assisted in weight loss. In addition, it has been used to promote the reactive qualities of the antihistamine.

Vibrates to the number 5.

DELHAYELITE [Astrological Sign of Cancer]

DELHAYELITE - $(Na,K)_{10}Ca_5Al_6Si_{32}O_{80}(Cl_2,F_2,SO_4)_3$ ♥ $18H_2O$ or $(Na,K)_{10}Ca_5Al_6Si_{32}O_{80}Cl_6 3$ ♥ $18H_2O$; Hardness unknown; Locality: Chibiny, Russia. Imaging by HP Scanjet, Assisted by Bob Jackson and ♪ Melody ♬; Collection of ♪ Melody ♬, Applewood, CO, USA.

Delhayelite crystallizes in the orthorhombic system as masses. The colour range includes colourless, white-grey, and green-brown. The mineral was first described by Th.G. Sahama and K Hytönen in 1959; it was named for F. Delhaye.

This mineral has been used by the ancient native cultures of Zaire (currently The Republic of Congo, and previously The Belgium Congo) in sacred ceremonies which were conducted to provide information concerning "lost" things. Delhayelite was placed in a grid configuration, using four pieces, such that the one was located in the southwest, one in the southeast, one in the northwest, and one in the northeast. A circle was drawn in the middle of the grid and the shaman stood within the circle, where he/she received the information.

Delhayelite has also been used in healing to promote receptivity to radionic treatment. In addition, during radionic analysis [where one holds a sample specimen and places a sample on the witness], or when used as a pendulum, the energy of the stone permeates the energy of the user and points to the problem[s] involved and/or to the answers required. radionic analyses

The mineral assists one to facilitate "upswings" in the mood (e.g., providing an immediate swing from despair to hope, from terror to courage....). It does not eliminate the return to the "down-mood", but maintains the "upswing" for the length of time the user holds it. It further assists one in seeing the beauty in everything, and in enjoying the beauty that is within.

Delhayelite promotes caring about others with no equivocation or hypocrisy in the affection. It assists one in being both lovingly strange and complex, and at the same time, burningly simple, such that one is sufficient unto himself/herself and does not allow happiness to rest with that which others are or that which others effect.

It furthers smiling with the whole being, from the heart, and to the eyes. The mineral acts to stimulate verity in the expression of happiness.

Delhayelite brings an energy which produces moral strength and a single-minded dedication to ones purpose. It assists one in dismissing from ones thoughts any area of concern and/or choosing when and if one will think about the concern and when and if one will not think about the concern.

It makes the action second-nature to one to find the words to courteously say nothing. The mineral actually brings the energy for the secret of "charm" - not so much an intrinsic quality in a person, as an outgoing one, since it depends for its effect upon the reception by another and an openness of another. Since "charm" does not exist in a vacuum, the energy of the mineral produces an inherent "charm" within the user which draws other particles of our universe to it.

Delhayelite has been used in the treatment of CMV virus and herpes, in inhibition of tumor growth, and in the amelioration of radiation damage.

Vibrates to the number 7.

DEVILLINE - CaCu$_4$(SO$_4$)$_2$(OH)$_6$♥3H$_2$O; Hardness 2.5; Locality: Laurion, Greece. Imaging by HP Scanjet, Assisted by Bob Jackson and ♪ Melody ♫; In the Collection of ♪ Melody ♫, Applewood, CO, USA.

Devilline crystallizes in the monoclinic system as a light-blue, blue-green, and pearly green bubbly mass. The mineral was first described by F. Pisani in 1872.

This mineral has been used to enhance the "madly, truly, deeply" positive emotional states which one experiences. When, and if, a situation is perceived as negative, the energy also assists one in dissipation of same.

Devilline has been known as "a stone of dispersion", bringing dispersal and a breaking-up of old patterns and modes of behavior. It assists one in recognizing unfulfilling and undesired behavior, and assists one in the reformation and/or modification of the behavior pattern.

It can be used to rid oneself of unwanted "things" (e.g., circumstances, people, objects, etc.); the energy actually acts to repel that which is unwanted. It should be noted that one needs to take care in the decision-making process which determines that which is not wanted (i.e., "be careful what you ask for").

Devilline provides the energy of protection to businesses, the protection specifically applicable to the unseen and unknowable. It also provides stimulus, with the protection, for the inspiration of avantgarde actions and instills the necessary courage for one to attempt new "things".

It further dispenses courage to the leader and the innovator, such that forays into the unknown are without anxiety. The mineral also can be used to stimulate the prosperous conduct of business and the attainment of the material aspects of this reality. Devilline has also been used to assist in the study of religion, sociology, and the humanities.

Devilline is a "stone of transformation" and could be considered one of the requisite minerals for ones collection because of its predisposition for reconstruction during the transformation process. It is a mineral to stimulate transformation while bringing a continuity of tenacity to expedite and to ease the process of the renewal of the self. The theory of incentive and stimulus for action are revealed in this energy.

The mineral is one for gradual and steady change, assisting one in progressing movement in all aspects of life. It promotes the understanding that one need not resist existence or non-existence; it helps one to both relax and accept the creation of personal reality. It further assists one in listening to the melody of life, eliminating discordance while instruct in that which is of the nature of perfection. It further assists one in surrendering to creation, assisting in the spontaneity of transformation to spontaneously, and inspiring the completion of cycles.

Transformation of disorders has been facilitated with Devilline, allowing the tension causing the disorder to be discharged. It has also been used to enhance Calcium assimilation, and in the treatment of degenerative dis-ease, lung dis-ease, cancer of the organs.

Due to the softness of this mineral, do not prepare an elixir of this mineral via the normal method.

Vibrates to the number 2.

**"ALL THINGS IN THE UNIVERSE
HAVE THE ENERGIES
OF THE UNIVERSE
COMING FROM THEM
AND PASSING THROUGH THEM...
AS DO THE STONES OF THE EARTH."**

Paul Ellerman
Colorado, USA

ELPIDITE

ELPIDITE - $Na_2ZrSi_6O_{15}$♥$3H_2O$ (it occasionally contains titanium); Hardness 7; Locality: Gobi Desert, Mongolia. Imaging by HP Scanjet, Assisted by Bob Jackson and ♪ Melody ♫; Collection of ♪ Melody ♫, Applewood, CO, USA.

Elpidite crystallizes as fibrous crystals and masses. The colour range includes white, brick-red, and orange/brown. The specimen in the image shows Elpidite with Arivedsonite. The mineral was first described by G. Lindström in 1894 and was named for the Greek word meaning "hope", given the desire to find additional rare minerals in the original location of occurrence of Elpidite.

This mineral can be used to stimulate the base, sacral and crown chakras, both opening and bringing clarity to those domains. It further can be used to cleanse the areas from intruding ethereal "cords" (c.f., "Love Is In The Earth - Laying-On-Of-Stones").

Elpidite has been used to bring faith in the future and can advance exploration in all areas. It has been used by book-scouts to assist in encountering rare books, in mine exploration, in the "hunt" for new places of residence, etc.

It is a mineral which delivers the message of subtlety, and has been used to soften communications, to bring calm to argumentative situations, to assist in negotiations, and to promote the attainment of contacts within business situations.

Elpidite has been used to assist one in finding a direct route to a goal (instead of maintaining a circuitous itinerary). It tends to focus one on the avenue for success while removing blockages on the path, promoting continuity in travel. The mineral has also been used as an equalizer, to provide an "edge" which balances pressure and tensions. It further secures a constant between the areas of constraint and freedom within ones life; the constant bearing an energy to advance the compounding of the steady-state of action between the two.

It has been used to further analytical pursuits in the study of both geometry and trigonometry, topology, and Lebesque theory; it stimulates the thought-processes and brings solutions to the forefront, such that one may recognize and resolve.

Elpidite brings the energy of development and abiding change throughout all times is focused with persistence of both the expedition and the ease of reformation of the self. The objectives of motivation and stimulating movement are exhibited in the energy of the mineral.

It has been used to promote clarification of issues within groups and between two or more people, such that during discussions, there is no divergence from the subject which is to be rectified.

The energy brings the elimination of omissions from topics of consideration, assuring that all subsets and relevant ideas are addressed; it has also been used to eliminate confusion during discussion and to remove obstacles which would occur during same.

Elpidite can be used in the treatment of strains, sprains, skin eruptions, Epstein Barr, and tumors. It has been used to enhance ones peripheral vision, and in the treatment of disorders of the structure of the veins. It has been carried by athletes to preclude dehydration.

Vibrates to the master number 44.

EMERALD - CAT'S-EYE

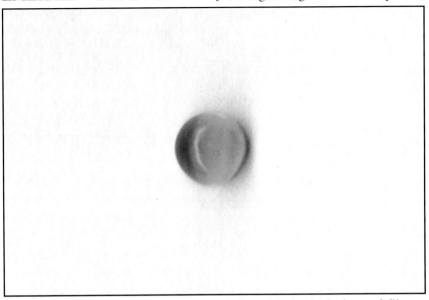

CAT'S-EYE EMERALD - $Be_3(Al,Cr)_2Si_6O_{18}$ with the inclusions of fibrous structures which provides for the Cat's-Eye effect; Hardness 7.5 - 8; Locality: Espirito do Santo, Brasil, South America. Imaging by HP Scanjet, Assisted by Bob Jackson and ♪ Melody ♫; Collection of ♪ Melody ♫, Applewood, CO, USA. Gift of Kim Sang, Goias, Brasil.

Cat's-Eye Emerald is a form of beryl and crystallizes in the structure of prismatic crystals, sometimes vertically striated and terminated by small pyramid-like faces. The colour is emerald green. The mineral was first described by Kim Sang and the name was chosen to reflect the Cat's-Eye chatoyancy of appearance. The following properties are in addition to the properties listed in the EMERALD and CAT'S EYE sections of "Love Is In The Earth - A Kaleidoscope Of Crystals Update".

This mineral has been used to promote the extension of occurrences to advance knowledge with spontaneity and proficiency such that strategy for each event/condition/experience is with absolute exactness and beneficial construction. The mineral actually furthers the approach to situations and circumstances via the implementation and the utilization of strategic techniques.

Holding the Cat's Eye Emerald has produced conscious THETA brain-wave patterns, activating a deeper state of ESP and prompting a level of consciousness which is conducive to psycho-kinesis [PK]; it has further facilitated painless surgery and dentistry.

It has also been used in the furtherance of the culinary arts and to assist one in the development of innovative and original creations.

Although green in colour, it has been used to enhance the third-eye chakra, provides a mixture of both indigo and green colours to the area of the third-eye. This enhancement to the intuitive energies brings an excellent energy for the awareness and for the promulgation of diagnosis for healing. One can perform the exercise for the self and/or for others by holding the mineral at the area of the third-eye.

It is an excellent mineral for stimulating the crown chakra, elevating ones clarity and lucidity. It tends to produce a transparency in information that his not totally correct so that the user may "read between the lines" and eliminate deception.

Cat's Eye Emerald has been known as a "stone of truth", exhibiting an energy which precludes non-truths being reported to the holder of the stone. Hence, it is excellent for negotiation, for relationships, and for teaching situations.

Reminiscent of an all-seeing configuration, it acts to capture the energies of eternal meditation, bringing a selectiveness to the choices in ones path. The configuration further allows one to recognize that the study of what is beautiful can never be wasted, especially if one is seeking to understand and to preserve it, and assisting one in seeing all aspects of a situation.

The Cat's Eye Emerald has been used to draw-out infection, to block pain, and to decrease muscular tension. It has been used in the amelioration of near-sightedness, the grogginess which occurs after surgery, disorders of the brain, and varicose veins. It has also assisted in the expedition of healing after intrusive surgery.

Vibrates to the master number 55.

**"IT'S ESSENTIAL TO BELIEVE IN MAGIC...
THE REST I CAN'T REMEMBER"**

Eliud Ferres (SALIM)
Espirito do Santo, Brasil

FERRIMOLYBDITE

FERRIMOLYBDITE - $Fe_2(MoO_4)_3$ ♥ $7.5H_2O$; Hardness 1 - 2; Locality: Yavapai Co., Arizona, USA. Imaging by HP Scanjet, Assisted by Bob Jackson and ♪ Melody ♫; In Collection of ♪ Melody ♫, Applewood, CO, USA.

Ferrimolybdite crystallizes as elongated crystal fibers and acicular crystals; it also occurs in small amounts as an oxidation product of molybdenite. The colour range includes earth-yellow to sulphur-yellow. The mineral was first described by P. Pilipenko in 1914; it was named by Pilipenko to distinguish it from molybdenum trioxide.

This mineral has been used to provide for the vitality and virility of youth, heightening the essence of ones nature and providing a "hard hat" for protection against pernicious opinions, impaired precision, and psychic attack. It stimulates both the base and sacral chakras, bringing an intelligence to understanding the pathway to health and longevity.

Ferrimolybdite brings uniformity, continuity, and conscientious to ones actions. It assists one in fulfilling commitments and in formulating a goal such that one may adjust the goal each day, and such that one may control ones responses and gain knowledge to think positively. It brings an impetus for one to maintain a journal and to verify daily progress (or regress) in the attainment of same. It acts as a catalyst to maintain that which one has and dispenses an energy of balancing to ones life. It has been used to balance the chakras, the bodies, and the mind. It further fills voids in the aura and stimulates an electric charge to provide symmetry and rationality in all areas of ones life.

An effective utilization of the energy is facilitated by allowing the mineral to remain in ones energy field; this provides for supplemental influx of energy and an alignment of ones energy paths. It is not necessary that one be aware of the presence of the mineral in order for the balancing and for the alignment and the support to occur.

It has also enhanced contact between the Conscious Self and the Inner Self, promoting the transfer of necessary information to the conscious portion of the brain such that one may assist the self in healing and in actualization of that which one desires. It stimulates the opening of the pathway of transfer of information within the self.

Ferrimolybdite produces a pathway of energy between the physical realm and the auric bodies to stimulate the movement of electrical charges. The movement of the energy has been shown to strengthen the connection such that when the auric bodies are cleansed, the physical body is energized. It can decrease turbulent/disorderly activity within the body.

The mineral produces an ardent wish-fulfilling energy which assists those who wish to establish new lives, assisting in the stabilization of the positive portions of ones being and in consecrating the new. It actually expedites ones progression from one perception to the next.

Ferrimolybdite has been used in the stimulation of the circulatory system, to stabilize the dispersion of oxygen within the body, to treat conditions associated with the immune system, blood disorders, and muscular atrophy. It can also be used to strengthen the reproductive system.

Due to the softness of this mineral, do not prepare an elixir of this mineral via the normal method.

Vibrates to the number 8.

"FLOWER STONE"

"FLOWER STONE" - $(K,Na,Ca,Ba,NH_4)(Si,Al)_4O_8$ (Feldspar), with Granite/ Basalt; Hardness 6 - 6.5; Locality: Texada Island, British Columbia, Canada. Imaging by HP Scanjet, Assisted by Bob Jackson and ♪ Melody ♫; In Collection of ♪ Melody ♫, Applewood, CO, USA. Gift of Pierre Stéphane Salerno, Alberta, Canada.

"Flower Stone" crystallizes as masses with phenocrysts exhibiting a flower-type structure. The background colour ranges from dark green to blackish-green; the colour of the flower configuration ranges from white to greyish-white. The mineral was first brought to the attention of the author in 1998, and has been used widely in Canada for many years.

This mineral can be used to empower one to "see the puddle" instead of being in the mind-set to only "see the ocean". It assists one in attention to detail and in the realization of all sub-parts of reality.

It helps to remove the negative traits of cynicism and to train the user in the contrast between beliefs and "knowing".

The "Flower Stone" assists one to maintain balance in relationships and cooperative efforts, facilitating savoir-faire and discretion in all matters of import. It also enables one to "nip" disagreeable situations at the onset, defeating negativity with ease. It produces an energy which promotes "noblesse oblige", furthering correctness in action in discriminating situations in which correct action will further ones plans.

It has been reported that the "Flower Stone" also brings one an increase in money; the mineral inducing recognition of, and generous overtures to, the user.

It has been used for dowsing, to enhance creativity, to enhance fertility in both mind and body, and to bring long life.

It has further assisted in translation of symbology and ancient languages which are not constructed with the normal English letters, has been used to advance automatic-writing, and has facilitated ease of translation of other current languages.

It also tends to reverse "declarations of intolerance" such that one is provided with patience when necessary. However, the energy of the mineral is such that patience is seldom needed; the actualization is not dependent upon patience or persistence, but rather on intent.

The "Flower Stone" brings the message that one need never "grow-up", and that one only needs to continue growing while remaining in a state of joyful, fun-loving, innocence. It also helps one to understand that the flower is always within the self; both prior to and after, as well as, during ones physical experience on this plane. It brings the message to enjoy each moment, allowing one to both recognize and to understand that time, so often, does not become precious and cherished until it is already past.

The mineral has been used in the treatment of disorders associated with the hair, face, and head.

It has been used to balance white cell count, to lessen traumas associated with physical growth, and to ameliorate dyslexia and muscular inflexibility, and in the stabilization of conditions promulgated through the AIDS virus.

Vibrates to the number 8.

FOSHAGITE

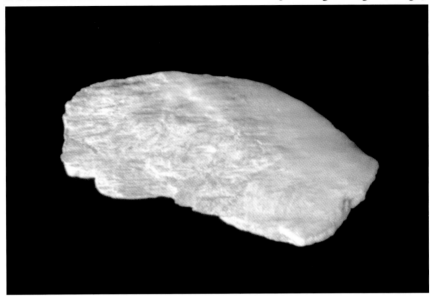

FOSHAGITE - $Ca_4(SiO_3)_3(OH)_2$ or $H_2Ca_5(SiO_4)_3$ ♥ H_2O or $H_2Ca_5(SiO_4)_3$ ♥ $2H_2O$; Hardness 5 - 6; Locality: Riverside, California, USA. Imaging by HP Scanjet, Assisted by Bob Jackson and ♪ Melody ♫; Collection of ♪ Melody ♫, Applewood, CO, USA.

Foshagite crystallizes as white compact fibers. The mineral was first described by A.S. Eakle in 1925; it was named for W.F. Foshag.

This mineral has been used to increase ones will-power, assisting one in speaking "no" and in resisting temptation.

It has enhanced safe delivery of mail both to and from the user.

Foshagite has been used to grid farmlands and ranches to enhance the protection of animals. In these cases, it has acted to produce a protective barrier and has been found to produce an energy which can prevent disease and abduction of the animals.

Gridding in urban areas has also resulted in stabilization of soils and has decreased movement in structures. It has been used in Feng Shui arrangements to dispel negative intrusions of non-symmetry.

Foshagite can be used to clear the judgment of inconsequential matters. It provides for the equilibration of both sentiments and sexuality, for the awakening of both inspiration and ingenuity, and for a advantageous channel for desire. It has been used to assist one during intervals of change and provides for a multitude of insights with respect to the accessible alternatives.

It brings the energy to actualize proficiency in acting and in participating in the dramatic aspects of situations; providing, in addition, it furthers the necessity to laugh at the trivial aspects of the drama.

Foshagite can also be used to enhance ones abilities in the pursuit of mathematics, stimulating logical thinking and inducing the mental state required for problem-solving.

It provides for sincerity and for conformity to the truth of ones nature. It affords the ability of accuracy when one is participating in ceremonial activities and when one permeates the spirit world or initiates contact with other physical presences from other worlds.

It promotes fluency in self-expression, in presentations and speech-making, and in reporting the details of visions, intuitive encounters, and psychic experiences. It further allows one to understand the meanings inherent to these activities.

It has been used to stimulate the throat chakra and the hand and feet chakras, bringing action to verbalization.

Foshagite can be very helpful in the treatment of recurrent and chronic dis-ease.

It can also be used in the treatment of intestinal absorption problems, viral disorders, and bacterial infections. It can enhance stability in ambulatory disorders, can help to correct posture, and has been used in the amelioration of asthma, emphysema, blood disorders, excess mucus, and disorders of the spleen. It has furthered improvement in the saturation levels of nutrients, vitamins, and minerals.

Vibrates to the number 9.

FOSSIL PINE CONE [Astrological Sign of Libra]

FOSSIL PINE CONE - An ancient pine cone which has been fossilized; i.e., wherein a mineral [e.g., quartz, calcite, opal, pyrite, agate, jasper, etc.] infiltrated the empty cellular spaces in the pine cone, such that some of the original organic matter retained, and the pattern remained as, the original cellular structure; Hardness 3 - 7; Locality: Washington, USA. Imaging by HP Scanjet, Assisted by Bob Jackson and ♪ Melody ♫; Collection of ♪ Melody ♫, Applewood, CO, USA.

Fossil Pine Cone crystallizes as masses with the pattern and structure of the pine cone remaining. The colour ranges from tan/brown to black. The following properties are in addition to the properties listed in the FOSSIL section of "Love Is In The Earth - A Kaleidoscope Of Crystals Update".

This mineral has been used when one is at an impasse in decision; specifically, when one cannot determine whether to defend the self or whether to investigate methods of handling an offender more effectively. The energy assists one to examine the behavior of another with respect to ones reaction to the behavior, such that one can determine the method to acquire closeness to others. The intriguing aspect of the energy is the acknowledgment that control over another cannot exist in a loving social structure and that one can only advise (but cannot expect the other to obey). It further assists one in the realization that "turning back the clock" is futile - when one acts in a certain manner, one has lessons to process and to learn.

The Fossil Pine Cone has further been used to assist one in the prevention of delays - in ones life, in each moment.

It is an excellent mineral to assist one in maintaining dependable relationships with ones relatives; it acts to bringing camaraderie to situations involving relatives to promote an understanding bond. It further helps one to realize that all people do not wish to have the same patterns in life; and that for some, there is a major difference in choices and in actions. The mineral produces an energy which instills sufficient sensitivity to assure the appreciation of different ways of life.

The Fossil Pine Cone has also been used to dispel bigotry and prejudice, alleviating the reasons for bias and discrimination. The energy further induces one to rise above the basic insecurities which instill these detrimental feelings, further assisting one in being open to differences between the self and others, between options, between privileges, and within ones mind.

It has been used to eliminate trivial sophistry, the beguiling, generally fallacious method of reasoning, which places one at a definite disadvantage in progressing toward the release of karmic debts.

The Fossil Pine Cone can also be used to assist one in access to information relevant to the karmic burdens incurred during past-lives, helping one to both recognize and understand the "easy" lessons which can cancel the karma. It has been used to access future lives and to understand that which must be accomplished in this life in order to eliminate the need to repeat harsh lessons.

The mineral has been used in the treatment of restrictions in veins, atrophy, decreased sense of smell and response to scent, allergies of the senses, age-related disorders, hardening of the arteries, osteoporosis, and dis-ease related to being within the Agent Orange environment.

Vibrates to the number 8.

FOSSIL ALGAE [Astrological Sign of Sagittarius]

FOSSIL ALGAE - A combination of Jasper (SiO_2 with impurities) and Hematite Iron ore (Fe_2O_3) replacing the Stromatolite Algae; Hardness 5 - 7; Locality: The Mary Ellen Mine, Minnesota, USA. Imaging by HP Scanjet, Assisted by Bob Jackson and ♪ Melody ♫; Collection of ♪ Melody ♫, Applewood, CO, USA. Gift of Peter Giangrande, Minnesota, USA.

Fossil Algae is the world's oldest megascopic fossil; it is also known as Algae Iron and is a Minnesota Stromatalite. The colours include red, black, white, yellow, etc. The mineral was first brought to the attention of the author in 1997, and has been used widely in Canada and the northern Mid-West for many years. The following properties are in addition to the properties listed in the FOSSIL, JASPER, and HEMATITE sections of "Love Is In The Earth - A Kaleidoscope Of Crystals Update".

This mineral has been used to bring the power to create wisdom and to not destroy that which is beneficial. It assists one in recognizing that freedom from the rigid is a crucial issue in daily living, and provides for freedom from the orthodox that ossifies the faculties of invention and discovery. It further conveys the energy of understanding that one is a creature full of the power of the mind, assisting one to free the mind from the shackles of fear. The mineral can be used to rid one of suspicion built on the past, combatting a primitive instinct which sometimes is truer than reason.

Fossil Algae facilitates the discernment that mistakes, as such, hold no bearing on ones future; it serves one in the area of discovery and in the naming of "new" truths for the self, while disentangling one from the timidness and apprehension to initiate adventures into unknown regions of thought or knowledge. It acts to release the condemnations (self-righteous, of course) of those experiences which one has never had the opportunity through which to participate or to complete.

The mineral has been used to assist one in contemplating "the smallness of the craft" in which one is a passenger; the energy brings the realization that one is a small part of the vast universe and that one truly contains a complete universe within the self and is precious in the sight of creation and is greatly loved. It helps one in the art of seeing that which is required in order to facilitate that which is desired.

It acts as an energy to cleanse the environment in which it rests and is an excellent mineral for use in purifying (environments, "things", minerals, foods, etc.). It has been said to bring good luck to fishermen, divers, and explorers of the sea.

Fossil Algae helps one in the attunement to the requisites of others and inspires prudence during the evaluation of problems. It promotes the equilibration of ones needs with the necessities of the day, allowing one to acknowledge and to care for that which is of prime significance to well-being. It provides for amiability and openness in opinions, and for allegiance in commitments. It provides companionship for those who are alone and/or lonely, and stimulates a beneficial behavior modification for children.

The mineral has been used to transmute of disordered energy into healing energy. It has been used in the treatment of infection, scleroderma, and high cholesterol, to assist in spinal alignment and assimilation of iron and Vitamin A, and in the elimination of toxicity from the body.

Vibrates to the numbers 1 (Algae Iron) and 7 (Fossil Algae).

"FRANKLINORE" [Astrological Sign of Sagittarius]

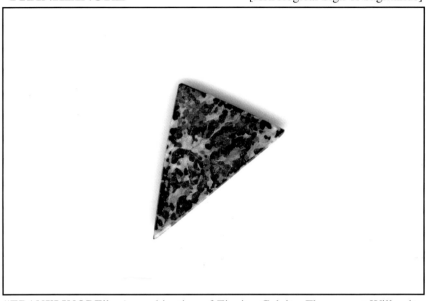

"FRANKLINORE" - A combination of Zincite, Calcite, Fluorescent Willemite, Fluorescent Franklinite, Friedelite; Hardness 3 - 6.5; Locality: Franklin, New Jersey, USA. Imaging by HP Scanjet, Assisted by Bob Jackson and ♪ Melody ♬; Collection of ♪ Melody ♬, Applewood, CO, USA. Gift of Bob Jackson, Colorado, USA.

"Franklinore" crystallizes as masses which have a beautiful green fluorescence on short-wave ultraviolet. The colour range includes black, white, tan, and red. The mineral was first brought to the attention of the author in 1994, and was discovered in the early 1800's. It was named by Bob Jackson to represent the fluorescent ore from the tailing's piles in Franklin, NJ.

This mineral assists one in expression of life's ambiguities. It brings thoughts which are felt to be "seven-feet above", to the realm of the conscious logical mind.

"Franklinore" can be used to assist ones brain-response to the electrical waves positioned when an object is viewed and encourages two or more people to see "things" in the same manner, with the same image, and with the same thought patterns. Hence, it has been very conducive to gaining and maintaining agreements between the self and others and between factions of varying opinions. This is not to say that one will change ones opinion, but that ones opinion will meld with the opinion of another.

The mineral holds the energy to assist in the amelioration of Self-organized criticality; it has been used to relieve the structural disorganization which has caused complex dynamic phenomena like earthquakes and devolution. "Franklinore" contributes a dynamic energy to stabilize the various magnitudes and frequencies which occur when a situation or a structure reaches a "critical value". (Note: the situation or structure is said to be "self-organized" because it reaches the critical state without outside influence, and it is said to be "critical" because of the absence of a single well-defined length or time scale.)

Simply stated, the energy of "Franklinore" assists "smaller" events to relieve the pressure which is necessary to cause "larger" events. Hence, during the tendency for devolution, for example, one may experience small set-backs, but not large ones; and, during the structural organization which would allow a major earthquake, a smaller earthquake would assist in the relieve of the energy such that a larger earthquake would not be as probable.

The mineral is actually one which introduces a weakness in the actualization of the theory of "self-organized criticality" such that one may experience indications of larger problems, but not the disastrous consequences of the same larger occurrences. (For example, the difference in the feeling of indignation versus the actualization of furious action).

"Franklinore" promotes the "smile of the cheshire" during ones evolution and stabilization in the advancement-areas of ones life. It truly fosters increase in a step-by-step progression.

The mineral has been used to induce stability in personality disorders, to treat disorders associated with the teeth and gums, and to stabilize degeneration of the body. It can be used in a homeopathic manner for illnesses related to body structure and function.

Vibrates to the number 6.

FRIEDELITE

FRIEDELITE - $(Mn,Fe)_8Si_6O_{15}(OH,Cl)_{10}$ or $Mn_8Si_6O_{15}(OH,Cl)_{10}$ or $H_7(Mn,Cl)Mn_4Si_4O_{16}$; Hardness 4 - 5; Locality: Kalahari Area, Republic of South Africa, Africa. Imaging by HP Scanjet, Assisted by Bob Jackson and ♪ Melody ♫; In Collection of ♪ Melody ♫, Applewood, CO, USA.

Friedelite crystallizes as tabular crystals and masses. The colour is a rose-red. The mineral was first described by E. Bertrand in 1876; it was named for Ch. Friedel.

This mineral has been used by the Zulu tribe in Africa to assist in "bringing in the harvest", serving to promote expediency in action and quality of the harvest. It has been known as a "stone of fertility" and a "stone of stamina."

It has also assisted in bringing faith in the self to oneself - a very necessary quality since, as the Chinese proverb states "those without faith in themselves cannot survive".

Friedelite acts to dispel anxiety and the consciousness of inadequacy when one is involved in the nature of loving another. It assists those who are beginning to love to be aware of themselves and the other, and to, concurrently, be aware of the "two-ness". The energy assures no "loss of balance" (which "falling" in love implies), and serves secure individual self-sufficiency and the knowledge that ones happiness truly rests within the self (not in anything outside of the self).

The mineral assists two people in looking together in the same direction, inspiring compatibility in the physical, emotional, and intellectual planes.

In addition, it assists one in obtaining a love-relationship; the energy of the mineral, when directed toward the goal, provides for an all-consuming intent and purpose, and an overwhelming passion which brings that which is desired.

Friedelite has been used to assist in the study of the French language (to expedite studying and comprehension of details) and in managing situations with the French populace when one does not speak the same language (to increase knowledge associated with aesthetics).

The mineral is also one to bring surprises. If one is melancholy, it is a lovely stone to hold - insights, solutions, and surprises do, indeed, invariably occur.

In addition, it has been used by many soccer players to advance agility, gain, and acumen during the game. It tends to act as guidance in instinctual actions, providing "the edge".

Friedelite has been supportive to educators and lecturers, providing for an augmentation of the expertise required to arouse understanding in audiences, and consigning the faculty to preserve audiences in a state of steady, sensible rationality.

The mineral has been used in the treatment of spasms, fevers, and disorders of the reproductive system and the internal digestive organs. It has been used to enhance the sympathetic nervous system [activating involuntary muscles which enhance the mobilization of the physical body].

Vibrates to the number 3.

FRONDELITE

FRONDELITE - $Fe^{2+} Fe_4^{3+} (PO_4)_3(OH)_5$ [re: Dana]; Hardness 4.5; Locality: one location in Minas Gerais, Brasil, South America. Imaging by HP Scanjet, Assisted by Bob Jackson and ♪ Melody ♫; Collection of ♪ Melody ♫, Applewood, CO, USA. Gift of Daniel Foscarini de Almeida, Minas Gerais, Brasil, South America.

Frondelite crystallizes in the orthorhombic system as botryoidal and nodule-like masses and in radial-fibrous configurations, occasionally with a drusy surface. The colour ranges from brown to yellow-brown to orange-brown and exhibits pleochroism. The mineral was first described by C. Frondel in 1949; it is named for C. Frondel. Frondelite is similar to Rock Bridgeite in physical and chemical properties; the only difference being that the primary cation is Manganese (in Frondelite) and Iron (in Rock Bridgeite).

This mineral is one of "noblesse oblige", fostering honourable conduct and distinguished and refined action. It serves to bring one to the realization that one may live ones days upon the Earth in a "long and good" manner, while still having the experiences ones desires (and participating in these experiences without guilt). The mineral further assists one in recognizing that "Too much of a good thing is wonderful!" and expedites the "wonderful" elements while dispelling the negative.

It provides for a strong dispersion of ones "old ways" such that one is unable to remain in the past and to dwell on same, but, instead lives in the moment and recognizes that the "future is now" - bringing actions to match ones thoughts and feelings.

Frondelite has been used as a bridge to other worlds, assisting one in maintaining the brain-wave states which are necessary, and to overcome any fear-based limitations which can preclude contact.

It assists one in entering into chaos without form such that chaotic actions are understood and such that one does not experience the disorder, discord, or turmoil. It brings a coherence to thoughts which are filled with inchoate confused, eliminating bewilderment and providing solutions via rudimentary application of fundamental knowledge.

The mineral has been used to assist one in solving puzzles - mathematical problems, crosswords, chess, bridge, etc., and in "winning" in competitions involved in same. It also brings an energy to assist one in determining the "whys" of any given situation which one does not consciously understand.

It has been used to smooth the aura, to sooth the chakras, and to open and to activate the solar plexus chakra. The mineral is one which will automatically align the chakras, without conscious direction. It never needs clearing or cleansing.

Frondelite has been used as an emissary, sending an energy of an agent to assist one in the furtherance of ones missions within the world. When directed to further ones "causes", the energy tends to be sent to, and to permeate, the area which requires diplomatic enhancement of the sender. It has also been used to assist one in qualifying for endeavors in which one wishes to participate. The mineral can be used to eliminate objectionably avuncular tones during verbalization of issues with others - both in the speaking of others and in the replying/speaking of the self.

It has been used in the treatment of carpel tunnel, drug-less healing, ear-nose disorders, and is currently being used in the treatment of AIDS.

Vibrates to the number 9.

"YOU ARE THE SPARK
OF INITIATION,
OF BECOMING..."

Gary "Horsefeathers" Wallace
Maryland, USA

GARNET In SILLIMANITE   [Astrological Signs of Aries & Leo]

GARNET IN SILLIMANITE - $(Ca,Fe,Mg,Mn)_3(Al,Fe,Mn,Cr,Ti,V)_2(SiO_4)_3$
(Garnet) with Al_2SiO_5 (Sillimanite); Hardness ranges 6.5 - 7.5; Locality: In Minas
Gerais, Brasil, South America. The Imaging by HP Scanjet, Assisted by Bob Jackson
and ♪ Melody ♫; Collection of ♪ Melody ♫, Applewood, CO, USA.

Garnet in Sillimanite crystallizes as masses of Sillimanite with Garnet
attached; if the garnet becomes detached, a "key" configuration remains
at the area of detachment. The colour of the Garnet is normally a very
deep red; the Sillimanite normally ranges from white to yellow/tan.

Although both Garnet and Sillimanite have been reported previously
and separately in "Love Is In The Earth - A Kaleidoscope Of Crystals
Update", this combination is quite unique and is, hence, reported here.
The following properties are in addition to those listed in the GARNET
and SILLIMANITE sections of "Love Is In The Earth - A Kaleidoscope
Of Crystals Update".

This combination of minerals has been used to assure the detection of
humour in instances when dispositions indicate that solemnity would
be prevalent. It further assists one in providing surprising answers to

ingenuous questions, serving in situations of conflict to expedite replies which are relevant, unanticipated, and unforeseen. Bringing clarity to situations so that one is not hopelessly mis-read, the energy also supports the reassertion of intelligence over emotion.

Garnet in Sillimanite has been used to provide one with the impetus to proceed in plans which have been delayed by the self; hence, dispelling complacency and discontent via action.

It can help one to recuperate from both "life in the fast lane" and from slow movement in change (e.g., "changes in the slow lane").

Providing a steady "always-there" energy, it assists one to adopt a steady and continuous tempo; providing a steady "always tenacious" energy, it serves one to maintain patience and rectitude.

The combination has been used to reveal information pertaining to healing concepts and to features of oneself which are inclined to be elusive. It can also support the retrieval of information concerning questions relative to the reasons behind ones belief that one is unable to perform in a certain manner.

Garnet in Sillimanite also assists one in gaining information with respect to that which is obscure or indefinite in any situation. One can place the mineral upon letters, photographs, etc., in order to gain admittance to concealed or hidden meanings and information which are intrinsic.

It can further be used to expedite rational and systematic resolutions of problems; placing the mineral upon a textbook, which contains the information necessary to arrive at a solution, has stimulated the inner knowledge of the answer.

Garnet in Sillimanite has been used to promote inner cellular awareness such that each cell affected by a disorder can singularly, and collectively, recognize the reason for the malfunction and then release the anomaly, facilitating both alignment with the perfect self and the healing state. It has also been used to promote control of dizziness and tinnitus.

Vibrates to the number 8.

GARNIERITE

GARNIERITE - $(Ni,Mg)_3Si_2O_5(OH)_4$; Hardness 2.5 - 4; Locality: Noumea, New Caledonia. Imaging by HP Scanjet, Assisted by Bob Jackson and ♪ Melody ♫; In the Collection of ♪ Melody ♫, Applewood, CO, USA˙

Garnierite crystallizes as masses and is an ore of nickel consisting primarily of hydrated silicates of magnesium and nickel. The colour ranges from bright apple-green and pale green to nearly white. It is also known as Noumeite. The mineral was first described by W.B. Clarke in 1874; it was named for J. Garnier who described the mineral prior to analyses.

This mineral has been known as a "stone of acquisition" and "a stone of accumulation". It can advance ones storage and maintaining of goods and can promote increase in assets.

It has ben used to assist in the unleashing of magnificence from within a structure or within a person. It further brings the energies of recognition and of appreciation to the forefront so that one may recognize magnificence within the other and within the self (hence, enhancing self-esteem and self-confidence).

Garnierite has been used to stimulate and to activate the heart chakra and to support healing on all levels via the heart center, allowing for the love of the universe to permeate the entire cellular structure of the subject.

The mineral can be used to cause suspension in gossip and to ameliorate scandal. It acts to bring forth a barricade which obstructs the continuance of negative communication. If one has a proclivity for gossiping, or if one knows another who has the proclivity for gossiping, it can be placed in the environment of the person and will act to thwart the action.

It has been used in gaming to enhance "winning"; it has been placed in the coin-catcher of slot machines to bring funds to same. Please note that the mineral is soft and it is best to place it in an area which will not be besieged when the coins fall.

Garnierite has also been used to dispel martyrdom and to instill self-esteem. The energy actually tends to bring the message of compassion with no regrets, and action with no lamentation. It helps one to remember the laughter and the comradeship, the absurdities and the fierce sentimental moments, while retaining the joyfulness of self-love.

It further acts to prompt one to have the qualities of a friend: honor without pomposity, generosity without condescension, humour without malice, and courage without cruelty.

The mineral assists one in releasing the barren ground of resentment and despair.

It has been used to facilitate one in the confidence and self-sufficiency essential for single-parenting and/or single-living. It helps one to be conscious of the self as an exhibit of the perfect Creator, promoting loving command and organizational and interactive capabilities.

Garnierite has been used in the treatment of disorders associated with the wrists, the vertebrae and the spinal cord, the forearms, and the secretion and manufacture of bile. Overall, it enhances ones recuperative and regenerative capabilities.

Vibrates to the numbers 3 (Noumeite) and 7 (Garnierite).

GENEVITE

GENEVITE - A silicate of Calcium and Aluminum; Hardness 5.5 - 6.5; Locality: Dalmar, Morocco. Imaging by HP Scanjet, Assisted by Bob Jackson and ♪ Melody ♫; Collection of ♪ Melody ♫, Applewood, CO, USA˙

Genevite crystallizes as masses with tetragonal and prismatic cleavages. The colour ranges from black to grey. The mineral was first described by L. Duparc and M. Gysin in 1927; it was named from Geneva, Switzerland.

This mineral has been used to control emotions which are prevalent in confrontations, anger, and uncontrolled fury. It produces an energy which tends to "reach-out" and calm the participants in same, allowing any negativity to flow into the ethers after transformation to positivity.

Genevite has been used to instill rhythm in dancing and in musical endeavors.

It brings an appreciation of the "old", and has been used to assist one in the collecting and in the marketing of antiques, assisting one in both location and negotiation. It can further assist in the acquisition of material wealth and is a stone which has been used to provide security to ones precious objects within ones environment. Placed in an area of the objects, it brings a protective force to same. It has been placed upon a photograph/image of an antique object to encourage the manifestation of the object; this application has been utilized to assist one in obtaining specific articles for antique collections.

Genevite acts to quicken ambition, sincerity when sincerity is necessitated, light-hearted behavior when seriousness is not required, organizing capabilities, and preservation of resources [e.g., decrease in spending, reduction in over-use of the natural resources of the Earth, etc.].

It further stimulates the discernment of the subversive actions of others, providing insights to allow for the detection of any potential harmful actions against one and promoting guidance in regulation of the effects in a positive manner.

Genevite has provided for contact with spiritual guides who are versed in the enlightened rites and rituals of the archaic orders of Freemasons. The information is usually granted during the meditative state when the participant holds the mineral, but has also been given during periods of time in which the user is in a "waiting" mode (e.g., traffic signals, market lines, etc.).

When utilized for the purpose of insightful guidance and/or to facilitate contact with the freemasonry spiritual guides, it is recommended that the mineral be placed in the hands.

The energy has also stimulated insights relative to the basis for, and the use of, the Runes; further producing understanding of the general data of the Runes, and application of this information to specific circumstances.

Genevite has been used to assist one in understanding dis-ease and in allowing the dis-ease to depart. It can be used when one is performing "bodywork" on another, helping the other to be receptive to releasing blockages and to the supplementary energies which are being applied. It has been used in the promotion of successful chiropractic manipulation.

Vibrates to the number 6.

GEODE - CHALCOPYRITE [Astrological Signs of Scorpio & Leo]

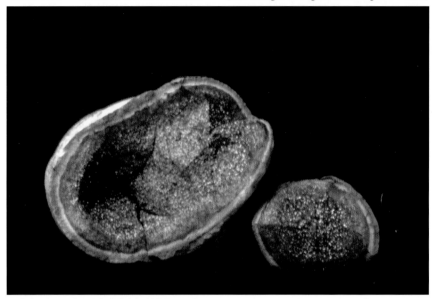

GEODE - CHALCOPYRITE - CuFeS$_2$ (Chalcopyrite) with a fine-grained sedimentary geodic over-covering; Hardness 3.5 - 4; Locality: Russia. Imaging by HP Scanjet, Assisted by Bob Jackson and ♪ Melody ♬; Collection of ♪ Melody ♬, Applewood, CO, USA. Gift of Steve Goins, Oklahoma, USA.

The Chalcopyrite Geode crystallizes with the Chalcopyrite in the form of tetrahedrals with sphenoidal faces, in octahedrals, and compact botryoidal or reniform masses. The Chalcopyrite colour range includes brass-yellow which may tarnish to green or iridescent. It often occurs with copper and/or zinc. The geode structure is irregularly spherical and contains a cavity lined with the crystalline Chalcopyrite and projecting into the hollow interior.

Although both Chalcopyrite and the Geode have been reported previously and separately in "Love Is In The Earth - A Kaleidoscope Of Crystals Update", this combination is quite unusual and is, hence, reported here.

The following properties are in addition to those listed in the CHALCOPYRITE and GEODE sections of "Love Is In The Earth - A Kaleidoscope Of Crystals Update".

This combination has been used to provide for the recognition of action/ thought patterns that are beneficial, promoting the liberation of the detrimental modes of being and the retention of the quality patterns.

It has been used to promote the governing of emotional responses via prompting one to center the self prior to reply and/or "reaction". It assists one in the discovery of the appropriate protocol for any given situation or circumstance.

It has been used in office environments to stimulate both clarity and business opportunities.

The Chalcopyrite Geode can also be used to open, to cleanse, and to energize the hand and the feet chakras.

In addition, it has been used to energize, and occasionally, to improve the taste of foods/drinks. This has been facilitated via placing the mineral beneath the bottle or the food for a period of 1-2 hours.

One piece held by two people can serve to help each of the participants to understand a complete and loving platonic relationship. It can also be used for further contemplation of the other, providing for understanding of the depth and/or the superficial components of the personal structure.

It has been used to provide one with "permission" to accept the positive sides of self-indulgence, to be kind to the self, and to indulge the self with care.

The Chalcopyrite Geode has been used to protect from radiation in the environment and to assist in the recovery from penetrating radiation from radiation treatment.

This mineral combination can be used to assist in the relief of arthritis, rheumatism, frostbite, numbness, infectious disorders, premature aging of the skin, skin cancer, bruises, and metabolic disorders. It has been used in the treatment of Alzheimer's dis-ease.

Vibrates to the number 9.

GEYSERITE

GEYSERITE - Siliceous sinter (a chemical sedimentary rock which is deposited as a hard incrustation on the ground by precipitation from mineral waters) which constitutes concretionary deposits in proximity to geysers; Locality: Yellowstone, Wyoming, USA (during road construction such that the Yellowstone Park was not disturbed). Imaging by HP Scanjet, Assisted by Bob Jackson and ♪ Melody ♬; In the Collection of ♪ Melody ♬, Applewood, CO, USA.

Geyserite crystallizes in the form of beautiful white to greyish porous, stalactitic, filamentous, cauliflower-like forms, compact masses, and scaley-masses. The mineral was first described by J.C. Delamétherie in 1812; it was named from the original locality of Geyser, Iceland.

This mineral acts to stimulate endurance and tenacity in action. It can initiate passive resistance with articulate verbalization of ones feelings during conflicts, helping others to diminish aggressive behavior.

Thoroughness, reliability, and steadfastness are qualities which can be enhanced. It assists one in following an activity to completion, promoting mental recall of lessons learned and encouraging the sharing of these details with others.

It has also been employed to help one to enjoy busy circumstances, to excel in over-populated areas, and to enhance success and security in ones career and in "life after work".

It can also be placed upon a photograph/image of a subject or a facsimile of a plan to encourage additional information, care in tactics and subsequent ease of action.

Used to grid a garden, or a photograph/image of same, germination, abundance, and dis-ease resistance can be furthered.

Geyserite can also assist one in understanding the disadvantages of possessiveness, facilitating one to work toward building a tangible and reliable reality, while allowing one to remain open to the transformative processes.

It can act as a stimulant for releasing and/or resolving that which is unattainable - the unattainable being defined as that which is desired, and at the same time, not desired.

It has been used in gridding areas of the Earth, to assist in the stabilization of those areas of unrest [e.g., areas of volcanic or earthquake potential] which are below the surface.

It can also work with the pyramidal structure to assist in preservation and stability of foods, elixirs, tinctures, etc.

The mineral can be used to assist in the cleansing of arteries, to inhibit the formation of plaque on the teeth, to ameliorate chromosomal imbalance, glandular swelling, the lack of the sensation of taste, and circulatory disorders. It can also be used in the treatment of disorders related to the vertebrae, the teeth, Parkinson's dis-ease, and child-birth. Overall, it has been used to enhance ones recuperative abilities.

Due to the solubility of this mineral, do not prepare an elixir via the normal method.

Vibrates to the number 5.

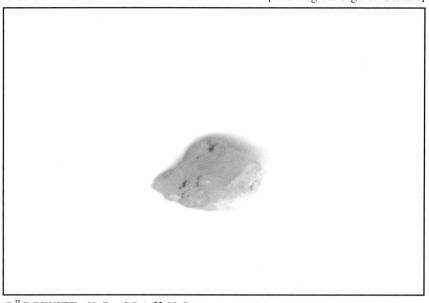

GÖRGEYITE - $K_2Ca_5(SO_4)_6$ ♥ H_2O; Hardness 3.5; Locality: Lake Inder, Kazakhstan. Imaging by HP Scanjet, Assisedob Jackson and ♪ Melody ♫; In the Collection of ♪ Melody ♫, Applewood, CO, USA.

Görgeyite crystallizes in the monoclinic system in the colours ranging from colourless to white to yellowish. The mineral was first described by K. Mayrhofer in 1953; it was named for R. Görgey von Görg.

This mineral brings one of the messages of Goethe; it assists one in realizing that whatever one can <u>do</u>, or dream that he/she can <u>do</u>, one needs to begin <u>doing</u>, since boldness has genius, power, and magic within it. It is a "stone of confidence", bringing reliance and trust in oneself and furthering ones endeavors.

Görgeyite assists one in maintaining the "work ethic", serving to provide impetus, stimulus, and forward motion in ones career, trade, or vocation.

It can be used to assist one in the manifestation of the qualities representing the intellectual nature which is inherent in humanity; it acts as a stimulus to incite the varying intellectual activities. It promotes both the mentality and the spirituality, providing insight with respect to purpose while promoting ones incentive toward integrity. The energies operating through the mineral tend to awakening the vitality which leads to innovation and action. It also provides insight by which to measure ones progress.

Görgeyite serves to enhance the morality and to initiate guidance with respect to the definition of and reasons behind ones principles.

It further assists one in flowing with the times, encouraging one to be less inflexible, less demanding, and less structured; it can assist one in the actualization of the independence of the "free spirit".

It has been employed to arouse the instinct and to expedite the accomplishments which bring value and contribution to the furtherance of unconditional love.

It can also be used to assist one in accessing and interpreting ancient writings during the meditative state and can provide for stimulus to inspiration. It acts to sharpen the quality of perception, to enhance writing and/or speaking abilities, to promote opportunities for traveling, and to provide for increased protection for passengers during travel.

It can also help one to understand another with respect to versatile relationships, and acts to change ones reality (when consciously directed) so that commitment to another and from another is feasible.

It has been used to assist in the re-birthing process, helping traumatic events and conditions of the past to become obvious and assisting one in the release of same [it is an excellent mineral in cooperative re-birthing].

It has also been used to energize crystal elixirs.

Görgeyite can be used to assist in the relief of personality disorders, nervous disorders, the organs related to speech, and respiratory malfunctions due to nervous afflictions. It has been used to assist in the assimilation of Potassium and in balancing the Sodium within the body.

Vibrates to the number 3.

"THE NATURE OF THE CRYSTAL IS THE ART OF DIVINE PERFECTION"

Bill Hagestein
Cambridge, New Zealand

HERDERITE - PURPLE

HERDERITE - PURPLE - CaBePO$_4$(OH,F); Hardness 5 - 5.5; Locality: In Minas Gerais, Brasil, South America. The Imaging by HP Scanjet, Assisted by Bob Jackson and ♪ Melody ♫; Collection of ♪ Melody ♫, Applewood, CO, USA. Gift of Ligia Barbosa, Minas Gerais, Brasil, South America.

Purple Herderite crystallizes in the monoclinic system in the form of fibrous aggregates, and prismatic and tabular crystals. The mineral was first described by W. Haidinger in 1828; it is named for S.A.W. von Herder. Herderite has been reported in "Love Is In The Earth - A Kaleidoscope Of Crystals" in the colour range of pale yellow and green; the reporting herein is solely for the unique colour purple.

This mineral has been used to incite ones latent forces into action; assisting one in recognizing and in taking appropriate action during the "turning points" in ones life. It furthers impulsive and innovative adventures, and promotes motivation and courage.

It has also been employed to arouse the pursuit of goals and the awareness of ones personal potential, helping one to remain aware of individual objectives. It can also be used to assist one in identifying and removing obstacles which are in the path of ones progression. It furthers ones access to desired seclusion which can be utilized for spiritual, intellectual, or emotional renewal·

Purple Herderite has been used to stimulate control of the fires and to bring spiritual renewal of that which is consumed. Used when engaged in fire-walking, it has served to bring success.

With the mineral, the movement of the Kundalini can be initiated and/or stimulated to continue upward toward the crown chakra. It can also be used to open, to activate, and to energize the crown chakra.

It can be used to enhance the expression of consideration of others, concurrent with personal exhibition of assertiveness. It actually assists one in seeing beyond the situation, and in delving into the ethers for knowledge.

Purple Herderite has also acted to dispel partiality and bias.

This mineral has also been used to assist one to eliminate somnambulistic "consciousness", to be attentive to the moment, and to connect in the conscious state to the present moment. It has acted to bring memories of past-lives when present situations will benefit.

It assists one in being conscious of, and in assimilating, the unusual; again via exploration of the ethereal portion of both ones consciousness and the consciousness of that which is unusual.

Purple Herderite his been used in the treatment of capillary disorders, to relieve of vertigo, intestinal upset, insomnia, migraine headache, and cerebral congestion. It can also be used in the treatment of disorders associated with the adrenal glands, the cerebrum, the retina, and the structure consistency of the teeth. It can assist in the assimilation of Potassium and Iron.

Placement of the mineral upon an area of the body after physical surgery can assist in recovery.

Vibrates to the number 9.

HURÉAULITE - $(Mn,Fe)_5H_2(PO_4)_4 \heartsuit 4H_2O$ or $Mn_5(PO_3OH)_2(PO_4)_2 \heartsuit 4H_2O$; Hardness 3.5; Locality: Mangualde, Portugal. Imaging by HP Scanjet, Assisted by Bob Jackson and ♪ Melody ♫; Collection of ♪ Melody ♫, Applewood, CO, USA.

Huréaulite crystallizes in the monoclinic system. The colour range includes brown, orange, and red. The mineral was first described by F. Alluaud in 1825; it is named for the locality (Heréaux, St. Sylvestre, Haute-Vienne, France, of first discovery.

This mineral has been used to support the removal of the dis-ease from the organs of the body which are located below the waist; one travels with the mineral to the specific affected organ of the body and visually brings the affectation to the surface, surrounding and transmuting it into white light.

Huréaulite holds an energy of action and reaction, conveying strength, daring, physical stability, and constructive and autonomous self-reliance. It helps one to understand the difference between action and reaction, teaching that re-action is that which occurs when one is not centered, and assisting one to remain centered in situations which may require action.

The mineral serves one in maintaining a concentrated focusing during the course of ones daily activities.

It can assist one to shift the mind "out of the way" of growth, bringing insight to the restrictions imposed by the mental processes, and allowing one to open to the actions gleaned from the intuitive realm.

It can also be employed to rid one of deep-seated anger, resentment, hostility, and inner discord.

It has been used to provide for the enhancement of yang qualities and to help one to exercise control over uncontrolled emotions. It further assists in providing courage and endurance.

It can also be used to open, to activate, and to energize the base and sacral chakras.

Huréaulite has also been placed on a written statement of "that which is impeding ones progress" [a written missive is included which states the reason that the barrier is non-functional]; the resultant reward being the dissolution of the impediment.

If ones power animal is an eagle or a hawk, the mineral can stimulate ethereal and/or dream visits by same. The visitations have been conducive to healing and/or to the awakening of the inner forces to actualize that which is desired. It has been reported that the power animal has remained, in some instances, to act as a guide and protector.

The mineral has been used to bring praise to the user, acting to enhance ones stature and prominence.

Huréaulite can be used in the treatment of disorders of the haemoglobin and organs of the lower body, in cleansing the body of toxins, and in detoxification of the lymphatic system. It has been used to assist in ease of child-birth and to ameliorate loss of vitality. As an elixir, it has been used to stimulate hair growth. It has also been used to assist in the assimilation of both Iron and Protein.

Vibrates to the number 3.

♪ FOR EACH REALITY,
THE PATHS ARE MANY ♫

JADE - BOTRYOIDAL

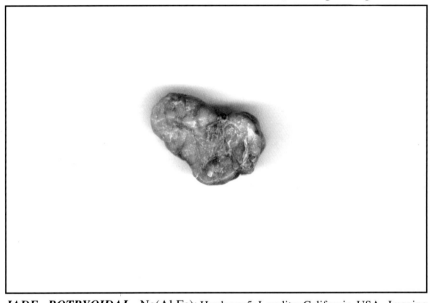

JADE - BOTRYOIDAL - Na(Al,Fe); Hardness 5; Locality: California, USA. Imaging by HP Scanjet, Assisted by Bob Jackson and ♪ Melody ♫; Collection of ♪ Melody ♫, Applewood, CO, USA. Gift Jim Cowan, Oregon, USA.

Botryoidal Jade crystallizes as botryoidal masses. The mineral was first brought to the world by Michael Hendrix; it was named to reflect the botryoidal appearance. The following properties are in addition to those listed in the JADE section of "Love Is In The Earth - A Kaleidoscope Of Crystals Update".

This mineral acts to stimulate the initiation and/or renewal of relationships and partnerships. It imparts versatility to varying circumstances such that one does not feel trepidation, but becomes even more focused when working to re-construct and to re-build that which has degenerated.

Botryoidal Jade can also be used to assist one in the accomplishment of artistic endeavors and scientific quests, via the amplification of ones literary skills. It helps one to conceive novel concepts and theories, furthering the talent for perceiving the a situation in its entirety prior to concluding what the resolution will signify; it stimulates "choice selection", providing insight to the many and varied options which are available in any given circumstance. It can also be used to open, to cleanse, and to energize the heart chakra, providing one with an enhanced appreciation of beauty and the willingness to acknowledge same.

It can also be used to stimulate interactions and/or romance, cooperative efforts [especially for group endeavors], and conflict resolution.

It further promotes the awareness of the cooperation between the Conscious Self and the Higher Self, stimulating the continuance of the direct conveyance of information.

It soothes the chakras and the energies of the body, assisting in the elimination of energy blockages, elevating ones sense of well-being.

Botryoidal Jade has been used to awaken the automatic-writing capabilities and to provide for the reception of information from those involved in the construction and use of ancient structures.

The mineral has been used to promote ease in the attainment of the meditative state and in the performance of yoga, and other meditative arts. It can also sustain a balanced emotional nature, precluding a despondent temperament and assisting one in understanding the inner reasons for depression and/or resentment.

Placement of Botryoidal Jade upon a contract or upon legal papers which represent litigation can serve to promote the positive outcome of same.

It is a configuration for the atmosphere, stimulating cleansing and purification; it has been used in gridding to assist in the stabilization of the total auric field; the arrangement can also be used in conjunction with radionics to facilitate similar results.

This mineral has been used in the relief of Bright's dis-ease, imbalance in the equilibrium, and in the treatment of disorders of the liver, kidneys, the ductless glands, fallopian tubes, and the top portion of the brain.

Vibrates to the number 6.

JASPER - WILLOW CREEK [Astrological Sign of Pisces]

JASPER - WILLOW CREEK - SiO$_2$ with impurities; Hardness 7; Locality: Willow Creek, Idaho, USA. Imaging by HP Scanjet, Assisted by Bob Jackson and ♪ Melody ♫; Collection of ♪ Melody ♫, Applewood, CO, USA. Carving by Bob Rolen, Oregon, USA.

Willow Creek Jasper crystallizes as masses in the colours ranging from light tan to grey to rust. Jasper was first described by J.D. Dana in 1837 and was named from the Greek word for "an opaque coloured variety of quartz". Willow Creek Jasper was named for the locality of origin. The following properties are in addition to those listed in the CHALCEDONY and JASPER sections of "Love Is In The Earth - A Kaleidoscope Of Crystals Update".

This mineral has been used to enhance ones imagination, energy, and evolution. It assists one in attaining resolution to problems, guiding one toward the answers which are available.

Willow Creek Jasper is also quite effective for assisting one in obtaining an elevated state of meditation, inducing higher spiritual powers and promoting spiritual investigation and progression. It precludes indifference to pedantry, and encourages the exploration of the unknown areas of knowledge from which order arises from chaos, and through which enigmatic issues can be understood.

The mineral can also promote the furtherance of leisure time and the enjoyment of same.

It has been an excellent energizer for mineral elixirs, can be used for gridding springs, lakes, and water bottles, bringing the abundant energies and life forces to the composition of the water.

It is an energy for the stabilization of the oceans and waters of the Earth.

It also serves to provide for receptiveness to joint channeling, enhancing both telepathic communication and receipt of information. It has also stimulated the merging of one or more mental and spiritual selves (in rather an ethereal grouping).

Willow Creek Jasper also can provide for insight to the shared soul-connection, assisting in managing circumstances and conditions which arise during the cooperative enterprises which are encountered. It further provides one with a lovely radiant glow, " ... like unto a stone most precious, even like a jasper stone, clear as crystal" (Revelation 21:11).

It further assists participants in a group to maintain receptivity to the other, to be open to compromises, and to speak from the heart with an understanding which is furthered by the energy.

It is a lovely mineral for gridding fish tanks, to further the well-being of the inhabitants.

It has been conducive to the furtherance of absent-healing and to facilitate diagnostic endeavors.

Willow Creek Jasper has been used to balance the fluids of the body, to ameliorate dehydration, and in the treatment of tumors, gout, internal poisoning, pleurisy, and disorders associated with the mucoid membranes, and the synovial fluid. It has assisted in the assimilation of Vitamin A.

Vibrates to the number 7.

**"IS IT CONSCIOUS CONSIGNMENT,
OR CONSCIOUS ALIGNMENT?"**

Gary "Horsefeathers" Wallace
Maryland, USA

"KEYSTONE" - Occurs in many forms, with many chemical compositions and a variety of hardnesses, in many colours, and in many localities; A detailed description is difficult to report; however, it is guaranteed that the reader, guided by wisdom, will intuitively recognize the stone when permitted the encounter; Imaging by HP Scanjet, Assisted by Bob Jackson and ♪ Melody ♫; Collection of ♪ Melody ♫, Applewood, CO, USA.

The "Keystone" shown in the image has been sculpted to resemble a true key. "Keystone" was first coined by several mineral dealers during a mineral show many years ago.

The energies of those participating in the contemporary movement which involves merchandising of minerals to the widespread public have led the "true merchant" to be attracted to "Keystone".

It seems that the moment one definitely commits oneself, then providence moves to the situation and assists one in arranging a transaction which is quite beneficial monetarily and a true benefit to ones stability in prosperity. It truly expands and amplifies one resources in all avenues of acquisition.

The "Keystone" is a "stone of preference", providing encouragement for, and assisting in, ones increase in resources and in the increase of both abundance and the knowledge of acquisition.

It is both a "merchant's stone" and a "consumer's stone". It assists the merchant in providing bargains and provides the consumer with the ability to manifesting discrimination in spending and to recognize the best deals. It is never necessary for the consumer to negotiate when the "Keystone" is present.

The energies assist in the refinement of selection, the discernment in choice, and the discretion in judgment.

The energies are also helpful in bringing very pleasant surprises to those who have never experienced the manifestation of the "Keystone".

The "Keystone" can help one to understand that concepts of expertise and insignificance exist only within ones mind; It furthers the ideals of details and brings an energy of advantage "to leave no stone unturned".

Finding a "Keystone" is a true indication of ones astuteness in business, for the "Keystone" is a true sign of the ever-prevailing easily facilitated compromise that is recognized by few.

It is an excellent energy for the rectification of indecisiveness. It further provides for the development of solutions in arbitration.

It has also been used to stabilize currency exchange and to increase the value of money which is being used as an implement of trade.

It brings an excellent energy to facilitate agreements between parties with respect to "give and take" issues, allowing each of the parties to "come to terms" with the other.

The "Keystone" has been used in the treatment of disorders associated with acceptance of the lesser states. It can also assist in the remediation of half of any situation and/or state of being.

Vibrates to the master number 33 and to the ruling number 1/2.

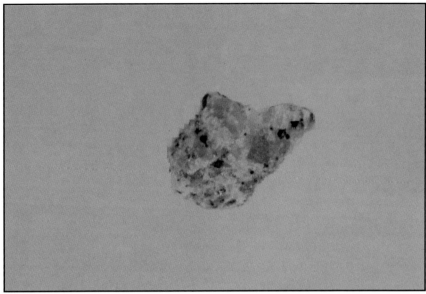

KIMZEYITE - $Ca_3(Zr,Fe,Ti)_2(Si,Al,Fe)_3O_{12}$ or $Ca_3(Zr,Ti)_2(Si,Al,Fe^{+3})_3O_{12}$; Hardness 7; Locality: Magnet Cove, Arkansas, USA. Imaging by HP Scanjet, Assisted by Bob Jackson and ♪ Melody ♫; Collection of ♪ Melody ♫, Applewood, CO, USA. Gift of Bob Jackson, Lakewood, Colorado, USA.

Kimzeyite crystallizes in the cubic system as masses and in garnet configurations. It is actually a zirconiferous garnet with the colour ranging from brown to grey to black. The mineral was first described by C. Milton and L.V. Blade in 1958; it was named for J. Kimzey. The following properties are in addition to those listed in the GARNET section of "Love Is In The Earth - A Kaleidoscope Of Crystals Update".

This mineral can be used to "open the door and let the future enter". It acts to illuminate one from within the center of wisdom, and lights ones path to that which is impending. It also assists one in clarifying and brightening the paths of others, bringing insight for assistance to those on the paths.

It tends toward bringing a freshness to personal relationships and assuring virtuous conduct in the balance of the universal forces.

Kimzeyite acts to eliminate the entrapments of the world of Maya, known to be the ancient world of day-dreams and non-actualization. It furthers the annihilation of old patterns and limitations and assists in the achievement of goal-setting and step-by-step progression.

The mineral serves to help one to recognize karmic situations and to go through these situations unscathed - learning via "seeing" instead of via re-experiencing.

This mineral promotes affiliations and unions: physical, mental, emotional, spiritual, etc. It assists in raising the energies of the base chakra to a higher level of intensity. It creates a dynamic "knowing", via the intuitive self, and allows for the recognition of the areas available (and conducive to ones growth) for travel and adventure.

It also acts to increase ones hardiness and to facilitate continuity in endeavors.

Kimzeyite symbolizes the central energy of the universe, a force constant and perpetual, which is synonymous with the appreciation and with the understanding that one is truly a part of a super-structure which is omniscient and benevolent. It is here to remind us of our goals upon the stairs of progression, and within the human realm.

It also symbolizes impeccability, uniformity (matching the action to the word), and fidelity.

Kimzeyite brings a charisma to the user, assisting one in the smiles of sincerity, the caring of the heart, and the service-orientation of honesty and openness.

In addition, it can be used to provide assistance in the treatment of disorders of the degenerative muscular disorders, carpel tunnel syndrome, the liver, pancreas, and the nerve structures of the lungs. It provides for help in increasing bone stability and in the mending of bones and muscles. It is currently being used in the treatment of macular degeneration.

Vibrates to the number 6.

KINGITE

KINGITE - $Al_3(PO_4)_2(OH,F)_3$ ♥ $9H_2O$ or $Al_3(PO_4)_2(OH)_3$ ♥ $9H_2O$; Hardness Unknown; Locality: Robertstown, South Australia, Australia. Imaging by HP Scanjet, Assisted by Bob Jackson and ♪ Melody ♫; Collection of ♪ Melody ♫, Applewood, CO, USA.

Kingite crystallizes in the triclinic system as masses in a white to grey/tan colour. The mineral was first described by K. Norrish, L.E.R. Rogers, and R.E. Shapter in 1956; it is named for D. King.

This mineral supports one in thinking, that which no one has yet contemplated, about that which everyone has seen. It actually brings the ability for one to have a novel look at an old situation/thing/concept.

It further produces a sensation of discovery which is initiated in the depths of ones consciousness, providing an impetus for, and impression that "things are moving". Moreover, the thin curtain between the distress of ignorance and a very clear vision, is dispelled.

Kingite represents growth and acts to bring happiness and virtue. It assists in producing the actualization of ambitions, calmness and balance in decision-making, and discrimination in actions.

It can be used to inspire "returning" to ones origin, the origin being that which is immediately prior to this lifetime. It assists one in recognizing the karmic patterns and the lessons one has chosen, promoting acceptance of responsibility for ones reality.

It assists one in building structures within ones life, in organizing systems, and establishing basic foundations for personal development. It can also be used to assist one in the conservation of resources and in the attainment of prestige via tenacity and continuance of action. It assists in the relief of inhibition, providing for equilibrium of the emotions.

If ones power animal is an snake or a spider, the mineral can stimulate ethereal and/or dream visits by same. The visitations have been conducive to healing and/or to the awakening of the inner forces which are conducive to the actualization of that which is desired. The messages may also supply information concerning deception or duplicity. In the situation of the snake, the movement of the Kundalini can be initiated and/or stimulated to continue upward toward the crown chakra.

Kingite can further assist one in understanding limitations and in subsequently removing same; it can also be used to produce the acceptance of trust, responsibility, and practicality.

The mineral can assist in the control of the emotional nature and can stimulate patience and perseverance. It has been used to grid places of ritual and ceremony to bring protection. It has also been used to grid vegetation, to produce bountiful and healthy yields.

It is a mineral which brings an energy of defining and correcting, of defining and acting.

Kingite has been used in the treatment of disorders associated with the bladder, spleen, acid formations in the joints, the sympathetic nervous system, kidneys, gall bladder, liver, transverse colon, and the pneumogastric nerve. It can also assist in the amelioration of CFS, polio, ruptures, gangrene, and epilepsy. It can be used to stimulate the growth and maintenance of hair and beards.

Vibrates to the number 3.

KURNAKOVITE

KURNAKOVITE - $MgB_3O_3(OH)_5 \heartsuit 5H_2O$); Hardness 3; Locality: Kern Co., California, USA. Imaging by HP Scanjet, Assisted by Bob Jackson and ♪ Melody ♫; In Collection of ♪ Melody ♫, Applewood, CO, USA.

Kurnakovite crystallizes in the triclinic system as masses in colours ranging from clear to white to yellowish-white. The mineral was first described by M.N. Godlevsky in 1940; it is named for N.S. Kurnakov.

This mineral is one for combining the energies of the solar plexus with the crown chakra, stimulating the mind to instill both wisdom and theoretical judgment.

It assists one to recognize that which misleads, both within the self and within others; it further supports ones decision-making process when one is beset by skepticism such that one regains confidence in personal abilities.

Providing liberty from that which restricts, and from the conventional which ossifies the skills of innovation and discovery, it facilitates the command of the mind to free it from anxiety and concern.

Providing an energy for one to evaluate mistakes, it helps one to discover new insights and to avoid the resultant fear which could impede one in the commencement of new thinking.

The energies of Kurnakovite are said to be equal to Socratic methodology, such that the focus of "questioning" all and everything is encouraged and latent ideas and concepts are developed. It also tends to bring the knowledge of the "right" questions and facilitates "the asking" when one is beset by confusion propagated by another.

The mineral serves to release one from outmoded methods and acts to steady the intellect, helping to free one of negative thought patterns. It helps one to identify and to apply that which is consequential to further ones progress along the spiritual path, functioning to discontinue any sensation of confinement, even if physical confinement is a reality. With Kurnakovite, seclusion and hermetic activities, are a pleasure.

It has also been used with horses, cows, mules, and bulls to allay anger, stubbornness and fear.

It tends to contribute a certainty to feelings the self and helps one to courageously brave any danger which is in ones path; it also provides for realization of the wisdom to prevent dangerous situations.

Acting initially at the crown chakra, it can also be used to align the chakras with the subtle bodies, enhancing physical stability.

Kurnakovite acts to bring the energy to assist one to enhance conservation within ones life, and to facilitate acceptance of obligations. It provides a greater than gentle reminder of ones economical condition and serves to guide one toward reconciliation of ones funds.

It has been used in the treatment of disorders related to elimination, and to assist in bringing the energy to facilitate cleaning of arteries. It can also be used to support the elimination of fatty deposits, to regulate cholesterol, and to diminish the conditions relative to leukemia and toxicity of the intestinal tract and the liver.

Vibrates to the number 3.

KYANITE - With FUCHSITE [Astrological Sign of Libra]

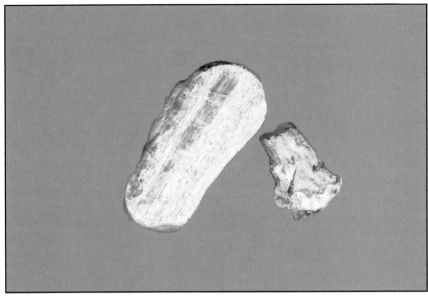

KYANITE With FUCHSITE - A combination of Kyanite (Al_2SiO_5) and Fuchsite (($H,K)AlSiO_4$ with Chromium); Hardness 2-2.5 (Fuchsite) and 5.5 - 7 (Kyanite); Locality: Russia (left specimen); New Zealand (right specimen). Imaging by HP Scanjet, Assisted by Bob Jackson and ♪ Melody ♫; Collection of ♪ Melody ♫, Applewood, CO, USA. Gifts of Water Levin, USA (right specimen) and Craig M. Williams and Andrew Hodge, New Zealand (left specimen).

Kyanite with Fuchsite crystallizes as a combination of twisted fibrous structures/masses/blades and plates/scales/masses. The colour range is a amalgam of blue and green, sometimes including the other varying colours of Kyanite.

Although both Kyanite and Fuchsite have been reported previously and separately in "Love Is In The Earth - A Kaleidoscope Of Crystals Update", this combination is quite unusual and is, hence, reported here.

The following properties are in addition to those listed in the KYANITE and FUCHSITE sections of "Love Is In The Earth - A Kaleidoscope Of Crystals Update". This combination brings an energy of harmony and commonality within the self, and between the self and others.

♪ 156 ♫

It acts to bring both love and beauty to the exterior and the interior of ones being while providing for magnetic attraction between kindred spirits. It furthers the forming of attachments and the continuity of love affairs, bringing the actualization of "love is the victor over all". It opens, energizes, and cleanses the heart chakra and the throat chakra, providing for speaking words of love and kindness.

It further acts to align all chakras and to bring life to social and emotional situations. It provides for the activation of both receptivity and dynamic attraction, assisting one in recognizing that which is being attracted via emotional actions and guiding one toward the furtherance of attracting that which is desired.

It can be used to help one attract people, experiences, or objects which have been defined as necessary to ones growth, stimulating ones creative emanations and furthering creativity in a simplistic manner.

Kyanite with Fuchsite can be used to enhance ones attributes, to provide for diplomacy between the self and others, to facilitate the vocalization of ones thoughts and feelings, and to assist in the resolution of personal conflict. It can serve to permeate the mystique which surrounds another, allowing for the recognition of the bases of action and subtleties.

It has been used for enhancing both the yin and the yang qualities, to balance any divisions in same, and to dispel disparities in ones being.

When more than one person holds the mineral, it can be used to promote recognition of the love connection between the physical manifestation of each and the spiritual being of each.

The Kyanite with Fuchsite combination is an excellent energizer for salves, elixirs, and tinctures.

The energy of the mineral has been applied to the re-establishment of the freedom of movement in the body, assisting the body in self-healing. It can be used to stimulate the thymus, and in the treatment of lower back pain, TMJ syndrome, obesity, and nervous system/veinular dysfunctions.

Vibrates to the number 5.

"GIVE ATTENTION TO CONTEXT, NOT MEANING."

Lynn Fielding
Washington, USA

LINDGRENITE [Astrological Sign of Aquarius]

LINDGRENITE - $Cu_3(MoO_4)_2(OH)_2$; Hardness 4.5; Locality: Pinal Co., Arizona, USA. Imaging by HP Scanjet, Assisted by Bob Jackson and ♪ Melody ♬; Collection of ♪ Melody ♬, Applewood, CO, USA.

Lindgrenite crystallizes in the monoclinic system as masses and small acicular crystals with the colour range including green and yellow-green. The mineral was first described by C. Palache in 1935; it was named for W. Lindgren.

This mineral provides for a total healing and protective environment, acting to transmit a green healing essence around the user and/or the area where the mineral is placed.

It serves to stimulate altruistic pursuits, providing insight with respect to the ideal toward which the world would progress in order to produce a loving environment and humane-ness to all. It allows one to recognize and to practice that which would bring the highest good to the reality of this lifetime, and can be used to inspire persistence in following a chosen course of action; it has been used in promoting convergent concepts and in the development and in the implementation of ideas, further serving to

♪ 160 ♬

assist one in the correlation of information and application of same to systematic approaches.

Lindgrenite can promote visions of ideas, allowing for the reception of visionary concepts of the future such that one can implement the concepts while maintaining a view of personal goals; the insight produced serves to teach one that charitable goals are compatible with personal goals.

It can be used to add the quality of "faith" to ones nature, to facilitate an enhanced appreciation of life, to promote logical and intelligent thinking and speaking, and to stimulate the skills of communication and, of interaction. The mineral actually helps one to speculate, anticipate, foresee, and foretell.

Lindgrenite promotes the knowledge and the amplification of abilities for, the disciplines of astrology, astronomy, theosophy, and astral travel. It assists one in the exploration of the ethers and promotes the access to, and the understanding of, the Akashic records.

The mineral also promotes attracting and maintaining loyalty to, and from, friends and acquaintances. It assists one in the reduction of social obligations, producing an appearance of options for the user.

It has also been used to, via placement upon travel itineraries, to promote safe and enjoyable travel.

Lindgrenite can serve to promote tolerance of others, assisting one to gain emancipation from restrictive situations via the recognition, understanding, and application of charitable feelings and actions.

It further assists in the appreciation of paradoxes and in the continuance of the free will. It has been used to assist groups in celebrating together that which will allow them to promote the highest good for humanity.

Lindgrenite has been used in the treatment of arthritis, the liver, silicosis, irregularities in heartbeat, and anemia. It can be used to smooth and soothe the skin and to lessen wrinkles in the skin.

Vibrates to the number 9.

"LINGHAM"

"LINGHAM" - A Jasper (SiO_2 with impurities) which is found in a tributary (Narmado River) to the Ganges River and in the Ganges River in India; Hardness 7; Imaging by HP Scanjet, Assisted by Bob Jackson and ♪ Melody ♫; In the Collection of ♪ Melody ♫, Applewood, CO, USA. Gift of Michael Flaherty, Minnesota, USA.

The Lingham crystallizes as masses which are configured as a solid tube, rounded on both ends - the smoothness of the structure is due to natural river-tumbling. It is also known as the "Shiva Lingham"; the correct name being the "Narmadeshvara Lingham". It should be noted that the buyer should "beware" - many Linghams are currently being fabricated and represented as natural.

This formation is a "stone of the Kundalini", and is defined in Eastern Indian philosophy to be the sleeping serpent which rests at the base of the spine, dwelling deep within the confines of ones being. It serves to activate the movement of the sacred energy which is slumbering within the self, so that one may comprehend the profound mysteries of enlightenment which lead one to spiritual consciousness and to the actualization of perfection. The Lingham stimulates the conduction of the energies of the body into a subtle channel which traverses the interior of the spine, awakening each of the major energy centers on the path to the crown chakra. As each major energy center is awakened, the energy flow emanates through the body, additionally activating the minor chakras.

Utilization of the formation provides for the upward movement of a concentration of energy, which stimulates and opens each chakra during the successive progression. One will become aware of the location of placement for the "Lingham" via recognition of the following indications:

♥   Movement through the first three chakras: awareness to properly regulate and to direct ones experiences upon the physical plane.

♥   Movement through the heart chakra: awareness of the world divinity.

♥   Movement through the throat chakra: recognition of a oneness with the ethereal body, conveying purification and renewal of the physical body.

♥   Movement through the third-eye: freedom from the limitations of the senses, understanding of the Higher Self, and maintenance of distinction between the Conscious Self and the Higher Self.

♥   Movement into and through the crown chakra: transcendence of the action and knowledge of duality, merging with "All That Is" and with the fulfillment and dissolution of the worlds of sound, form, and the mind.

Each application of the "Lingham" will provide for the progression of the movement of the Kundalini through the chakras such that ultimately one may feel the movement from the base chakra to the crown chakra.

The "Lingham" is also auspicious for construction and for conquest, and has been used to balance the male qualities (yang).

This formation can also be used to balance the fluids of the body, to alleviate back pain, and to assist in the alignment of the spine. It has additionally been used to relieve menopausal symptoms, to increase fertility, and to dispel frigidity in males, and in the amelioration of disorders of the prostate.

Vibrates to the numbers 1 (Lingham), 6 (Shiva Lingham) and 8 (Narmadeshvara Lingham).

LITHARGE

LITHARGE - PbO; Hardness 5.5 - 8; Locality: Belmont Mine, Tonopah, Arizona, USA. Imaging by HP Scanjet, Assisted by Bob Jackson and ♪ Melody ♫; Collection of ♪ Melody ♫, Applewood, CO, USA.

Litharge crystallizes in the tetragonal system as masses and scales. The colour range includes yellow-orange, orange, and red. The mineral was first described by A.S. Larsen in 1917.

This mineral has been used to access ones secondary origins; specifically, providing <u>not</u> past-life information, but information with respect to where ones commencement into <u>this</u> world began (i.e., ones first life in <u>this</u> world). Additionally, as directed, it can provide information with respect to ones first life in other worlds. (The operative word is "first").

Litharge assists one in recognizing others who have shared ones first-lives, further defining multiple-souls (same soul, different bodies) during those first-lives such that one knows with whom, and for what, ones experiences are focused. Expediting the gaining of knowledge with respect to the issues and situations one planned to learn throughout the cycle from first to last lives, it also serves one in recognizing which issues and which situations and lessons have not yet been completed during this life.

This mineral is a practical grounding stone and allows one to feel relaxed and "at-home" in all environments. It is a useful stone for business-travelers, as well as pleasure-travelers. It allows one to easily adapt to conditions and to modify ones behavior, as required; it enables one to realize that change is transient and helps one to be accommodating.

Providing for the effectiveness to manage the conditions of ones reality, it allows one to recognize that which one can change and assists one in releasing that which one chooses to release from ones being.

Litharge mineral encourages growth and acts to augment the strength of wisdom to all areas of relationships. It can be utilized to help one with decision-making and to initiate contrasts in ones life. It can be use to alleviate introversion, to provide tact, and to instill cooperation. It is excellent to use in the ceremonial aspect, promoting a bond between participants while sustaining grounding of the energy centers. It also provides for guidance and assured-ness to activities.

Litharge is excellent in both inspiring and intensifying communication; it is quite favorable to all facets of correspondence. It also assists one in the art of unabridged listening. It has been used to balance the left-brain and right-brain, supporting originality in the intellect as well as supporting intelligently directed creativity.

It helps to align the network of the nervous system and to provide for free flow of energy.

Litharge has been used in the treatment of insomnia, in disorders affecting the coordination of voluntary movements, and to ameliorate mental discontinuity, and to reduce fleshy areas of the body. It can provide strength and renewal to the inner organs and skeletal system, and has been used to "draw-out" energies of toxicity and disorderly growth.

Do not prepare an elixir via the normal method.

Vibrates to the master number 44.

"...And blessed be my rock..."
Psalms 18:46 and 2 Samuel 22:47

"...And upon this rock I shall build my church..."
Matthew 16:18

"...And it fell not, for it was founded upon a rock."
Matthew 7:25

MENDOZAVILITE

MENDOZAVILITE - $Na(Ca,Mg)_2[Fe_6(PO_4)_2(PMo_{11}O_{39})(OH,Cl)_{10}]♥33H_2O$ or $NaCa_2Fe_6(PO_4)_2(PMo_{11}O_{39})(OH,Cl)_{10}]♥33H_2O$; Image shows mineral in molybdate-schorl matrix; Hardness 1.5; Locality: Rustler Mine, Tooele Co., Utah (Second World Occurrence - 1st in USA). Imaging by HP Scanjet, Assisted by Bob Jackson and ♪ Melody ♫; Collection of ♪ Melody ♫, Applewood, CO, USA.

Mendozavilite crystallizes as masses with the colour ranging from yellow to orange. Although it is not a molybdate, it occurs naturally with same. The mineral was first described by S.A. Williams in 1986; it is named for H. Mendoza Avila.

This mineral supports one in concern for the other, bringing an energy which furthers both empathy and compassion for the crises and dilemmas which occur outside of the self.

It has been used to facilitate continuity when one experiences a break in ones "train of thought", bringing the consciousness in focus with the initial issue of communication (internal or external). Specifically, it furthers continuity of concentration, deliberation/problem-solving, and attentiveness.

Mendozavilite can be used to both repel and protect against negativity. It acts to guard one from victimization by the negative energy of another and/or by the negative energy of a situation. It has also been used as an energy deflector, being an excellent stone for those with potential for exposure to excessive amounts of radiation.

It provides for an increase in ones physical vitality, emotional stability, and intellectual acuity, and can maintain ones "spirits" even in conditions which appear to emit the messages of sorrow or despair.

As a protective stone against "spells" which are cast by the negative side of another, during the time period of practicing shamanism, it was a special stone to the Ute Indians; not only dissipating the "spell", but energizing the intended target and increasing the vitality of same. It was also used by these tribes in exploration of lands, assisting in guiding the user to the desired location.

It is also used to activate grounding between the intellect and ones sexuality, producing a mindfulness concerning safe-sex and procreation. It can further assist one in considering the benefits, rewards, and/or detriments of action or non-action.

The mineral can also be used to enhance the force of ones personal action. It acts to teach one to initiate optimistically, attaining independence, while maintaining the pioneering spirit of innovation.

Mendozavilite can instill a bond between the two people such that a recognized identical pathway to a specific goal is delineated as a clearly marked step-wise methodology.

It has been used to stimulate the building of the body, in the treatment of constriction and blockages in the veins and blood flow, to balance the acidity/alkalinity of the body, and to eliminate free-radical oxides. It has also been used in the amelioration of disorientation, and in the balancing of the adrenal glands.

Do not prepare an elixir via the normal method.

Vibrates to the number 2.

MICA - GREEN With QUARTZ   [Astrological Sign of Aquarius]

MICA - GREEN With QUARTZ - CaMgAl(Al$_3$SiO$_{10}$)(OH)$_2$ (Clintonite) with SiO$_2$ (Quartz); Hardness 3.5 - 6; Locality: Minas Gerais, Brasil, South America. Imaging by HP Scanjet, Assisted by Bob Jackson and ♪ Melody ♫; In the Collection of ♪ Melody ♫, Applewood, CO, USA.

Green Mica is Clintonite (in the Margarite subgroup of the Mica group) which crystallizes as a trioctahedral mica with distortion of the layer units. The colour is a beautiful lime green. Lime-coloured Mica was first described by E.S. Dana in 1892. Margarite was first described by J.N. Fuchs in 1823; it was named from the Pearl-Mica which had been described by F. Mohs. Clintonite was first described by W.W. Mather in 1828; it was named for DeWitt Clinton. The following properties are in addition to those listed in the MICA, MUSCOVITE, and QUARTZ sections of "Love Is In The Earth - A Kaleidoscope Of Crystals Update".

This mineral represents the personification of the Earth and the physical world. It can assist one in dispensing with irregular patterns and in attainment of universal consciousness. It enables one to move beyond the typical realm of actualization and to expand awareness of that which is available in the kingdom of perfection.

Green Mica with Quartz can further one in the courage to be "different", acting as a catalyst for the manifestation of the unique aspects of oneself and for ones personal growth and the empowerment for one to go beyond that which is common and ordinary. It promotes experimentation and enhances spontaneity, bringing a unique perspective to ones visions and actualization of the future.

It further promotes ones detachment as an observer, allowing one to remain detached and assisting one in decision-making. It helps one to experience a total departure from ones lifestyle, enhancing the commencement and continuance of a fresh and dynamic life.

The mineral can also facilitate the accomplishment of changes which will enable one to progress toward reward. It encourages articulation of ideas, independence, and the elimination of compulsions; it assists in investigations and debating. It can be used to enhance the protective forces when one is physically moving, and serves to assist one in safety during aviation, bicycling, and motorcar driving. It facilitates competency in the chiropractic field and in the realms of chemistry and alchemy.

It has been used to grid areas, written missives explaining the disorder, and/or photographs/images of areas of disorder, bringing a reflection via the third-eye which assists in stabilization and ease of transition.

Unconventional attachments and ideas can also be discerned, evaluated, and rectified via the assistance of the mineral. It has also been used to enhance education in the geological sciences, and to furthering the pursuits of attorneys and statesmen.

Green Mica with Quartz can help one to attain a constitution which defies physical disorders. It has enabled one to consume alcohol without exhibiting the effects. It has been used to protect/improve the liver. It can also be used to assist in lessening fatty deposits and restrictions in the joints. It has been used in the treatment of malaria/fever-producing disorders, electrolytic imbalance, and to ameliorate conditions of malnutrition. It is an excellent mineral to be used with drug-less healing.

Vibrates to the numbers 7 (Green Mica-Quartz), 1 (Green Margarite-Quartz), and 3 (Green Clintonite-Quartz).

MICA - YELLOW

MICA - YELLOW - $KAl_2(Si_3Al)O_{10}(OH)_2$ (Muscovite) with minor Fe, Na, Mg, and P, and with traces of Ca, Mn, and Ti, and with slight enrichment with H_2O (Water), and with slight enrichment by 13 elemental metals; Hardness 2.5 - 3; Locality: Minas Gerais, Brasil, South America. Imaging by HP Scanjet, Assisted by Bob Jackson and ♪ Melody ♫; Collection of ♪ Melody ♫, Applewood, CO, USA. Gift of Bonnie and Marv Seeman and Annette Blansett, Texas, USA.

Yellow Mica is a general Muscovite sheet silicate which crystallizes as plates, scales, and masses. Muscovite was first described by J.D. Dana in 1850; the name was derived from Muscovy glass. The colour is due to oxidized Iron. The following properties are in addition to those listed in the MUSCOVITE and IRON sections of "Love Is In The Earth - A Kaleidoscope Of Crystals Update".

This mineral brings the qualities of balancing of the inner masculine self, the nurturing of the self and/or environment [e.g., via gridding], the stabilization of fluctuations in the body, mind, and/or emotions, and the stimulation of the self toward growth of the inner child.

In Zen practice, the mineral has been used to assist one in attainment of oneness with nation. Meditation and opening the self to spiritual development can also be facilitated. It has been used to stimulate the opening of the pathway to the Higher Self and to subsequent renewal of all aspects of the physical self.

It has been used in telepathic communications to bring information from those who have been separated by thousands of miles. It further encourages a pragmatic approach to ones efforts.

Yellow Mica tends to further ones knowledge and to support a beneficial outcome during activities involving speculation.

It has been used to discourage introversion, to encourage the acceptance of self-approval, and to stimulate the aspects of creativity, delineating the experiences and realities that are conducive to the awakening of the personal self, and the expansion of ones "glorification" via the actualization of ones innate attributes.

The mineral can be used to further the development of personal power, to stimulate generosity, and to mobilize of the features of "luck". It truly facilitates the continuance of states which are attained.

Yellow Mica is currently being used to assist in the physical renewal of the rain forests in South America.

The mineral can stimulate peaceful transformation of the imbalances in ones physical and emotional bodies and can assist in the elimination of pre-judgment tendencies and in the furtherance of correspondence between all involved. It also fosters cooperation in the environment of social gatherings.

This mineral can be used to assist in the relief of burns, inflammation, dizziness, skin eruptions, hot flashes, and tremors. It has been used in the treatment of disorders associated with the bone marrow, the pituitary gland, the adrenal glands, and the endocrine system. It can facilitate the recuperative processes, and the assimilation of protein. It has also been used to grid areas to protect against plagues.

Vibrates to the number 1 (Yellow Mica), and the master number 66 (Yellow Muscovite).

MORAESITE

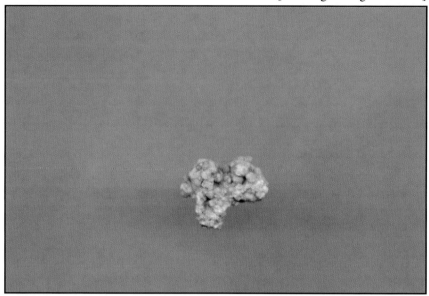

MORAESITE - $Be_2PO_4(OH)$ ♥ $4H_2O$; Hardness Unknown; Locality: In Minas Gerais, Brasil, South America. The Imaging by HP Scanjet, with assistance by Bob Jackson and ♪ Melody ♫; Collection of ♪ Melody ♫, Applewood, CO, USA.

Moraesite crystallizes in the monoclinic system as white-to-tan acicular crystals. The mineral was first described by M.L. Lindberg, W.T. Pecora, and A.L. de Barbosa in 1953; it is named for Dr. L.J. de Moraes.

This mineral has been used by merchants to dispel "lookers" - those people who have nothing better to do than to pretend interest and have no interest at all. It can also bring the same effect when one is beginning a relationship.

It is a "stone of abundance", abundance in remembering dreams, expanding the mystical side of the self, and enhancing the psychic abilities. It assists one in maintaining concentration, in utilizing intuition and telepathy, and in attaining proficiency in mysticism and the metaphysical arts. It has also been used to stimulate the trance state and to produce medium-ship such that the medium is the observer and is in total control, with total memory, of all that transpires. It has been used to further ones proficiency in, and understanding of, the bases supporting alchemy, astral travel, access to the Akashic records, clairsentience, clairvoyance, visioning, divination, dream consciousness, future-telling, hypnotism, white magic, the I Ching, the tarot/Neo-tarot, telepathy, the use of talismen, psychic research, and psychometry. It furthers the study/ comprehension of esoteric theosophy and assists one in obtaining and maintaining contact with the ancient teachers of same.

Moraesite further assists one in the transcendence of barriers and in the exhibition of confidence to heal, to be healed, and to accept the unification with "All That Is" as perfection. The mineral brings the knowledge that "the universe will provide", helping to actualize that which is necessary and sufficient for the furtherance of the perfect self. It also assists one in the application of pantheistic philosophy to ones life, providing insight to the actualization of flawlessness and the connection between the universal power and the self.

It can assist in the decline of claustrophobia and can promote the desire for freedom and independence. It furthers the situations which will be conducive to attaining total emancipation.

It can also assist in the transition from one state to another on the physical, emotional, and/or spiritual planes. It also stimulates entry to, and maintenance of, the meditative state, allowing for connection and interaction between the Conscious Self, the Inner Self, and the Higher Self.

The mineral can assist one in attaining and maintaining the trance state, allowing for the alliance between the self and those of other planes and spiritual worlds; it has successfully promoted contact with the ancient teachers from Atlantis, Lemuria, and Mu. It has also been used to contact those spiritual guides who have provided information and guidance from the days of the Mound Builders and the Mayans.

Moraesite can be used in the treatment anorexia, excess weight-loss, and disorders the parathyroid system, the pituitary gland, and the pineal gland. It can also assist in the amelioration of addictions, lethargy, catalepsy, mononucleosis, and to provide a barrier against contagious dis-ease.

Vibrates to the number 6.

MOZARKITE

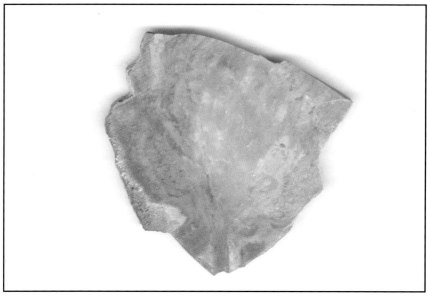

MOZARKITE - A multi-coloured chert from the Ozark Mountains; Hardness 6 - 7; Locality: Ozark Mountains, (Missouri and Arkansas) USA. Imaging by HP Scanjet, Assisted by Bob Jackson and ♪ Melody ♫; Collection of ♪ Melody ♫, Applewood, CO, USA. Gift of Leslie "Wild Child" Bowen, Arkansas, USA.

Mozarkite is the state rock of Missouri and is a vari-coloured Ordovician Chert. It crystallizes as masses and is named for the Ozark Mountains in Missouri. The mineral was first described in Lapidary Journal in 1977. (Mozarkite has sometimes been known as "Ozarkite"; however, "Ozarkite" is actually a white Thompsonite.) The following properties are in addition to those listed in the CHERT section of "Love Is In The Earth - A Kaleidoscope Of Crystals Update".

This mineral has been used to carry awareness and communication from one point to another, stimulating both communication and connections. It assists one in rational thought, in mental concentration, and in the refinement and understanding of information.

It is an energy for the "seeker", supporting one on the many paths through which one may venture. It assists one in astral travel and enhances ones psychic awareness. It has also been employed to stimulate rapid thought transfer, providing the sender with energies to expedite the mental transmittal of messages.

It serves to kindle the intellect and to provide stimulus to intelligent articulation and to comprehensive understanding during listening, bringing the cognitive processes toward the maximum proficiency. As Plato said, "thoughts rule the world" and this mineral is used as the cerebral activator and the teacher that "thoughts are things".

It enables one to understand that one is the totality of thought, feelings, and actions; it allows one to recognize that experience grows from thought and that experience can be changed to the actualization of all positive incidents as choices upon which ones life is built.

Mozarkite can be also be used to stimulate "right-brain" creativity and receptivity. It is excellent for reinforcing public communication and interaction; introversion is diminished and interactive-ness is maintained.

It furthers pursuits in astrological fields, sharpening the senses and perceptions.

It further has enhanced precision in creativity and exactness in performance.

It has been used in a dowsing activity where it is placed upon a photograph/image and the thoughts of the person and/or the environment in the photograph/image are brought to the mind of the user.

Mozarkite has been used to promote the alleviation of worry, such that one may "put away" the concern for a period of time.

This mineral has been used to assist in relief from vertigo and nervous disorders, promoting composure. It can also be used in the treatment of speech impediments, lassitude, disorders of the vocal cords, to promote manual dexterity and motor skills, and to dispel the fear of needles. Recreational drug-usage has been suspended via the energy of Mozarkite.

Vibrates to the number 1.

MURMANITE

MURMANITE - $Na_2(Ti,Nb)_2Si_2O_9nH_2O$ or $Na_3(Ti,Nb)_4O_4(Si_2O_7)_2$ ♥ $4H_2O$; Hardness 2 - 3; Locality: Julianehaab District, Greenland. Imaging by HP Scanjet, Assisted by Bob Jackson and ♪ Melody ♫; Collection of ♪ Melody ♫, Applewood, CO, USA. Gift of Don Toth, Ohio, USA.

Murmanite crystallizes in the triclinic system as tabular masses in the colour violet. The mineral was first described by A.E. Fersman in 1923; it is named for the Murman Coast in Russia, where it was first discovered.

This mineral has been used in the authentication of intent and in the presentation and fortification of ones personal intentions. It assists one in minimizing arrogance and haughtiness with respect to ones abilities and/or possessions.

Providing a stimulus for the mind, it further enhances ones structure of thought, adaptability, and consistency, it is also a stone for expression, reflection, and writing. It assists one in charismatically attracting that which is desired and in amplifying practicality and freedom. It further acts to reduce ingratiating behavior.

Removing the ambiguity from ones nature, it fosters the ability to dispel hesitancy, vacillation, and uncertainty in ones conclusions, decisions, and actions.

It assists one to act in a gentle, kind, and free manner, bringing romance to ones life, through the stimulus of courtesy, accommodation, and refinement - without co-dependency.

Murmanite been said to have been used by the early civilizations of Greenland to bring both riches and comfort, and has promoted contact, during meditation, with the ancient civilizations of same.

Carrying the mineral has assisted in the increase of "reading" people and in understanding exactly what is being communicated (on the "silent" level). The mineral has further assisted one in the ability to empathize with others and to understand exactly what is being felt, more on a spiritual plane; subsequently, the application to the mental and material plane is enhanced.

It can be used to stimulate reasoning capabilities and is excellent in promoting success in rationality. It tends to provide the energy to assist ones intelligence to reassert itself over emotion, no matter how objectionable ones position is at the time.

It has been shown to bring a violet ray to the aura in such a way that even if the colours of the aura are not predominately in this range, the violet tends to be revealed through the veil of the other colours. In addition, a layer of violet is shown to underlie the aura of the total body. (Kirlian photography has been used to determine and to validate this occurrence).

Murmanite has been used in the treatment of emotional disorders, to ameliorate disorders associated with the regulatory organs, and elevated body temperature. It has also been shown to stimulate the production of negative ions to assist in the maintenance of well-being, to assist in the assimilation of minerals, and to support treatments for cellular cancer and multiple sclerosis.

Vibrates to the number 6.

**"DON'T JUDGE YOURSELF
BY WHAT YOU DON'T DO,
BUT BY WHAT YOU DO!"**
Julie Murphy
Washington, USA

NATROJAROSITE [Astrological Sign of Capricorn]

NATROJAROSITE - $NaFe_3(SO_4)_2(OH)_6$ or $Na_2Fe_6(OH)_{12}(SO_4)_4$; Hardness 3; Locality: Lincoln County, Nevada, USA. Imaging by HP Scanjet, Assisted by Bob Jackson and ♪ Melody ♫; Collection of ♪ Melody ♫, Applewood, CO, USA.

Natrojarosite crystallizes in the rhombohedral system in minute tabular crystals and a glistening powder comprised of these minute crystals. The colour ranges from yellow to brown. The mineral was first described by W.F. Hillebrand and S.L. Penfield in 1902; it is named as the sodium analogue of Jarosite; Jarosite was named for Z. Jaros.

This mineral can be used to stimulate sensitivity and responsiveness, encouraging behavioral adjustments and banishing insecurities.

It serves to activate the conscious awareness of dreams, assisting in the interpretation and providing insight to action. It promotes psychic receptivity, medium-ship, and extra-sensory perception.

It has been used to provide illumination to both universal mysteries and to those mysteries which are a part of ones reality, being conducive to stimulating images of the answers and solutions to the puzzles. It helps one to look at the overall picture as parts which are manageable and understandable.

It has also been employed to stimulate emotional support and physical support. It can be also be used to initiate change in stressful and/or pleasant situations of which one is a part, and has assisted in relief from emotional trauma.

Natrojarosite can be used for expansion of ones receptivity to metaphysical occurrences, such that one is aware of the occurrence.

Specific information from the Mayan civilization, with respect to the ancient methods of healing and prevention of dis-ease, has been made available during the utilization of this mineral.

The mineral has been used to promote weather stabilization and to incite specific weather changes, when directed.

The energy of the mineral has acted to bring success to activities associated with preservation (of foods, flowers, the self). It has also been used in a dowsing mode to determine whether a food which is labeled as "natural" is, indeed, natural, with no preservatives. It has been used to secure "food storage", mini-storage, and storage of seasonable materials (e.g., clothing).

Natrojarosite brings the energy of purification and protects against contamination. It further assists one in being in the natural state of beauty (i.e., no camouflage of the self or deception by the self) and in harmony with the Earth.

The mineral can be used to assist in the relief of allergies and asthma. It has been used to prevent dehydration of the body, to balance the blood serum level and the basic minerals of the body, and to ameliorate female disorders, infertility, measles, and disorders relative to myopic and near-sighted conditions.

Do not prepare an elixir via the normal method for the powdered form.

Vibrates to the number 3.

"NEBULA STONE"

"NEBULA STONE" - A combination of Aegirine ($NaFeSi_2O_6$), Potassium Feldspar (general formula $(K,Na,Ca,Ba,NH_4)(Si,Al)_4O_8$), Quartz ($SiO_2$), and traces of Epidote ($Ca_2FeAl_2(Si_2O_7)(SiO_4)(O,OH)_2$); Hardness 6 - 7; Locality: North America (further locality information is proprietary). Imaging by HP Scanjet, Assisted by Bob Jackson and ♪ Melody ♫; Collection of ♪ Melody ♫, Applewood, CO, USA. Gift of Ron and Karen Nurnberg, Arizona, USA.

The "Nebula Stone" crystallizes as smooth-rounded masses, is a black-green/grey stone with green rounded spherules; the formation of the stone was due to metamorphic conditions, providing sufficient high pressure to affect the configuration. Comprised of Aegirine, Potassium Feldspar, Quartz, and traces of Epidote, the Aegirine exhibits pleochroism and is clustered in a feather structure. It was first described by Ron and Karen Nurnberg, and was named by them.

The following properties are in addition to those listed in the AEGIRINE, FELDSPAR, QUARTZ, and EPIDOTE sections of "Love Is In The Earth - A Kaleidoscope Of Crystals Update". The Nebula Stone has been shown to assist the mind in remembering small kindnesses during times of tragedy, further assisting in the sustainment of the physical form to facilitate and assist the user to adhere to the memory during the confusion and despair of these events.

It has been used to maintain freedom from the rigid and the orthodox belief structure that diminishes the faculties of invention and discovery, assisting one in realizing that he/she is a creature full of the power of the mind, and freeing the mind the bonds of fear. It allows one to recognize that mistakes are important only when, in the end, one discovers and names a "new" truth. The energies provide for courage to undertake adventures into unknown regions of thought and knowledge.

The Nebula Stone has assisted one in accessing information from both the ancient sacred texts and the akashic records, providing for lucidity in transliteration with respect to the writing and furthering the clarification of that which is written. It has further promoted both seeing and "reading" the aura and conscious channeling.

Dowsing with this stone can assist in determination with respect to whether an "organic" food is truly "organic".

At times of numb tragedy, the Nebula Stone assists the mind in remembering the smallest kindness, allowing one to reflect upon the positive amid the confusion and despair of events.

It is a mineral which brings the concept of self-preservation, promoting the recognition of injustice which is beyond the boundary of reason, and promoting the study and understanding of that which is beautiful. The mineral further acts to stimulate kindness to the self.

The energy of the Nebula Stone will make continue to impart a significant contribution to humanity in the healing realm.

It has been used in the treatment of macular degeneration, herpes, and bronchitis. When used as an elixir, it has also been used to facilitate the cleansing of the kidneys and the purification of same. It has been used to reveal the location of areas of obstruction to the flow of blood in the body. It is currently being used in the treatment of AIDS.

Vibrates to the number 2.

NONTRONITE

NONTRONITE - $Na_{0.3}Fe_2(Si,Al)_4O_{10}(OH)_2 \heartsuit nH_2O$; Hardness 2.5 - 4.5; Locality: Pima Co., Arizona, USA. Imaging by HP Scanjet, with assistance by Bob Jackson and ♪ Melody ♫; Collection of ♪ Melody ♫, Applewood, CO, USA.

Nontronite crystallizes as compact masses. The colour ranges from pale yellow to canary-yellow to green. The mineral was first described by P. Berthier; it is named for the locality of first discovery, Notron, France.

This mineral brings the energy of "timing", assisting one in the selection of the "right" time for manifesting ones personal and unique potential; it helps one to operate in accordance with ones personal inner "designating" force and inspires the recognition of, and the methodology by which to eliminate, the imposed boundaries of another.

Nontronite has facilitate continuance of ones goal, providing the courage and boldness for one to say "no".

It has been used to produce a connection between the self and another and has stimulated the feasibility so that one may recognize the methodology through which one may attract that which has been destined.

Nontronite can be used to promote healthy plants and to protect both humans and animals from the acquisition of contagious disorders. It is an excellent energy for animals.

The mineral has also been used to allow for the recognition of the deeper ties between souls prior to their entry to the Earth plane, promoting the inner knowledge of this life condition and the experiences chosen from other realities.

It can be used to assist one in the recognition of similarities between the self and another, to provide awareness of the other on a spiritual level, and to allow the extending of the self to the other in total identification.

It can also be used to facilitate psychic interaction between those involved. It can assist the participants in straightforward and prompt receipt and transmission of feelings to/from one another. It can also assist one in discovering that which is hidden about another; in addition, it promotes flexibility in relationships. It further assists one in "completing the circle".

The energy represents the entrance to the upper realms of ones being, and acts to provide one with the ability to transcend the material essence of the body, bringing about prompt response to healing situations.

Nontronite has been likened to the "spark of inspiration", bringing one to the zenith of ones manifestation.

It acts to stimulate the receipt of information conducive to the facilitation of the realization of ones fantasies. It further serves to initiate the pursuit of spirituality and assists one in progressing toward enlightenment via the opening and energizing of the third-eye.

It has been used in the treatment of cysts, lumps, and acne, to facilitate flattening the abdomen, to remove cellulite, and to promote ease in child-birth. It can also be used in Diagnostic Imaging, providing third-eye "pictures" of that which is currently provide via the mechanisms of ultrasound, CT scans and MRI's.

Vibrates to the number 9.

NOVACULITE

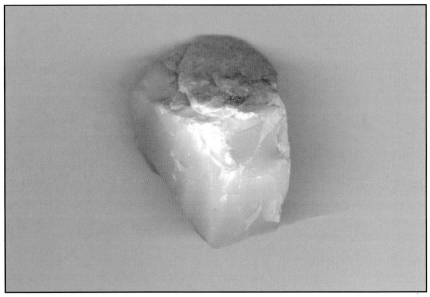

NOVACULITE - A sedimentary mineral composed almost entirely of microcrystalline quartz (SiO_2); Hardness 6 - 7; Locality: Ouachita Mountains, Arkansas, USA. Imaging by HP Scanjet, Assisted by Bob Jackson and ♪ Melody ♬; Collection of ♪ Melody ♬, Applewood, CO, USA. Gift of Jimmy Fecho, Arkansas, USA.

Novaculite crystallizes as finely-grained to porous masses with a waxy to dull luster; the colour ranges from white to greyish-black. The mineral has been reported extensively by the Geological Commission in Arkansas, USA, and is recognized world-wide in its use as whetstones and oilstones. Novaculite is named from the Latin word "novacula", meaning "razor stone". It has also been known as "Arkansas Stone" and "Washita Stone", depending upon its porosity and its luster.

The mineral has been used for weapon-making since the early 1700's by the early Native Americans who inhabited in Arkansas. It was also considered a stone to "cut through" problems, to smooth pathways, and to promote the advancement of solutions.

Novaculite can be used to polish the sharp edges of personality, bringing a constant placidity when placed in ones environment. It has been used to lift one from the "depths of despair" and to bring celebrative energies to situations which one may otherwise consider to be misfortunate (assisting the user in identifying the positive aspects of situations).

Allowed to rest in ones environment, it provides a structural energy which provides cohesiveness and solidity.

It has been used to assist in the removal of the ethereal "cords" which one sends to another (not the ones coming from another to the self). Holding the mineral at each of the chakra locations, one experiences an ease of detaching from another. Conversely, it has been used to further connections in the world of trade, bartering, and commerce; when the mineral is placed upon a description of that which one wishes to trade/barter/sell, the energy tends to focus on a recipient with the same/similar wishes. It is used by those who offer personal services to stimulate business and to enhance profitability with respect to the associated service and/or merchandise which is available.

Novaculite can also be used to open, to activate, and to energize the chakras to promote the removal of energy blockages and to promote the subsequent free flow of the electromagnetic forces through the body. It further acts to bring a personal magnetism to the user.

It has facilitated contact with those of the stars, facilitating contact specifically with those who have not previously visited the Earth. It seems that with each birth of a star, new contact is promoted and new information is obtained. It is also helpful in channeling information and in deciphering ancient languages.

Novaculite can be used to introduce a freshness to ones life - acting to bring new perspectives, new adventures, and new situations to ones personal sphere of action. It is excellent for psychic-surgery.

The mineral has been used in the treatment of chills, to assist in building cellular structure and to firm the skin, and to further toning for health. An elixir placed in a salve is excellent for the renewal of skin.

Vibrates to the numbers 1 (Washita Stone), 4 (Arkansas Stone), and 5 (Novaculite).

NUNDERITE

NUNDERITE - A combination of Andalusite (Al_2SiO_5), Quartz (SiO_2), and Epidote ($Ca_2FeAl_2(Si_2O_7)(SiO_4)(O,OH)_2$); Hardness ranges from 6 - 7.5; Locality: Nundle, New South Wales, Australia. Imaging by HP Scanjet, Assisted by Bob Jackson and ♪ Melody ♫; Collection of ♪ Melody ♫, Applewood, CO, USA. Gift of Bill Hagestein, New Zealand.

Nunderite crystallizes as masses with the colour ranging through the green spectrum. The mineral is accepted by the mineralogical community in Australia and New Zealand, but has not been yet described in the United States. Nunderite is named from the locality of first discovery, Nundle, NSW, Australia.

This mineral can promote protection from discovery; this can be quite helpful for underground activities, clandestine affairs, and secret societies. It can also be used to grid areas and photographs/images of areas which are of interest to the user.

It has been used to increase the abilities and the safety of those involved with water travel, sailing, submarines, etc., furthering knowledge of, and awareness in, same.

Nunderite has been used to assist one in manifesting the chameleon effect when desired, promoting the blending with the environment when one wishes to remain unnoticed.

The mineral can act to promote instruction from the "fathering" portion of ones Higher Self, bringing insight to new traditions which can bring meaning to relationships. It stimulates hindsight prior to the passing of events, subsequently reducing "failures" and disappointments. It helps one to discern responsibility and to augment the abilities required to support ones accountability.

It has been used to further the recording of diaries, histories, journals, chronicles, and original prose, poetry, and music. In addition, it brings an energy to assist one in remembering the oral versions of that which is to be recorded.

Nunderite is an excellent mineral for "cloud-busting" - placed in both ends of a rod, it acts to bring the accumulation of negative ions to within the rod and further acts to direct the force to the area where rain is desired.

The mineral is one which instills forgiveness of others, with respect to all things; further providing for memory of same, but without malice or anger. This energy is conducive to the non-repetition of the same lessons and serves as a permanent diplomatic representative.

Said to have been taken to Europe in the 1800's, it is reported to have been one of the stones of the "Holy Alliance"; the thought being that the energy of Nunderite would assist in the preclusion of revolution and would assist in the establishment of brotherhood.

Nunderite has been used to assist one in seeking cures for the self, and by the self. It has been used in the treatment of parasitic infection, candidiasis, and sterility. It can also be used as a free-radical scavenger, and as an effective adjuvant in enhancing immunity to murine babesiosis. It has been used to support the reduction of morbidity after major surgery.

Vibrates to the number 2.

**"FIND YOURSELF
AND YOU CAN FIND ANYTHING YOU WANT"**
Jose Luis
Washington, USA

OBSIDIAN - GREEN With PERLITE   [Astrological Sign of Pisces]

OBSIDIAN - GREEN With PERLITE - Obsidian is a vitreous lustrous volcanic glass; Perlite is volcanic glass which has a perlitic texture and, generally, a higher water content than Obsidian; Hardness 5 - 5.5; Locality: Paraná, Brasil, South America. Imaging by HP Scanjet, Assisted by Bob Jackson and ♪ Melody ♫; In Collection of ♪ Melody ♫, Applewood, CO, USA. Gift of Orizon de Almeida, Minas Gerais, Brasil, South America.

Green Obsidian with Perlite crystallizes as masses containing Perlite; the Perlite has a grey to white pearly texture and has formed due to contraction/fracturing during cooling of the Obsidian, the fractures forming small spheruloids. Perlite was first described by J.D. Dana in 1837, the original name being Pearlstone; in 1887, T. Egleston reported the mineral as Perlite. Obsidian was first described by Pliny in 77 A.D. and named for its resemblance to a stone found in Ethiopia by the Roman, Obsius (aka Obsidius); the name was also reported since Medieval days through the authors of natural history documents. The following properties are in addition to those listed in the OBSIDIAN section of "Love Is In The Earth - A Kaleidoscope Of Crystals Update". Please note that the buyer should "beware"; there is currently some green slag from the United States, and which resembles this transparent obsidian, which is being advertised and sold "on the market" as "Green Obsidian". It is difficult to determine the difference unless the Perlite is present; however, when the Green Obsidian is from the formation in Paraná, it has been found that all sizes of the mineral (e.g., pieces without the Perlite), contain all of the energies of the total configuration, although each mineral may not be exhibited separately.

This mineral has been used to convey the energies of a "guardian angel" to others. The process is simple; one selects the piece of Green Obsidian with Perlite and states: "The angel of (your location) brings (whatever one desires to send - e.g., peace, love, healing, protection, etc.) to the angel of (location of the other)."

Green Obsidian with Perlite also assists one in reasoning, auric reading, visioning, past-life ascension, conscious channeling of ones spiritual counselors and benevolent astral entities, psychometry, clairvoyance, astrological prediction, lucid dreaming and solution-dreaming, mysticism, and all psychic and metaphysical arts. Note that during channeling activities, the array stimulates the preservation of command by the self such that one is an observer and translator with total memory recall. *It acts to dissolve all boundaries and enhances ones trust in oneself in all circumstances.* It is an excellent array for use during sessions involving ascension and meditation, providing for clarity via calming of the mind. It has been used in dowsing, where it is necessary only for one to hold the mineral and to ask the question - the answer is given via the third-eye and/or is written etherically within the stone such that the stone reflects the solution to the user. It can also be used to promote automatic-writing.

Green Obsidian with Perlite provides for intellectuality and has been used to enhance study and to bring successful results when one must undergo testing. It acts to bring an ethereal low-voltage energy charge which connects the intellect with the intuition, promoting the "seeing" of the answer to any problem. It is a stone which never needs cleansing or energizing and has been used to further healing and well-ness on all levels. It has been used to enhance the assimilation of Vitamin A, and to protect from infection due to insect bites.

Vibrates to the number 9.

OBSIDIAN - GREEN SHEEN   [Astrological Sign of Sagittarius]

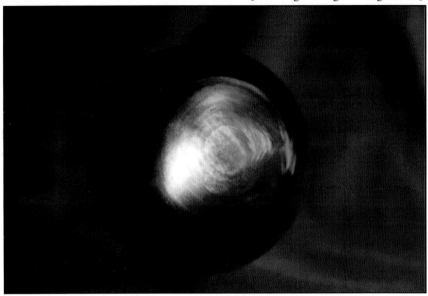

OBSIDIAN - GREEN SHEEN - A lustrous volcanic glass, exhibiting an internal sheen (caused by various needle-like inclusions) which is reflected in the colour green; Hardness 5 - 5.5; Locality: Mexico. Imaging by HP Scanjet, Assisted by Bob Jackson and ♪ Melody ♫; Collection of ♪ Melody ♫, Applewood, CO, USA.

Green Sheen Obsidian crystallizes as masses which exhibit an internal sheen. The colour is represented by a black background of Obsidian and a green sheen iridescence reflecting from the background; the sheen portion actually modifies the surface luster and is a very thin layer. Obsidian was first described by Pliny in 77 A.D. and named for its resemblance to a stone found in Ethiopia by the Roman, Obsius (aka Obsidius); the name was also reported since Medieval days through the authors of natural history documents. The following properties are in addition to those listed in the OBSIDIAN and SHEEN OBSIDIAN sections of "Love Is In The Earth - A Kaleidoscope Of Crystals Update" and in the SHEEN OBSIDIAN section of "Love Is In The Earth - Kaleidoscopic Pictorial Supplement A".

This mineral has been used to facilitate safety during celebration and has been used by many during Carnival, Fat Tuesday, and Mardi Gras, to protect one from theft, from attack, and from the detrimental effects of merry-making. It one with "permission" to accept the positive sides of self-indulgence, to be kind to the self, and to gratify the self with care. It promotes second-sight for the heart, opens and energizes the third-eye with respect to healing, and furthers the pursuit of "truth". Green Sheen Obsidian further helps one to surmount limitations [self-imposed or other-imposed] *and* to bring ones idea to realization. Placement of the mineral at the heart chakra enhances and stimulates polarity within the body such that the alignment of the outer bodies with the physical body is can be manifested.

It has been used by the Aztecs to induce visionary experiences and to provide information concerning medicine practices from the shamen of that ancient society. It further brings the continuance of the shamanic guide to assist in the healing activities and to assist in protecting and guiding one during the daily events and circumstances which one encounters. Green Sheen Obsidian has been used to assist one in looking deep within the physical eyes of the other, promoting insight into the true feelings of another and also assisting in the field of iridology. It can be used for "gazing" and for "journeying"; bringing "future scenes" and, via application to the shamanic and the healing arts, providing for the recognition of the areas within the emotional, physical, and/or intellectual bodies which are creating dysfunctional events/ conditions. The energy transfer, being simultaneously in all directions, has easily facilitated the trance state.

The mineral has been used to encourage good timing, to bring "luck" in games of chance, to stimulate publishing/publicity, and to stimulate foreign trade. A very interesting exercise has shown that the utilization of this mineral for relieve of headache and until headache was gone, has prompt a change in the green colour to the "Melody Purple" colour; subsequently turning back to green. This has been verified in both incandescent light and sunlight.

It has been used to assist in the relief of tired and/or blood-shot eyes, degenerative disorders of the spinal cord and vertebrae, lumbago, baldness, and inflammatory disorders. It promotes the metabolism of fats.

Vibrates to the number 2.

OBSIDIAN - MIDNIGHT LACE   [Astrological Sign of Scorpio]

OBSIDIAN - MIDNIGHT LACE - Obsidian is a vitreous lustrous volcanic glass; Hardness 5 - 5.5; Locality: Oregon, USA. Imaging by HP Scanjet, Assisted by Bob Jackson and ♪ Melody ♫; Collection of ♪ Melody ♫, Applewood, CO, USA.

Midnight Lace Obsidian is a volcanic glass which has a pattern similar to lace; this pattern is due to the colour arrangement which was caused by the initial volcanic flow. The colours include black and white/beige. Obsidian was first described by Pliny in 77 A.D. and named for its resemblance to a stone found in Ethiopia by the Roman, Obsius (aka Obsidius); the name was also reported since Medieval days through the authors of natural history documents. The following properties are in addition to those listed in the OBSIDIAN section of "Love Is In The Earth - A Kaleidoscope Of Crystals Update".

This mineral has been used to facilitate both privacy and seclusion, when desired. It acts to bring solitude such that one is not disturbed by the outside world and such that one may accomplish tasks which require concentration and focus. It has also served to protect one from discovery during secret and/or clandestine activities - acting to shield the situation from those outside the self.

Midnight Lace Obsidian can produce an unreadable expression when one does not desire ones thoughts to be obvious; assisting in bringing a "cloak" to camouflage and to conceal ones feelings.

In times of crisis when a person reacts on instinct, the mineral has been used to produce the response which is most comfortable. In situations where one may experience momentary confusion rippling across the mind, information is processed with expediency and reply and action is facilitated.

It furthers the act of "seizing the moment" such that one can advance that which "the moment" brings. Specifically, it is a mineral which instills the energy to "be prepared" for any and all opportunities and situations in which one has the desire to participate.

Midnight Lace Obsidian has been used to dispel the insensibilities of both the male and the female. Acting to deliver the energy of diplomacy and discretion when one is faced with circumstances which involve the emotions. It further serves to assist one with correctness in providing a loving response to others, suspending sarcasm and derision from the situation.

The mineral can assist in the elimination of the energies which promote the misinterpretation of the intentions of another and/or in the misinterpretation of the actions of the user. It brings an understanding to conversations and a sensitivity to interactions such that clarity of meaning and definitions of significance of the conversations/interactions are promoted.

Serving to dispel invidious positions, it promotes popularity, affinity with others, charitable opinions, reconciliation, and composure. The energy brings discernment without intolerance and prejudice.

Midnight Lace Obsidian has been used in the treatment of insomnia, bursitis, neuritis, neuralgia, and internal poisoning. It can also be used to act as an anti-matter for toxins, insecticides, viruses, bacteria, and medicinal overdoses.

Vibrates to the number 7.

OLIGONITE

OLIGONITE - (Mn,Fe)CO$_3$; Hardness 3.5 - 4.5; Locality: Leadville, Colorado, USA. Imaging by HP Scanjet, Assisted by Bob Jackson and ♪ Melody ♫; In the Collection of ♪ Melody ♫, Applewood, CO, USA.

Oligonite crystallizes as pink compact and granular masses, botryoids, crusts, and, rarely, rhombohedral crystals with round faces. The mineral was first described as Oligonspath by A. Breithaupt in 1841; it was translated to Oligon Spar by J.D. Dana in 1844; and was renamed to Oligonite by J.F.L. Hausmann in 1847.

This mineral is one of love, devotion, and calm passion, bringing new energies to enable one to dismiss traditional issues and to create and to maintain love within ones life. It contains a pulsating electrical energy which emits the power of love, assisting in the creation of new worlds filled with love and dreams. It gently energizes and purifies the base chakra and the heart chakra, restoring balance in these areas and acting to both cleanse and renew.

It has been used to provide contact with the "fairy kingdom" of this world, bringing unobstructed receptivity.

It confers an invulnerability, and favorably influences the outcome of lawsuits, petitions, and judgments. It promotes dedication to ones vision of justice, eliminating thoughts and fears which crowd the mind, and bringing confidence and peace of mind.

Oligonite brings intellectual acceptance of situations which appear negative such that one actually understands the purpose behind the situation, and has been used to eliminate ones Golgotha (any area of suffering or sacrifice which is present due to perceived negative situations).

The mineral can also both gently and quickly balance the emotions, providing a stability, or order and structure, to the mind. It further assists in promoting the female aspects of ones character, supporting ones honesty in the emotional realm and promoting the exhibition of ones true feelings.

It also provides a loving masculine energy for the physical body, supporting a strong, clear, and tolerant energy.

Oligonite acts to alleviate memories, which are perceived as traumatic and/or negative, supplanting same with memories of purposeful lessons without actual detail of the "why", the "how", and the specific situation which induced the lesson. Specifically, it can erase disturbing memories while allowing the user to recognize the lesson learned and/or the karmic debt which has been repaid.

The mineral can be used to stimulate the energies of the body, encouraging the maintenance of the optimum state of health. It has a gentle balancing effect which can maintain the etheric energy at a beneficial level and can help to prevent sickness.

Oligonite serves to enhance the well-being of ones body chemistry. It has been used to discourage disorderly growth at the cellular structure. It has acted to further the assimilation of Iron, to ameliorate sinus infection, to stabilize the heart rate and the pulse rate, and promote the production of the proper range of gastric fluids to enhance digestion.

Vibrates to the number 2.

OMPHACITE

OMPHACITE - (Ca,Na)(Mg,Fe,Al)SiO$_2$O$_6$; Hardness 5 - 6; Locality: Nordfjord, Norway. Imaging by HP Scanjet, Assisted by Bob Jackson and ♪ Melody ♫; Collection of ♪ Melody ♫, Applewood, CO, USA.

Omphacite crystallizes in the monoclinic system as granular and foliated masses. The colour ranges from green to grass-green. The mineral was first described by A.G. Werner in 1815; it was named for the Greek word meaning "an unripe grape", due to appearance.

This mineral has been used to enhance the understanding of metamorphosis in ones life. As one is in the state of constantly experiencing change of form, structure, and substance, the mineral can be used to ameliorate the more trying transformations, especially with respect to relationships and heart-connections.

It brings an energy of the full moon, the completion of a cycle, assisting one in the completion with growth and with the furtherance of "causes".

It helps one to exercise pride objectively, providing both humility and respect for the superior exhibition of ones intelligence. It allows one to recognize that the strength of the opposition is less than that which is within oneself, such that one is the victor.

Omphacite also allows one to understand the duality within the self, further stimulates the retrieval of personal information concerning the singular duality and coupled pairing of both sides of ones nature.

It has been used to initiate charitable contributions, subsidy to ones cause or life pursuits, and endowments. It acts to bring the knowledge to others that wealth will remain and will gain when one gives to others.

It is also useful to those exploring the fields of accounting and mathematics.

The mineral has been used to dispel the feeling of external heat and has acted to support the maintenance of the visualization of the "icicle" within the body such that both the intellect and the physical body does not perceive excessive temperatures as excessive.

Omphacite is a facilitating mineral for meditation, providing for the initiation of a mantra and for the stamina to assure the continuance during mindful meditation with mantras.

In the realm of metaphysics, it has been used to overcome nullifidian opinions, bringing an action of "proof" such that the skeptic is provided with both evidence and validation. It has assisted others in "feeling" the energies of minerals and has encouraged future application of same.

It has further introduced the energy to convey prophetic signs which portend and signify the existence of that which is beyond ones normal range of experience. Hence, assisting one in "belief".

Omphacite has been used in the treatment of physical weakness, physiological and psychological disorders, and far-sightedness. It can be used to promote the assimilation of Vitamin C, Manganese, Calcium, and Iron. It has also been used in the treatment of bone loss, periodontal disorders, and in healing of deficiency disorders of the immune system.

Vibrates to the number 9.

OPAL - LIME

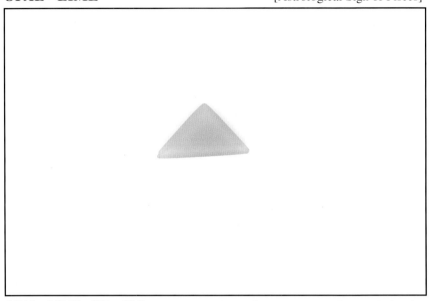

OPAL - LIME - $SiO_2 \cdot nH_2O$; Hardness 5.5-6; Locality: Nevada; Imaging by HP Scanjet, Assisted by Bob Jackson and ♪ Melody ♫; Collection of ♪ Melody ♫, Applewood, CO, USA. Gift of Bob and Micki Bleily, Montana, USA.

Lime Opal crystallizes in the form of delicious lime colour masses. It is uncertain who the first person was to describe Opal; however, it was named from "opalus", the ancient name for the mineral. The addition of "Lime" to the name was due to exhibition of the delicious lime colour. The following properties are in addition to those listed in the OPAL section of "Love Is In The Earth - A Kaleidoscope Of Crystals Update".

This mineral brings an approach life which is filled with an expectation of enjoyment; it assists one in being a pleasure in ones own right and assists one to act in such a way as to be sought by many. It is truly a "stone of popularity", bringing one to the condition of being "on the streets" instead of "off the streets".

The mineral assists in ridding one of fear and dispelling ones sense of isolation which is projected from within the self. When consciously directed, it also converts the energy of physical endurance toward the mobilization of the self toward non-restriction, and provides an energy to incite the awareness and subsequent response of choice, helping one to select and to be selected (due to physical, emotional, and intellectual attraction).

An adjuvant to memory, the mineral stimulates retrieval of information when one is unable to bring that image in front of ones eyes. The mineral is a "Gift of Memory", the mother of Muses, providing an unbounded power of concentration. It can transport one from the frowning action of forgetfulness to an astonished expression of "knowing".

Lime Opal assists in dispelling entropy, making ones physical potential unavailable energy available, and further supporting activities which require endurance of both the physical and/or the emotional.

The mineral also holds an aphetic energy, assisting one in "letting-go" of that which is unpleasant and/or unwanted and, further supporting the removal of same from ones life.

It can be used to cleanse the aura and to purify an area of negativity; it has been used to create sheltering ethereal enclosures to protect one from the influx of negativity.

Lime Opal has been used in the transference of healing energy to the self or another (with no residual unhealed energies returning to the user or remaining in the environment).

The mineral can facilitate the transforming of states from ALPHA, to BETA, to GAMMA, and to enhance lucidity in desires.

It has also been used to dispel estrangement and the attendant emotions of resentment and frustration which accompany dissociation/separation.

An elixir of the mineral has been used as an astringent in the treatment of internal ulcerations and external lesions, cuts, and abrasions. The mineral has also been used in the treatment of acidosis and toxicity.

Vibrates to the number 2.

OPAL - HYALITE

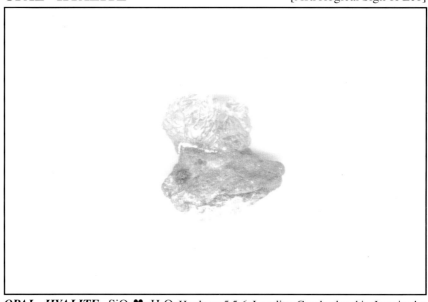

OPAL - HYALITE - SiO_2 ♥ nH_2O; Hardness 5.5-6; Locality: Czechoslovakia; Imaging by HP Scanjet, Assisted by Bob Jackson and ♪ Melody ♫; Collection of ♪ Melody ♫, Applewood, CO, USA.

Hyalite Opal crystallizes in the form of clear, translucent and colourless to white globular concretions, and crusts with a globular or botryoidal surface. It is uncertain who the first person was to describe Opal; however, it was named from "opalus", the ancient name for the mineral. Hyalite was first described by A.G Werner in 1794; it is named from the Greek word for "glass", due to the appearance. It is also known as "Muller's Glass". The following properties are in addition to those listed in the OPAL section of "Love Is In The Earth - A Kaleidoscope Of Crystals Update".

This mineral brings the brightness of the Sun which always follows rain. It acts to produce a splendor within ones life that is so dazzling that it illuminates far beyond that which one can normally see.

It serves to facilitate visions of ones personal future, bringing the information via a brilliant tunnel which appears before the eyes, and revealing the path which one had predetermined at birth and which one has forgotten from that moment; it further summons one to regain the divine origin which has been lost.

Hyalite Opal assists one in "watching", in hearing and in recognizing the "gypsy's warnings", and in acting on same. The protective energy it provides serves to bring information concerning risks and hazards to the user, such that the user may act to preclude the consequences of the danger.

The mineral can dispel stubbornness, abstinence, and intractability.

It acts to assist one in the effectual interaction with that which must be studied, such that one may become "one" with the subject, and can, hence, gain the depth of knowledge desired. It truly eliminates the "smoky brain" during in-depth study.

Hyalite Opal serves to allow one to see beyond illusionary identities and into the quintessence of the self. The energy brings an awareness of the insecurities which constrain the presentation of the perfect self. It further brings the reflection of ones self-image and the associated (and actual, currently-manifested) perfections or imperfections of the user. It can additionally be used to reflect the state of another (only with the consent of the other).

The mineral has also been used to locate "missing persons", assisting one in looking beyond the present situation and into the realms of that which occurred since the past situation. It further enhances clarity of the mind to ensure total reproduction of messages without any subtle self-held interferences.

It has been useful as an elixir to remove pesticide residues from fruits and vegetables.

Hyalite Opal has been used in the treatment of cuts, and in the prevention of allergies (promoting protection from pollen). It is quite useful in determining the cause of dis-ease.

Vibrates to the numbers 7 (Hyalite Opal) and 9 (Muller's Glass).

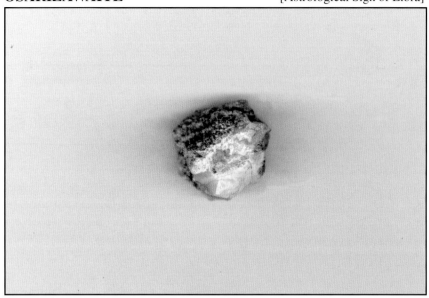

OSARIZAWAITE - $PbCuAl_2(SO_4)_2(OH)_6$ or $CuPb(AlFe)_2(SO_4)_2(OH)_6$; Hardness 3.5 - 4; Locality: Pina County & Yavapai County, Arizona, USA. Imaging by HP Scanjet, Assisted by Bob Jackson and ♪ Melody ♫; Collection of ♪ Melody ♫, Applewood, CO, USA

Osarizawaite crystallizes in the trigonal system as granular and fibrous masses and crystals. The colour ranges from an earthy greenish-yellow to a pale green. The mineral was first described by Y. Taguchi in 1961; it is named for the locality of first discovery (Osarizawa Mine, Akita Pref., Japan).

This mineral can provide protection by providing insight with respect to "what to say" when one encounters difficult communication situations which require response; hence, aiding the intellect in determining the best course of conversation, while allowing for the speaking of the many facets of the topic.

It assists one in facilitating an unsuspecting subtle attack toward the truth of a situation when one is overcome with curiosity. It is a "stone for clandestine activities", assisting one in satiating curiosity, staring in a discrete manner, watching surreptitiously, and further "leading one down the hallway and around the corner" to ultimate discovery. It is conducive to stimulating and to enhancing ones abilities of discretion and judgment.

Osarizawaite can also be used to hide ones thoughts, actions, and feelings, and to assist one in obtaining the look of innocence.

It can also be used to enhance diversification of activities and to produce a well-balanced character.

The mineral has been used to instill tactfulness, as well as cautiousness, when it is necessary for one to relate events of gossip or of that which could cause sorrow. It further produces a message and an action, when required, if it would be best for one to become or to remain silent.

Osarizawaite acts to bring an energy conducive to facilitating constructive criticism - not destructive criticism; it further prevails upon one to decease in badgering and/or heckling another. It has also been carried to obstruct and to thwart ridicule and teasing.

It holds an energy which is renewed by the call to action; hence, never requiring energization. It is an excellent stone for gridding the Earth.

It further facilitates an environmental consciousness (no more litter?).

The mineral has been used to eliminate confusion and grogginess when one is returning from a drug-induced state (the application being with prescription drugs and legal use of same). It has also assisted with dispelling the "morning stupor".

Osarizawaite has been used in the treatment of disorders associated with the thyroid, the ovaries, the prostate, and with the presence of fatty deposits, to rectify states of mental imbalance, and, as an elixir, for the skin and hair. It has also been used in amelioration of intestinal restrictions.

Do not prepare an elixir via the normal method.

Vibrates to the number 3.

OTTRELITE [Astrological Sign of Leo]

OTTRELITE - $(Mn,FeMg)Al_2SiO_5(OH)_2$; Hardness 6 - 7; Locality: Luxembourg, Belgium. Image shows a natural occurrence of Ottrelite in Schist. Imaging by HP Scanjet, Assisted by Bob Jackson and ♪ Melody ♫; Collection of ♪ Melody ♫, Applewood, CO, USA.

Ottrelite crystallizes as foliated masses, in scales and plates which are intermixed through the containing rock mass, and, rarely, in tabular crystals. The colour range includes dark grey, greenish-grey, greyish-black, yellow-green, black, and grass-green. The mineral was first described by A. Des Cloizeaux and A. Damour in 1842; it was named for the locality (Ottré, Belgium) of first discovery.

This mineral brings one to the realization of the "rainbow of the self", promoting a loving loveliness to all who are within the energy field.

It promotes intermixing on all levels - emotional, intellectual, physical, spiritual, assisting one in the recognition and the appreciation of that which is unlike the self.

It acts to help one to "bend" in ones structure of beliefs, allowing for the influx of "new" information such that one becomes less stringent in ones convictions and expectations (of others). It further dispels the brittleness of character and promotes elasticity in ones thoughts. It is rather like the "rolling stone", supporting one to have diversified experiences and diversified thinking (i.e., gathering no moss).

Ottrelite has been used to expedite proposal preparation and to bring an energy of gain and/or acceptance with the submittal of the proposal. The application has been successful in both the business and the personal worlds.

It can preclude the continuance of homilies, such that the one providing the discourse ceases in moralizing and admonition. It is an excellent mineral to use for terminating conversations and/or lectures which are judgmental and attacking in nature.

The mineral brings and energy for the reconciliation of family conflicts, and for quarrels with those outside the family (e.g., resolution of Hatfield/McCoy type feuds). It has also been used to end vendettas, bringing realization of that which is behind the problem (normally, something that is either truly simply and requiring only an apology, or something that is so small that it has been forgotten).

It is a stone which can actually distract others such that the thought of anger and/or revenge is no longer forthcoming.

It has been used to release an obligee, from being compelled by another to follow a specified course of action, when the obligation has been one which is not "of the light".

Ottrelite can also be used to promote the inheritance of admiral emotional and intellectual qualities. For this quality, one utilizes the mineral during both procreation (as an elixir) and during pregnancy (via placement upon the stomach).

It has been used in the treatment of oncological disorders, brittleness of nails and hair, liver spots, pancreas, and spinal dis-alignment and curvature.

Vibrates to the number 7.

"YOU ARE GOD'S GIFT TO YOU"
Perry Davis
Colorado, USA

PENWITHITE

PENWITHITE - $(Mn,Fe,Mg)SiO_3 \heartsuit H_2O$ or $(Mn,Fe)SiO_3 H_2O$; Hardness 3 - 4; Locality: Japan. Imaging by HP Scanjet, Assisted by Bob Jackson and ♪ Melody ♫; Collection of ♪ Melody ♫, Applewood, CO, USA.

Penwithite crystallizes as amorphous colloidal masses with no characteristic external form and which has no crystalline structure. The colour ranges from black to brown. The mineral was first described by J.H. Collins in 1878; it was named for the locality (Penwith, Cornwall, England) of first discovery, and is a synonymous mineral to Neotocite. Neotocite was first described as Neotokite by N. Nordenskiold in 1848; it was named from the Greek word meaning "of recent origin" being an alteration product. The name "Neotokite" was anglicized by J.D. Dana in 1868.

This mineral is one for change - bringing change through ones immediate environment such that one is prepared and comfortable for same.

It is reported to have been one of the stones of the "Holy Alliance"; the thought being that the energy of Penwithite would assist in the preclusion of revolution and would assist in the establishment of brotherhood.

Penwithite has been used to provide the neophyte with an inner knowledge for using the minerals of our Earth for facilitation of that which is desired. It acts to expedite results and to provide incentive for continuation of goals.

For those of recent origin (i.e., beginning the progression of lifetimes), it has acted to bring endurance against that which one perceives as negative and assists one in surviving difficult lessons.

The mineral has assisted in pursuits of creative and historic writing, supporting the user with innovative ideas and/or providing for opening of avenues of research.

When one feels that the light of ones inner life has been darkened by ones own cynicism and pragmatism, the mineral has granted optimism and exotic adventure.

It can be used to assist one in games where aim is important to target (e.g., games of darts, shooting, horseshoes, croquet, soccer, basketball, football, baseball, etc.).

Penwithite has been used to advance horizontal progression, bringing advancement in ones abilities with respect to that which one already knows.

It has also provided insights into the behavior of the young, heightening the understanding of the actions of the young and the triggers for those actions such that one may correct situations which are the bases for problem behavior. It can bring the energy of psychological counseling, providing answers which one may apply to care of the young.

The mineral has been used to assist in bending, to provide for comfort for the bedridden, and in the treatment of epidermal and endodermal disorders and dehydration, and to protect the skin from aging. It also tends to block the oxidation of tissue and has been used to treat chronic illnesses such as arteriosclerosis, cerebrovascular disorders, degenerative joint dis-ease, and strokes.

Vibrates to the numbers 3 (Penwithite) and 7 (Neotocite).

PERTHITE - A combination of Albite ($NaAlSi_3O_8$) and Orthoclase ($KAlSi_3O_8$); Hardness 6 - 6.5; Locality: Perth, Ontario, Canada. Imaging by HP Scanjet, Assisted by Bob Jackson and ♪ Melody ♫; Collection of ♪ Melody ♫, Applewood, CO, USA. Gift of Pierre Stéphane Salerno, Alberta, Canada.

Perthite crystallizes as a lamellar intergrowth in the form of masses which exhibit areas resembling strings, lamellae, blebs, and irregular veinlets; these areas occur due to the exsolving of the Albite. The colour ranges from light to dark orange. The mineral was first described by T. Thomson in 1843 and was named for the locality (Perth, Ontario, Canada) of first discovery. The following properties are in addition to those listed in the ALBITE and ORTHOCLASE sections of "Love Is In The Earth - A Kaleidoscope Of Crystals Update".

This mineral has been used to attend the maintenance of the molecular structure of the aura, enhancing stability and providing for continual cleansing of same.

It can be used to augment the energy field of the feminine soul such that the yin energy is stimulated and enhanced.

Perthite has been used to cleanse, to activate, and to energize crystals. it can both increase the energy and enhance the abilities of the healer.

It has also facilitated astral travel to the areas of the Indian Ocean where the vortices of Lemurian energy reside, assisting one in contact with those of the lost continent and in remembering the lessons of the enlightened members of that society.

Perthite provides for objectivity in conflict resolution and interaction between those involved. It has been used to bring a natural aptitude for logic.

The mineral has also been used to dispel ethnic and religious rivalries. Tending to dissipate the structured ordering and rigidity in religion, it brings a cohesiveness to group thoughts with respect to life-after-life and to life-before-life, and allows one to "sit back" and to contemplate and meditate on the wonders of that which occurred within the group.

It has also furthered the lucrativeness of seasonal employment.

It is an excellent stone for group re-birthing activities, bringing a steadiness in breath and an ease of recognition and processing of any trauma which is recognized.

It has been used to dissipate energy blockages, and to create harmony within the energy flow patterns. It further can be used to stimulate the Prana [breath of life] currents in the body to facilitate cellular balance and coordination.

It is an excellent energizer and stimulant for the germination of seeds, further assisting in the subsequent growth. When used for gridding, it further induces the replenishment of the ozone layer.

It has been used to assist in the assimilation of Potassium and to reduce excess levels of Sodium within the body. It has been used in the treatment of high blood pressure, Magnesium poisoning from antacids, aneurysms/blood vessel blow-out, and mobility problems.

Vibrates to the number 2.

PETRIFIED PALM - An ancient wood and/or root which has been formed by permineralization of the wood by chalcedony, such that the original form and structure of the wood/root has been preserved; Hardness 6 - 7; Locality: Wyoming, USA. Imaging by HP Scanjet, Assisted by Bob Jackson and ♪ Melody ♫; Carving by Bob Rolen, Oregon, USA; Collection of ♪ Melody ♫, Applewood, CO, USA.

Petrified Palm crystallizes as masses, both structured and geometric. The colour range is as shown in the image. The following properties are in addition to those listed in the PETRIFIED WOOD section of "Love Is In The Earth - A Kaleidoscope Of Crystals Update".

This mineral brings the energy of Ophiuchus, The Serpent Doctor. It assists one in full moon ceremonies and in time-travel. It is conducive to furthering pursuits in the study of history, traditions, customs, rituals, and Eastern religions.

The mineral has been used to assist in the discovery of mineral deposits and in the study of geology and geological forces. It can provide visions, given background information, with respect to locations of that which has not been discovered and/or that which has been "lost".

It has been used to initiate passive resistance and articulate verbalization of ones feelings during confrontations, helping others to diminish aggressive behavior.

Petrified Palm can also assist one in following an activity to completion.

It has also been employed to arouse the innate aptitudes to expedite financial gain, helping one to enjoy active circumstances, to excel in over-populated areas, and to enhance conquest and confidence in ones career and in ones life work.

It is an excellent stone for gridding during the art of massage, bringing calm and comfort to the subject.

The mineral has been used to assist one in climbing activities, in isometrics, and in parachuting. It acts to bring a courage and a knowledge of actions and reactions required for these endeavors.

The mineral represents a building block for new projects, new ventures, and new methods of progression; it provides a foundation for both the development and the construction of contemporary structures within ones life and further facilitates the stabilization and advancement of those pursuits. It has been used to assist one in building faith, character, relationships [removing pretenses], spirituality, and competence. It provides the basis for precision in, and preservation of, that which is constructed and represents the "source" from which the self would expand and flourish.

It brings an excellent essence for energizing ointments, conveying a lasting effect to the properties and the nature of same.

Petrified Palm can be used to assist in the relief of tonsillitis, heat prostration, sunstroke, chromosomal imbalance, gum dis-ease, head injuries, gluttony, abscesses, and atrophication of organs. It has been used in the treatment of disorders of the eustachian tubes, the optic nerves, and light sensitivity. It has also been used to enhance the absorption of Vitamin C and Protein.

Vibrates to the number 8.

PIEMONTITE [Astrological Sign of Sagittarius]

PIEMONTITE - $Ca_2(Al,Fe)_3Si_3O_{12}OH$ or $Ca_2(Mn,Fe)Al_2(Si_2O_7)(SiO_4)(O,OH)_2$; Hardness 6; Locality: Aosta Valley, Italy. Imaging by HP Scanjet, Assisted by Bob Jackson and ♪ Melody ♫; Collection of ♪ Melody ♫, Applewood, CO, USA.

Piemontite crystallizes in the monoclinic system as prismatic and acicular crystals exhibiting pleochroism (yellow/violet/red). The colour ranges from reddish-brown to reddish-black. The mineral was first described by A. Kenngott in 1853; it is named for the locality (Piedmont, Italy) of first discovery.

This mineral can produce an elevation in that to which one attunes it. It is truly a stone to experience in all aspects of one life where one wishes augmentation and improvement.

It acts to expel derogatory actions, to amplify acumen, to stimulate merging and unification, and to augment personal power.

It can also be used to assist one in realizing "the soul within the soul", assisting one to have the confidence such that outside approval is not required.

Piemontite has been used to further the success of litigation for "animal rights", and to assure accuracy and completeness of literature and legal documentation involving same. It has assisted one in understanding both the personal and the individual actions that one can take, and to enhance conscious realization by others, with respect to the conditions which are occurring.

It has been used to promote peacefulness in times and conditions of foreign unrest.

It has also been used to facilitate telepathic connections and can assist in bringing a specific person [or persons] to ones physical proximity. It can also be used to support "seeing" into the Inner Self of another, stimulating the opening of a pathway to the center of the other and facilitating wisdom and awareness with respect to past-life/future-life connections and condition, and personal thoughts and manifestations. It actually assists one in obtaining the same closeness to another that one has with oneself.

Piemontite can also be used to assist the participants of groups in the understanding of the ideal of freedom and autonomy in relationships, while continuing to promote actions of cohesiveness and collectivity.

It has been used to grid prisons to bring stability and to dispel unrest.

It has been used by the inmates of same to bring resolution to conflicts and to further the expediency of ones release, after lessons have been learned. In addition, it has been used by inmates of institutions to encourage learning trades and enhancing skills.

It has further been used in gridding to prevent wastefulness and extravagance in restaurants.

It can also be used in the treatment of disorders associated with the feet, the hands, the sacral region of the spine, the thighs, the hips, the liver, the hepatic system, bone fractures and separations, the brain, the nervous system, and the thyroid. It is also useful to combat dehydration.

Vibrates to the number 9.

PILSENITE

PILSENITE - Bi_4Te_3; Hardness 2; Locality: Ontario, Canada. Imaging by HP Scanjet, Assisted by Bob Jackson and ♪ Melody ♫; Collection of ♪ Melody ♫, Applewood, CO, USA.

Pilsenite crystallizes as foliated masses. The colour ranges from metallic silver to metallic white. (The image above shows Pilsenite with the metallic bronze-coloured Pyrrhotite.) Pilsenite was first described by A. Kenngott in 1853; in 1982, T. Ozawa and H. Shimazaki re-examined the mineral, and provided the correct chemical composition for Pilsenite. The mineral was named for the locality (Deutsch-Pilsen, Hungary) of first discovery.

This mineral favorably influences the outcome of lawsuits, petitions, and judgments. It has been used to augment and to amplify the qualities of diplomacy.

It acts as a link between the self and other cultures such that one may readily receive information. It is a "stone of the wizard", bringing information for the self and for others relative to the pre-programmed ethereal energies which are in ones energy field.

It manifests an energy which can uncover energy blockages and can open the crown chakra, allowing for release of blockages through the body and out through the crown, hence, fostering the cleansing and activation of all chakras concurrently. When used at the crown chakra, it can provide for the stimulation of total body energies, and can also increase ones emotional fields [this may/may not be desirable and is dependent upon ones emotional stability at the given moment]. It furthers one in the recognition of events which may require additional emotional attentiveness. It can also be used to transform the energy of the crown chakra to energize the base chakra [in contrast with most stones] and to activate both the instinctual energies of preservation and the authority of wisdom.

Pilsenite has been used in body-sectoring work, assisting the user to locate the area(s) which require restructuring and facilitating the transfer of modification to that/those area(s).

It can be used in the practice of reflexology to stimulate energy transfer and in cranial sacral therapy to expedite movement. It can balance ones volatility and can stimulate astral travel.

This mineral can be used to promote the actualization of an abundance of adrenalin during hostile situations and to encourage the protective mechanisms which are inherent within the self.

It also provides a malleability to ones nature, serving to purify the emotions and to encourage the release of buried emotions. It is also an expeditor for information exchange, bringing softness and subtlety to conversation.

Pilsenite has been used to stimulate the metabolic processes, to support ones life forces during surgery, to assist in the elimination of excess mucoid within the body, as an anti-bacterial agent, in the treatment of pneumonia and addictions, and as a cathartic and purgative in instances of poisoning.

Do not prepare an elixir of this mineral via the normal method.

Vibrates to the number 1.

PLATTNERITE

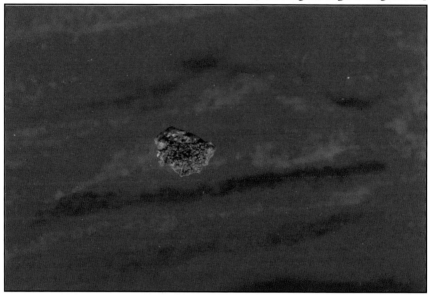

PLATTNERITE - PbO_2; Hardness 5.5; Locality: Mexico. Imaging by HP Scanjet, Assisted by Bob Jackson and ♪ Melody ♫; In the Collection of ♪ Melody ♫, Applewood, CO, USA

Plattnerite crystallizes in the tetragonal system as masses and, rarely, as small prismatic crystals and needles, although one will occasionally see the inclusion of the mineral in Quartz. The colour is iron-black with a submetallic luster; it further shows a greyish-white colour in reflected light. The mineral was first described by W. Haidinger in 1845; it is named for K.F. Plattner.

This mineral It has been known to represent both the needles of the seamstress, assembling the many segments of one life, hemming, tucking, and tacking. When found within Quartz, the ethereal aspects bring a foundation for love, an expertise in alteration, an adhesiveness and cohesiveness in ones unfolding, and uniformity in ones life.

It has been used for restoring and establishing symmetry within the aura via the removal of contrary energy. It affects the physical, etheric, and astral layers and assists one in recognizing the basic pattern of problems;

hence, providing for knowledge of the pattern of a dis-ease, so that one can redress the situation.

Plattnerite is a stone for stabilizing connections, marriages, mental processes, and for bringing unruffled emotions and material balances. It allows for the realization that each person is allocated the skills of the universe and the discernment of advanced environments of other worlds.

It also dispels unwanted interference from both the physical and spiritual worlds - in the physical world, it tends to eliminate circumstances which could encourage obstacles; and, in the spiritual worlds, the mineral directs a clear message that interference will not be permitted.

During astral travel and during "journeying", the mineral provides for insight into the reasons for visiting the sites and/or situations and for inspecting the scenes; it stimulates awareness of the connections between ones physical manifestation and the conditions which are surveyed.

The mineral contains three master numbers, bringing a trinity to the comprehension of the God within the self, the acceptance that God is in the totality of existence, and the understanding of the arrangement of the God outside of the self. It further produces an intermixture of these vibrations and assists one in the "realization" of the totality which is within the self. The access to parallel dimensions is opened and the totality of all of ones actions is both recognized and understood.

Plattnerite expedites revolution and evolution on all levels, and an energy of training which facilitates the insight into ones available paths to completion. Flexibility and variation in alterations are supported.

This mineral has been used in the treatment of neck pain, to promote the growth of existing hair, to regulate the production of hormones, to strengthen the walls of the blood veins, and to stimulate sexuality [when consciously directed]. It has also been used confer protection against a variety of biological insults.

Do not prepare an elixir of this mineral via the normal method.

Vibrates to the number 5.

POLYSPHAERITE

POLYSPHAERITE - $(Pb,Ca)_5(PO_4)_3Cl$; Hardness 3.5 - 4; Locality: Mexico. Imaging by HP Scanjet, Assisted by Bob Jackson and ♪ Melody ♫; Collection of ♪ Melody ♫, Applewood, CO, USA.

Polysphaerite crystallizes as globular and, rarely, in crystals. The colour range includes yellowish-grey, pale yellow to almost white, and varying shades of brown. The mineral was first described by A. Breithaupt in 1832; it is named from the Greek words meaning "many" and "a ball", referring to the usual globular form.

This mineral can be used to provide grounding and to enhance the unification of ones energies. It helps to open the pathway between the physical and ethereal bodies in order to allow for the alignment of energies and the stimulation of the nervous system.

It acts to bring accord to situations, further stimulating a blending of ideas and ideals and assisting in the decrease of self-limiting ideas.

It is quite helpful for those studying the field of medicine and can promote holistic, homeopathic, and herbal medicine studies, providing instinctive knowledge and, when required, the cynicism to provoke additional experimentation.

Polysphaerite can be used to incite deep relaxation and to engender ideas and solutions. It can facilitate the acquisition of awareness and can allow one to remain open to messages from the Inner Self and the Higher Self. It tends to release images from the unconscious mind and to assist one in achieving the BETA state. It is an excellent stone for meditation.

It has been used in healing situations to enhance the energy of the stones in use. Those minerals placed within the energy field of this stone become further stimulated to promote an augmentation to energy release.

It provides for oracular and prophetic abilities in matters of the humour and can stimulate ones level of personal energy, bringing a vigorous attitude and a novel direction. In addition, it has enhanced ones intuitive abilities, allowing one to distinguish between fraudulent and genuine friendships. With the energy of this mineral, ones inherent psychic qualities are manifested and information becomes readily available.

Polysphaerite has been used to provide increase; conscious direction of the energy to that which one wishes to increase is required. (Please note that a multiplication of ones "troubles" can be decreased via conscious direction of the energy to "increase the decrease....".)

It can also assist in "reading faces".

The mineral has been used in the stimulation of, and in the promotion of the release of blockages from, the triple-burner acupressure/acupuncture meridians. It can also be used to dispel unwanted micro-organisms from the blood, to aid in the proper assimilation of Calcium and the B-Vitamins, and to ameliorate degenerative changes in the gums and connective tissue between the stomach and duodenum. It can be used to inhibit the degeneration of cellular structures, to purify inflammations, and to balance the RNA/DNA structures.

Do not prepare an elixir of this mineral via the normal method.

Vibrates to the number 7.

"PRINTSTONE"

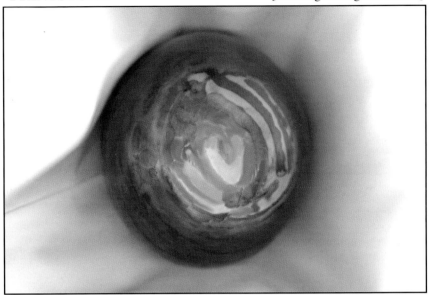

"PRINTSTONE" - A siltstone (with enriched bandings of Iron) whose composition is intermediate between those of sandstone and shale, and of which two-thirds is material of silt-size, contains hard, durable, thin layers, and, often, shows various primary current structures. Hardness variable; Locality: Brockman Station, North Western Australia, Australia. Imaging by HP Scanjet, Assisted by Bob Jackson and ♪ Melody ♫; Collection of ♪ Melody ♫, Applewood, CO, USA.

"Printstone" crystallizes as striated masses in the colour range of ochre to tan/brown to brown-violet, and was formed from cross-bedding in a still-water sedimentation environment. It was named in Australia for the geometric semi-linear, semi-circular "print" structure of the layers of flow which are exhibited.

This mineral has been used to assist one in the understanding of dualistic philosophy of Descartes which began with the famous phrase "cogito ergo sum" (I think, therefore, I am). It assists one in seeing the physical nature mechanistically such that one may apply rationalism and logic.

This mineral has been used to assist one in creation, to further adventures in visioning, and to provide an inner light during mindful meditation such that one may see the answers to problems and/or view situations in a more illuminating "light". It has also been used in the annual celebration of light (December) to enhance the spirit of ecumenical love during world meditation.

It is an energy which brings the knowledge that the "circle is unbroken" with respect to the return to the Earth for mundane lessons. It also acts as a reminder that the "circle" is broken when one has completed these lessons and that one then moves to another world, another series of lives, and another sequence of lessons, if one desires.

"Printstone" has assisted in one "aiming for the bulls-eye", acting to eliminate the confusion from the surrounding patterns of life and options, such that one can recognize, direct the attendant energies, remove the ambiguity, and obtain that which one desires.

It further promotes a single-minded focus to support ones dream, bringing the ability and the actualization to same. The mineral also assists one in determining the "single, most important" goal, and assists in the conscious programming array (See the "Gateless Gate" in "Love Is In The Earth - Laying-On-Of-Stones") such that one may clearly convey the goal to the universal energies of perfection. It acts to support clarity in specifics of the narrative, which describes that which one desires, despite any digressions of the mind which can bring doubt, imprecision, and apprehension.

The mineral has been used to assist one in both giving and receiving. It allows the user to experience joy in both areas and also brings loving acceptance and appreciation in receiving. It has been used to facilitate ease in decision-making and clear thinking, and provides insight into the "best", and probably most elusive, solution (for the person, at the time). It has been used to assist one in determining the "best" present to buy for another, the "best" electronic apparatus to buy for the self, the "best" course of action for an intended goal, etc.

"Printstone" has been used in toning the muscular structure, to facilitate re-shaping the form of the body, to enhance dexterity and agility, and to promote the assimilation of Iron.

Vibrates to the number 6.

PYROPHYLLITE   [Astrological Sign of Libra]

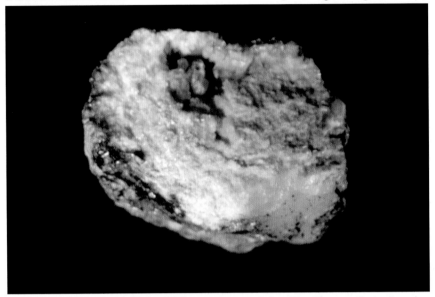

PYROPHYLLITE - $Al_2Si_4O_{10}(OH)_2$; Hardness 1 - 2; Locality: Caceres, Spain. Imaging by HP Scanjet, Assisted by Bob Jackson and ♪ Melody ♫; In the Collection of ♪ Melody ♫, Applewood, CO, USA.

Pyrophyllite crystallizes in the monoclinic system as two-layer and one-layer polytypes, whose different forms result from different stackings of similar atomic structural units.   The forms include foliated, radial lamellar, fibers, and granular to compact or cryptocrystalline masses. The colour range includes white, apple-green, greyish-green, brown-green, yellowish to ochre-yellow, greyish-white, and pale blue to greyish-blue. The mineral was first described by R. Hermann in 1829; it is named from the Greek words for "fire" and "a leaf", referring to the exfoliation of the mineral when heated. The compact massive type has also been known as "Pencil-Stone".

This mineral has been used to enhance, and to actually teach, automatic-writing. It provides a firm basis from which one may begin, and continue, to be receptive to the information available in the spiritual worlds and the worlds of the stars. It has furthered production of books, promoting the publishing and distribution of same.

Pyrophyllite can be used to align all chakras automatically and immediately, with no conscious direction. If directed with the consciousness of the user, it can also open the chakras. Conscious direction of the energy can also align the emotional, intellectual, physical, spiritual, ethereal, astral,.... bodies. It produces the alignment of the chakras with the grounding of ones being in a spontaneous and self-operating manner.

It can facilitate entering and maintaining meditation. The clearing effect of the mineral provides for a state of calm, while balanced state of the mineral provides for perpetuation of the centered alignment of ones being.

It is also quite useful when accessing the astral plane and when connecting with ones guides. It provides for balancing of the yin-yang energies, bringing an orderly growth to the intellect, emotions, and physical body. It dispels energy blockages, moving energy from the ethereal plane such that the physical plane feels immediate effects.

It can be used during radionic analysis; holding a sample and placing a sample on the witness or using a pendulum of this stone, the energy of the stone interferes with the energy of the user and points to the problem(s) involved.

Pyrophyllite has also assisted in the "asking of questions" such that one may interrogate via the conveyance of a comfortable "statement" rather than a prying inquiry; e.g., "so, you are not.....", "so, you are.....", "so, this (specifically) is the way it is".

The mineral has assisted in the subduing of those who are distressed and/or boisterous. It brings a comfort which relieves annoyance and serves to eliminate loud verbalization and/or loud anguish.

It can be used in the treatment of disorders of the muscular structure, the urogenital system, adrenal glands, burns, and the internal cellular structure. It has been used to ameliorate fevers. It is a beneficial stone to place between the base and third-eye chakras during the healing activities associated with the "laying-on-of-stones".

Vibrates to the numbers 1 (Pyrophyllite) and 6 (Pencil Stone).

"QUE A FONTE NUNCA SEQUE"

Daniel Foscarini de Almeida
Minas Gerais, Brasil

QUARTZ - "ARKIMER DIAMOND"   [Astrological Sign of Gemini]

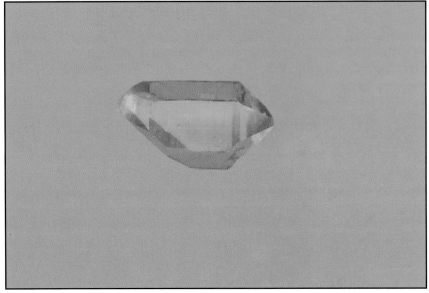

QUARTZ - "ARKIMER DIAMOND" - alpha-SiO$_2$; Hardness 7; Locality: Arkansas, USA. Imaging by HP Scanjet, Assisted by Bob Jackson and ♪ Melody ♫; In Collection of ♪ Melody ♫, Applewood, CO, USA. Gift of Bobby Fecho, Arkansas, USA.

The "Arkimer Diamond" is a unique form of quartz which crystallizes in the configuration of double-terminated short, stout, clear or included prismatic crystals. This mineral was given the name by the miners in Arkansas due to the diamond-like structure of this pseudo-diamond in Mt. Ida, Arkansas. The following properties are in addition to those listed in the HERKIMER DIAMOND section of "Love Is In The Earth - A Kaleidoscope Of Crystals Update".

This mineral has been used to convey the energies of a "guardian angel" to others. The process is simple; one selects the piece of Green Obsidian with Perlite and states: "The angel of (your location) brings (whatever one desires to send - e.g., peace, love, healing, protection, etc.) to the angel of (location of the other)."

It has been used as a "stone of attunement", one to another, and in the transference of healing energies during both present and absent-healing situations, and for thought transmission. The transmission of ones thoughts to another are reinforced via focus from the sacral chakra and subsequent dispatch to the location of the recipient. Thoughts of well-being, healthfulness, etc., may also be transmitted in healing situations. One of two effects usually result: if the recipient is not engaged in a definite thought pattern **and** the aura of same is clear of mental debris, the thought- form will discharge itself to the mental body; **or** if the recipient is engaged in definite mental activity, the thought-form will remain in the vicinity of the recipient until the mental body is sufficiently uncluttered - at the time of clarity, it will discharge itself to the mental body; this delayed action is dependent upon the sufficiency of the strength of the thought-form. If, however, the auric field/energy field of the potential recipient does not possess the capability of reception, the thought-form will be repelled and returned; for example, a thought form, which requires an action which is adverse to the potential recipient, will not be accepted. In addition, if one is protected from thought-entry via one of the various personal metaphysical protective mechanisms which are available, the thought will be returned to the source. With all of the loving protection which is being transmitted throughout the world today [e.g., during meditation, healing gatherings, retreats, etc.], any negative thought forms will, in all likelihood, be declined and reversed. Conversely, a consciously directed thought-form of love and protection will operate as a shielding and protective instrument, seeking all opportunities to benefit and defend the recipient; it will also strengthen the positive forces and weaken the negative forces which attempt to infringe upon the auric field. Hence, the positive thoughts tend to maintain a "guardian angel", ever near the recipient. This is an excellent stone for instilling protective force fields around persons, animals, plants, objects, and the totality of our Earth.

The "Arkimer Diamond", as a "stone of attunement" it has been used to assist one in maintaining a connection with another and/or with a group. It has also acted to "outlaw" secrets between those who are "attuned".

This mineral has been used to improve the odds on longevity and to reduce the ageing process. It has been used in hospital environments to provide protection from the communicable dis-ease which is prevalent.

Vibrates to the numbers 5 and 9.

QUARTZ - With CHERT

QUARTZ - With CHERT - alpha-SiO$_2$ (Quartz) with Chert (dense); Hardness ranges 6 - 7; Locality: Arkansas, USA. Imaging by HP Scanjet, Assisted by Bob Jackson and ♪ Melody ♫; Collection of ♪ Melody ♫, Applewood, CO, USA. Gift of Leslie Bowen, Arkansas, USA.

Quartz with Chert crystallizes as prismatic crystal clusters with a Chert matrix/base. Quartz was first described as "Crystallus" (representing the crystalline formation) by Pliny in 77 A.D. and was further described by U.R. von Kalbe in 1505 to present the history of the name. The name "Quartz" was originally spelled "Quertz" and represented Quartzite (the compact granular massive configuration); it was named for the Saxon word "cross-vein ore". In the late 1700's, the two configurations (crystalline and massive) were found by T. Bergman to have the same chemical composition and, hence, were consolidated and provided with one name (Quartz). Chert is a hard, extremely dense, compact microcrystalline/cryptocrystalline sedimentary rock, consisting, primarily, of interlocking crystals of quartz and impurities, with a splintery to conchoidal fracture. The following properties are in addition to those listed in the QUARTZ and CHERT sections of "Love Is In The Earth - A Kaleidoscope Of Crystals Update".

This mineral has supported the entry of records in both diaries and journals. It brings and energy which promotes ease and succinctness in managing ones records.

It can, in addition, stimulate ones growth toward the lunar side of ones nature, allowing for the pathway toward evolution to be clearly marked while providing grounding for the user. It cultivates a nurturing quality and assists one to grow in synchronicity with ones path. The energy is one of harmony, and is especially helpful during times of great stress. It helps to stimulate ideas and to give substance and continuity to thought. It is used to bring "delight" into ones life. It also allows one to recognize the "delight" inherent in each person and situation.

Quartz with Chert has been used by the Native Americans in the southeastern portion of the United States to grid villages and communities to protect against dis-ease and the infiltration of those which are of like-minds. It has also been used in ceremonial celebrations to provide success in battle. It is currently being used by one tribe such that each member of the tribe possesses one piece of the mineral and during religious ceremonies all are gathered together and programmed with the thought of "One".

It has also been used to initiate and to sustain a talk "over elixir" (of Quartz with Chert), similar to a talk "over coffee", during times when "a talk" is required to resolve issues which have been neglected with respect to relationships. It assists to bring decision to the situation such that both participants may either find a more pleasant way to be miserable together or such that there is mutual acceptance of incompatibility as partners. It further brings the insight to methodology for the actions which will support whichever resolution has been selected, guiding the participants in the accomplishment of same.

The mineral has been used to renew portions of the brain, in the treatment of disorders of the senses, speech, behavior, thought patterns, memory, paralysis, coma, burst arteries, high blood pressure, and build-up of fatty plaque in the arteries. It has been used in rehabilitation to improve physical ability and to reduce dependence.

Vibrates to the number 4.

QUARTZ - Chinese RED PHANTOM

QUARTZ - CHINESE RED PHANTOM - alpha-SiO_2 (Quartz) with inclusions of Red Hematite (Fe_2O_3); Hardness 7 (Quartz) and 5-6 (Hematite); Locality: China. Imaging by HP Scanjet, Assisted by Bob Jackson and ♪ Melody ♫; In the Collection of ♪ Melody ♫, Applewood, CO, USA. Gift of Ken Harsh, Ohio, USA.

Chinese Red Phantom Quartz is recognized by a burgundy-red to deep "red phantom" crystal form within the Quartz crystal. The phantom is comprised of a red Hematite and may be partial or complete. Quartz was first described as "Crystallus" (representing the crystalline formation) by Pliny in 77 A.D. and was further described by U.R. von Kalbe in 1505 to present the history of the name. The name "Quartz" originally represented Quartzite (the compact granular massive configuration) and was spelled "Quertz"; it was named for the Saxon word "cross-vein ore". In the late 1700's, the two configurations (crystalline and massive) were found by T. Bergman to have the same chemical composition and, hence, were consolidated and provided with one name (Quartz). The word "Phantom" was named for the Late Latin word "Phantasma", with usage in mineralogy beginning in the 1800's. The following properties are in addition to those listed in the QUARTZ And HEMATITE sections of "Love Is In The Earth - A Kaleidoscope Of Crystals Update".

It should be noted that the "Red phantoms" which have been reported previously contain a different chemical composition and are from an area in Minas Gerais, Brasil; the Chinese Red Phantoms have a different chemical composition and energy, and are, hence, reported here.

These crystals can be used to rekindle ones spirit such that the lack of energy and vigor in ones life is eliminated.

In cases where one would like more information of new businesses, it acts to provide rational insight into enhancing financial security and to promote analytical insight into the promotion of same.

It is an excellent mineral for the stabilization of the mountains, oceans, and waters of the Earth.

Chinese Red Phantom Quartz brings tranquility with an energizing effect to the entire physical being, with particular focus on the realm of activity. It stimulates physical awareness on all levels, dispels anger and frustration, and helps to facilitate physical activity with respect to the actualization of complex reasoning. It induces one to persevere in activities and in situation which would, generally, reduce ones strength; it provides a stimulating energy and supports one in the continuation of projects.

The crystal has also been used to promote protection the self by directing the energy to surround the physical body; it can also be accomplished by wearing or carrying the crystal. In all cases, when consciously desired, one tends to merge with the physical environment, becoming disregarded and/or un-seen. It facilitates a dematerialization, occurring on the ethereal plane, which allows one to remove ones essence from situations and locations where one does not desire recognition. It assists one (as Isaiah 2:10 states) to "Enter into the rock, and hide thee in the dust....." of the phantom.

The mineral has been used to bless and energize crystal elixirs and herbal tinctures. It has been used in the treatment of disorders of the reproductive system and to initiate generative energies.

Vibrates to the number 1.

QUARTZ - DRUSY BOTRYOIDAL   [Astrological Sign of Cancer]

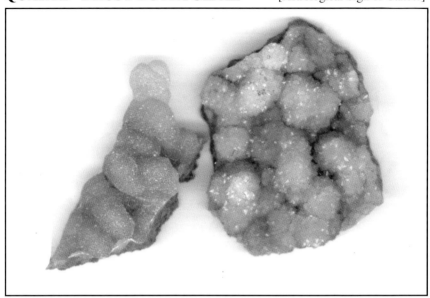

QUARTZ - DRUSY BOTRYOIDAL - alpha-SiO$_2$; Hardness 7; Locality: Missouri, USA (right), New Zealand (left). Imaging by HP Scanjet, Assisted by Bob Jackson and ♪ Melody ♫; Collection of ♪ Melody ♫, Applewood, CO, USA. Specimen on left is gift of Richard Two-Bears, New Zealand.

Drusy Botryoidal Quartz crystallizes as botryoidal masses of tiny Quartz crystals.   Quartz was first described as "Crystallus" (representing the crystalline formation) by Pliny in 77 A.D. and was further described by U.R. von Kalbe in 1505 to present the history of the name. The name "Quartz" was originally spelled "Quertz" and represented Quartzite (the compact granular massive configuration); it was named for the Saxon word "cross-vein ore". In the late 1700's, the two configurations (crystalline and massive) were found by T. Bergman to have the same chemical composition and, hence, were consolidated and provided with one name (Quartz). The following properties are in addition to those listed in the QUARTZ section of "Love Is In The Earth - A Kaleidoscope Of Crystals Update".

This mineral provides for the feeling of appreciation to the user if appreciation is lacking in ones life. It also enables one to smile and to laugh, for the sake of same, and at circumstances in which one has been overwrought and unnecessarily distraught. It can produce great inner strength, helping to sustain one during stressful and/or long-enduring situations.

Drusy Botryoidal Quartz is an excellent stone to use in the care of those restricted, either to bed, to home, or to an environment of confinement. It helps both the one confined and the one responsible for the care to manage and to cope with the unnatural-ness of the situation. It also promotes ideas for encouraging hope for ones day and for effecting the escalation of positivity. It further removes "edge" from situations.

It has been used to assist one to organize the mind, and can be used for mental adaptability, retention magnification, innovative thought, and for the furtherance of detailed knowledge. It assists one in pursuits in the fields of geometry and trigonometry, and in the development of both rational and manual dexterity.

While enhancing mental capability, it has also been used concurrently to create a calming atmosphere, and, in addition, to encourage one to undertake ventures which one has, in the past, felt to be beyond ones abilities. It helps one to realize that the only limitations which exist are those self-limiting concepts within the mind (it is an excellent stone to use when one is actively involved in "The Gateless Gate" exercises described in "Love Is In The Earth - Laying-On-Of-Stones").

Drusy Botryoidal Quartz has also been used to assist one in "sifting" the relevant from the irrelevant such that one may make immediate decisions (even concerning situations which are long-living).

The mineral can also assist one in the expression of sentiment and can facilitate the knowledge with respect to "how" one may make a gift of the self to another. Further bringing an appreciation of that which others "do" for one, it promotes thankfulness in ones life.

It has been used in the treatment of periodontal disorders, the fleshy organs, spurs, and gingivitis. It has also been used to assist in hair removal, and to ameliorate conditions of lethargy and depression.

Vibrates to the number 5.

QUARTZ - With EPIDOTE

QUARTZ - With EPIDOTE - alpha-SiO_2 (Quartz) with Epidote [$Ca_2(Al,Fe)_3(SiO_4)_3OH$ or $Ca_2FeAl_2(Si_2O_7)(O,OH)_2$]; Hardness 7 (Quartz) and 6 (Epidote); Locality: Minas Gerais, Brasil, South America. Imaging by HP Scanjet, Assisted by Bob Jackson and ♪ Melody ♫; Collection of ♪ Melody ♫, Applewood, CO, USA.

Quartz with Epidote crystallizes as Quartz crystals and masses which exhibit the Epidote covering and, sometimes interpenetrating the Quartz (shown in image above), or with the Quartz containing interpenetrating (normally green) Epidote crystals. Quartz was first described as "Crystallus" (representing the crystalline formation) by Pliny in 77 A.D. and was further described by U.R. von Kalbe in 1505 to present the history of the name. The name "Quartz" was originally spelled "Quertz" and represented Quartzite; it was named for the Saxon word "cross-vein ore". In the late 1700's, the two configurations (crystalline and massive) were found by T. Bergman to have the same chemical composition and, hence, were consolidated and provided with one name (Quartz). Epidote was first described by R.J. Haüy in 1801; it is named from the Greek word for "increase". The following properties are in addition to those listed in the QUARTZ And EPIDOTE sections of "Love Is In The Earth - A Kaleidoscope Of Crystals Update".

This mineral has been used in remote-viewing, assisting one to visit sites to observe and/or to transfer healing energy in situations of the existence of destructive influences and/or trauma associated with the area. It further assists one in the accurate reporting of that which is viewed.

Quartz with Epidote has been used as a refined "Delphi Oracle", such that the user may ask a question and receive the answer, the answer being relieved of ambivalence or the user being given the insight to eliminate the imprecision of the answer.

When there is Epidote which is totally enclosed within the Quartz, the combination man be used as a "Manifestation" crystal.

It has also been used between two people to assist in promoting insight into the uniqueness of the bond between the participants. It can also serve to enable one to maintain the understanding of the present while providing for the vision of the future, assisting the participants in understanding and experiencing common changes with ease.

Quartz with Epidote is also conducive to stimulating abilities to see the auric field, to open and to energize the third-eye, to receive telepathic messages, to initiate and strengthen the clairvoyant and clairaudient aptitudes, and to assist in the field of phrenology.

The mineral has provided for exhilaration during great times of activity, such as holiday seasons and travel situations. It assists one in maintaining direction and in accomplishing all that is needed to eliminate any crisis which could occur due to ones shortage of time available.

It further brings the energy to provide one with time for inner reflection, bringing and advent of revelation and visions specifically about the self.

It is an excellent healing stone, bringing a diagnostic energy with the transference of concomitant healing energy. It has been used in the treatment of disorders involving imperfect form and function. It allows one to recognize the perfection and beauty within the spiritual self and to manifest the totality externally and internally on the physical plane.

Vibrates to the number 6.

QUARTZ - GINGER \qquad

QUARTZ - GINGER - alpha-SiO_2 (Quartz) with alpha-Fe_2O_3 (Hematite), FeS_2 (Pyrite), and Fe_3O_4 (Magnetite); Hardness 7; Locality: Kazakhstan (formerly part of USSR). Imaging by HP Scanjet, Assisted by Bob Jackson and ♪ Melody ♫; Collection of ♪ Melody ♫, Applewood, CO, USA. Gift of Steve Goins, Oklahoma, USA

Ginger Quartz crystallizes with pyramidal faces and exhibits a ginger colour which is due to the inclusion of brownish-red to ginger-pink Hematite (curved wispy blades) and micro-pyrite (which can be seen under 50 power magnification. This book provides the first reporting of the chemistry of the mineral. Pliny first described Quartz as "Crystallus" (the crystalline formation) in 77 A.D.; U.R. von Kalbe, in 1505, presented the history of the name. In the late 1700's, T. Bergman found the crystalline and massive forms to have the same chemical composition and provided the name "Quartz". In 77 A.D., Pliny first described Hematite; it was named "Haematite" for the likeness to haemoglobin, etc.; In 1773, Romé de l'Isle changed the spelling to "Hematite". Pyrite was first described by Dioscorades in about 50 A.D.; named for the Greek word for "fire", it sparks when struck with steel. The term "Ginger" is used to represent the colour. The following properties are in addition to those listed in the QUARTZ, PYRITE And HEMATITE sections of "Love Is In The Earth - A Kaleidoscope Of Crystals Update".

This mineral has been used to eliminate the argument of emotion during times when "common sense" has no voice. Specifically, it acts to provide one with an energy of contemplation such that one will think prior to speaking.

Ginger Quartz has been used to enhance ones gentleness during care of the young, promoting the recognition of the fragility of the structure of esteem of the young and bringing an awareness of the loving actions required to stimulate the growth of the self-esteem, self-love, self-confidence, and self-reliance.

It can help one to connect with to others, in the spirit of "brotherhood" and love. It is expressive of cordiality and affability, promoting both altruistic tendencies and stamina against weariness from adulation.

Ginger Quartz has assisted one in studying emotions (anger, fear, passion, etc.) which appear as expressions on the face. It has quickened response time in recognizing the emotions and in acting "in the moment".

The mineral acts to bring expertise in activities involving both the legs and grace (e.g., skating, dancing, soccer, etc), assisting each endeavor to be one of beauty.

It has been used to eliminate over-booking in hotels and to support ninety percent occupancy in same.

It can also be used to facilitate gain during both dog-racing and horse-racing; the energy has acted to provide the number of the winning animal prior to the initiation of the race.

The mineral has also been used in gridding to preserve food.

Ginger Quartz has been used to enhance ones sense of taste, to balance hunger with optimum weight, and in the treatment of disorders related to tendonitis, "tight" shoulder muscles, and elimination. It has also been used to enhance physical stability and to prevent falls. In addition, it has been used as an elixir to eliminate candida.

Vibrates to the number 1.

QUARTZ - LIGHTNING   [Astrological Sign of Capricorn]

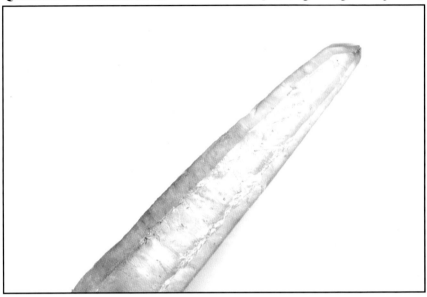

QUARTZ - LIGHTNING - alpha-SiO$_2$ (Quartz); Hardness 7; Locality: Bahia & Minas Gerais, Brasil, South America. Imaging by HP Scanjet, Assisted by Bob Jackson and ♪ Melody ♬; Collection of ♪ Melody ♬, Applewood, CO, USA. Gift of Joachim Karfunkel/Mário L.S.C. Chaves, Minas Gerais, Brasil, South America.

Lightning Quartz crystallizes as prismatic crystals, normally shaped as laser wands, with macroscopic deformation structures resembling irregular scratches (and not the same as natural etching). The configuration is also known as "FlashStone"and is the result of lightning energy on single quartz crystals which are found only in colluvial deposits. The terms "FlashStone" and "Lightning" were first used by Karfunkel, Chaves, Banko, Hadrian, Noack, and Schönau in a White Paper to describe the "Lightning" pattern on the crystal. The following properties are in addition to those listed in the QUARTZ and LASER WAND sections of "Love Is In The Earth - A Kaleidoscope Of Crystals Update".

Please note that encountering a "Lightning" Quartz crystal is similar in rarity to encountering a "Manifestation" crystal; currently the "Lightning" Quartz crystals are not separated by most miners and may be found in shops within their individual display of Laser Wands. This formation is a "Grand Formations" which can be used in surviving Earth changes and has been used to assist one in the recovery from shocks and traumas. It acts as a holophote, both focusing and transferring the light energy in the required direction. It has also been used to bring the energy of love like a lightning bolt.

"Lightning" Quartz has been used support swiftness in breaking the shackles of fear and dominion. Acting on the concept of inertia, it brings the energy of dispersion to the "still". It is an excellent stone for assisting in the modification of ones path, providing an energy to cut-through barriers and to clear-the-way for ones progression.

It has been used to transfer concentrated thoughts of the self to another location, such that ones form can be seen by those with intuitive and clairvoyant faculties and/or ones presence can be felt by those who are clairsentient. The hypothesis that "thoughts are things" explains the phenomenon as form created from ethereal and astral matter.

"Lightning" Quartz has been used to assist in the removal/relocation of poltergeists and spirits who are experiencing difficulty in the transition from the physical world to the spiritual world. It provides the message to "go to the light" in an expedient and rapid manner.

In addition to the Lemurian information which they have been reported to contain, they also contain an easily accessible knowledge of the healing techniques from other planetary worlds. This information is thought to have been transferred to the crystal by extra-terrestrial healers who are on-board ships in this select area of Minas Gerais; the transfer being accomplished with the energy of the lightning and during the progressive storms which are subsequent to same. The crystal has also exhibited speed during the facilitation of healing and in the advancement of contact with the extra-terrestrials.

The mineral has been used in the treatment of disorders involving deficiency in construction of ones body and in the functioning of the imperfect form. It can promote awareness by the cellular structure such that each cell affected by a dysfunction can singularly, and collectively, re-build and align with the state of perfection.

Vibrates to the numbers 5 and 2 ("Flashstone").

QUARTZ - With "LODALITE"

QUARTZ With "LODALITE" - alpha-SiO_2 (Quartz) with Illite [(K,H_3O)(Al,Mg,Fe)$_2$(Si,Al)$_4$O$_{10}${(OH)$_2$,H_2O} or (K,H_3O)Al$_2$(Si$_3$Al)O$_{10}$(H_2O,OH)$_2$] and Limonite [Fe^{3+}]; Hardness 7 (Quartz), 1 - 2 (Illite), and 5 - 5.5 (Limonite); Locality: Minas Gerais, Brasil, South America. Imaging by HP Scanjet, Assisted by Bob Jackson and ♪ Melody ♫; Collection of ♪ Melody ♫, Applewood, CO, USA.

Quartz with "Lodalite" crystallizes as prismatic Quartz crystals with "Lodalite" inclusions and with long hollow needles and needles filled with "Lodalite" within the Quartz. The "Lodalite" colour ranges from light to dark to reddish-tan. The mineral was first discovered by miners in Minas Gerais, Brasil; the name "Lodalite" was selected by the miners of Brasil from the word "Lodo" which is defined to be "mud", due to the light clay-like mud appearance. Quartz was first described as "Crystallus" (representing the crystalline formation) by Pliny in 77 A.D. and was further described by U.R. von Kalbe in 1505 to present the history of the name. The name "Quartz" was originally spelled "Quertz" and represented Quartzite (the compact granular massive configuration); it was named for the Saxon word "cross-vein ore". In the late 1700's, the two configurations (crystalline and massive) were found by T. Bergman to have the same chemical composition and, hence, were consolidated and provided with one name (Quartz). The following properties are in addition to those listed in the QUARTZ and LIMONITE sections of "Love Is In The Earth - A Kaleidoscope Of Crystals Update".

This mineral may be used to open the chakras and to perform psychic surgery. It assists in "surgically" removing attitudes, feelings, and attachments which may be causing or may potentially cause dis-ease. It should be noted that unless a person is willing to release the thought patterns, concepts, and self-constricting emotional patterns or ties, and to identify with a more positive self-image, the patterns may return and the person will be required to learn further lessons.

It has also been used to facilitate shamanic healing via the process of removing [by extraction] the unwanted condition from the physical form, and further transforming the condition to the state of purity.

Quartz with "Lodalite" can be used to ameliorate ones vulnerability when one encounters disappointment in affairs of relationships. It provides for the influx of distraction to ones life when ones ego has been damaged, and further assists one in surrendering to the outcome while maintaining an open-heart and while continuing progression on ones path. When used in these conditions, it brings an absorption of the distress and an emanation of an understanding of the concept of the "free spirit"; it further promotes the "giving of space" to the "free spirit".

The mineral also promotes the beginning in another act of the play of life, moving one from the "wings" of the stage to the new performance which will be commanded. It has also been used to stimulate "soft and smooth" and fascinating changes, providing the "right" time for life to take one to the newness of the adventure.

Quartz with "Lodalite" has furthered the activities of remote-viewing (such that one remains grounded and centered).

The mineral has been used in the dissipation of disorders of congestion and obstruction. It can also be used as an elixir to restore the body. It has been used in gridding during acupuncture.

Vibrates to the number 1.

QUARTZ - "METAMORPHOSIS"   [Astrological Sign of Scorpio]

QUARTZ - "METAMORPHOSIS" - alpha-SiO_2 (Quartz) with trace minerals; Hardness 7; Locality: Only from two mines, Minas Gerais, Brasil, South America. Imng by HP Scanjet, Assisted by Bob Jackson and ♪ Melody ♫; In the Collection of ♪ Melody ♫, Applewood, CO, USA. Gift of Daniel Foscarini de Almeida, Minas Gerais, Brasil, South America.

"Metamorphosis" Quartz crystallizes as masses and prismatic crystals which contain small amounts of Hafnium, Barium, Copper, Nickel, Strontium, and Aluminum. The colour is clear, yet foggy, and exhibits a controluz (a backlit opalescence). This book provides the first reporting of the mineral. The mineral was first discovered by miners in Brasil and the name was chosen to reflect the qualities of the stone which support the transformation to "Ouro Verde" Quartz (see pages 252-253) . Quartz was first described as "Crystallus" (representing the crystalline formation) by Pliny in 77 A.D. and was further described by U.R. von Kalbe in 1505 to offer the history of the name. The name "Quartz" was originally spelled "Quertz" and represented Quartzite (the compact granular massive configuration); it was named for the Saxon word "cross-vein ore". In the late 1700's, the two configurations (crystalline and massive) were found by T. Bergman to have the same chemical composition and, hence, were consolidated and provided with one name (Quartz).

The following properties are in addition to those listed in the QUARTZ section of "Love Is In The Earth - A Kaleidoscope Of Crystals Update".

"Metamorphosis" Quartz exhibits a back-lit opalescence which brings a "halo" to the mineral and has been used to automatically increase the range, the clarity, and the strength of ones aura. It has also assisted one in seeing the aura of others. It has performed as a spectrograph on the auric plane, bringing the entire spectrum into view.

This mineral is known as "THE stone of transformation", supporting the amplification of energy required for same. It assists one in replacing negative attitudes with positive direction and has been used as a mainstay and a foundation for one during changes. The mineral serves to prepare one for transformation, permitting the recognition of the obscure layers of "self-justification" which support the continuity of state of distress and dis-ease. It further assists one in releasing this justification; hence, reducing or eliminating the effects. It helps one to understand that any and all power is personal power and that in order to actualize ones full potential, personal action is required. It is truly a mineral to assist one in initiating and in persisting in changes, further supporting one during the process.

It has been used to direct one through the changes required to attain orderly situations while smoothing the state of change and dispensing a supplemental physical stamina and mental awareness to the user.

"Metamorphosis" Quartz has been used to assist one in intimacy. When one is preoccupied with outdated morality, it brings the energy to follow ones feelings (even if they change from day to day, hour to hour). It does not initiate immorality, but helps one to feel a commonality with being a part of life. It helps one to recognize that "if it feels good", and if it hurts no one (including the self), then one can do whatever it is and can enhance the self by "doing" and by "being".

The mineral is one for healing the self, on all levels. It has also been used in brain-wave stabilization and to ameliorate smoke inhalation and other maladies which block oxygen from reaching the bloodstream.

Vibrates to the number 4.

QUARTZ - "OURO VERDE"

QUARTZ - "OURO VERDE" - alpha-SiO_2 with trace elements and Gamma irradiation; Hardness 7; Locality: Only from two mines, Minas Gerais, Brasil, South America. Imaging by HP Scanjet, Assisted by Bob Jackson and ♪ Melody ♫; In the Collection of ♪ Melody ♫, Applewood, CO, USA. Gift of Orizon de Almeida, Minas Gerais, Brasil, South America.

"Ouro Verde" Quartz is a primary product after high-energy electron bombardment of "Metamorphosis" Quartz; the Gamma irradiation producing the golden green colour which results from an intense absorption in the ultraviolet range, actually acts to gently shift the electrical balance in the atomic lattice. The name "Ouro Verde" is the Brasilian portugues phrase defined as "gold green". This book provides the first reporting of the mineral. It should be noted that the Gamma irradiation of the "Metamorphosis" Quartz to produce the "Ouro Verde" Quartz does <u>not</u> confer a residual radiation; hence the mineral does not require "lockdown" prior to handling. The following properties are in addition to those listed in the QUARTZ sections of "Love Is In The Earth - A Kaleidoscope Of Crystals Update".

This mineral represents, Arcturus, the bright golden star which is known as the "guard of the Bear". It brings an energy of the first magnitude, never requiring cleansing or energizing, and additionally, providing a strength of protection to the user.

"Ouro Verde" Quartz assists in seasoning ones character to enable one to experience the deeper meanings of life. It also can assist one in applying the deeper meanings to superficial occurrences.

It has assisted one in the detection of Radon within ones environment and in the prevention of the uptake of radiation from both the state of nature and from the areas which reprocess radioactive materials and/or generate radioactive by-products.

It promotes maintaining a state of compliance with respect to exclusivity and with respect to adherence to rules and regulations. It has been used to alert one to restrictions which are in effect and to guide one in the fulfillment of requirements.

The mineral has assisted one in gaining information concerning the future, such that one is enabled in making correct choices and in gaining in same. It has been used in prediction for stocks and for games of chance such that one achieves the advantages for benefitting.

It is a stone which brings an actualization of prosperity - not a prosperity based solely upon the idea of being "calculator rich", but taking one from the calculation to the achievement.

The mineral has been used extensively to assist one in "shining" in whatever realm one pursues.

"Ouro Verde" Quartz acts to bring an energy which assists one in the identification of "triggers" to sporadic ailments (e.g., headaches), such that one can avoid the action and the repercussions of that action.

This mineral has been used in the treatment of disorders of pancreatic cancer, liver cancer, antibody-dependent cellular cytotoxicity (ADCCO), tumors, AIDS, herpes, and anaphylactic shock. It has assisted in the amelioration of allergies and has enhanced circulation to the feet,

Vibrates to the number 1.

QUARTZ - ORANGE With STARS [Astrological Sign of Taurus]

QUARTZ - ORANGE With STARS - alpha-SiO_2 (Quartz) with alpha-FeO(OH) (Goethite Starbursts), $KAlSi_3O_8$ or $CaCO_3$ (Adularia or Calcium Carbonate Rhombohedrals), Fe^{+++} (Iron), and Mn^{++} (Manganese); Hardness 7 (Quartz); Locality: The Republic of Congo, Africa. Imaging by HP Scanjet, Assisted by Bob Jackson and ♪ Melody ♫; Collection of ♪ Melody ♫, Applewood, CO, USA.

Orange Quartz with Stars crystallizes as prismatic crystals and clustered masses which contain metallic earth-black to brown Goethite starbursts <u>and</u> transparent to translucent white to colourless rhombohedral structures. The colour is a lovely "dreamcicle" orange, caused by the mixture of the iron and manganese. This book provides the first reporting of the chemistry of the mineral. The mineral was discovered in The Republic of Congo several years ago and the name was chosen to reflect the colour and the structure. Goethite was first described by J. Lenz in 1806; it was named for J.W. von Goethe. Quartz was first described as "Crystallus" (representing the crystalline formation) by Pliny in 77 A.D. and was further described by U.R. von Kalbe in 1505 to present the history of the name. The name "Quartz" was originally spelled "Quertz" and represented Quartzite it was named for the Saxon word "cross-vein ore". In the late 1700's, the two configurations (crystalline and massive) were found by T. Bergman to have the same chemical composition and, hence, were consolidated and provided with one name (Quartz). The following properties are in addition to those listed in the QUARTZ, MANGANESE, GOETHITE, and IRON sections of "Love Is In The Earth - A Kaleidoscope Of Crystals Update".

This mineral has been used to challenge the status quo, a task which must be performed in order to free one from the bondage to convention. It assists one in "looking" at emotional aspects of one life (e.g., fears, cravings, animosities, etc.) such that one can obtain mastery over these feelings. It further assists in the removal of deficiency in emotional intelligence. It subsequently assists one in a joyful focus on what is "right" with ones life and being, assisting one in embracing "who I am".

Orange Quartz with Stars has been known as a gift from the Pleiadians, assisting to those in that community to link with the "star people" of this planet and with those passive "star people" from the other realms. The coupling energy can advance physical perception and can help to bring those of corresponding minds into ones physical reality. It also acts to confer a coalition of the population, which shares experiences. The mineral assists one in recognizing "star people", the energy of the stone containing the genetic structure and cellular communication access, and providing for contact with those from other galaxies, as well as other planets in the solar system of the Earth. It contains an ethereal transmitting device which facilitates the connection. It should be noted that the number of "stars" within the structure is an indication of the number of different connections one may access.

It has been used to bring knowledge with respect to whether one is a "star person", to further define the lifetime in which one was a "star person", to discover the reasons for coming to Earth, and to ascertain the point of origin. It also facilitate inter-planetary and/or inter-galactic "party-line" communication.

Orange Quartz with Stars has been used in the treatment of degenerative and addictive behavioral disorders, in the amelioration of disorders of the skeletal and muscular systems, for dis-ease of the nervous system, and to eliminate neck pain due to whiplash.

Vibrates to the number 6.

QUARTZ - PYRITE INCLUDED [Astrological Sign of Scorpio]

QUARTZ - PYRITE INCLUDED - alpha-SiO$_2$ (Quartz) with Pyrite (FeS$_2$); Hardness 7 (Quartz) and 6 - 6.5 (Pyrite); Locality: Brasil, South America. Imaging by HP Scanjet, Assisted by Bob Jackson and ♪ Melody ♫; Collection of ♪ Melody ♫, Applewood, CO, USA.

Pyrite Included Quartz crystallizes as prismatic crystals with inclusions of Pyrite. Quartz was first described as "Crystallus" (representing the crystalline formation) by Pliny in 77 A.D. and was further described by U.R. von Kalbe in 1505 to present the history of the name. The name "Quartz" was originally spelled "Quertz" and represented Quartzite (the compact granular massive configuration); it was named for the Saxon word "cross-vein ore". In the late 1700's, the two configurations (crystalline and massive) were found by T. Bergman to have the same chemical composition and, hence, were consolidated and provided with one name (Quartz). Pyrite was first described by Dioscorades in approximately 50 A.D.; it is named from the Greek word for "fire" indicating the spark which occurs when Pyrite is struck with steel. The following properties are in addition to those listed in the QUARTZ and PYRITE sections of "Love Is In The Earth - A Kaleidoscope Of Crystals Update".

Pyrite Included Quartz is a "stone of manifestation", prompting the manifestation of abundance in ones life.

The mineral has been used to enhance ones introspective capabilities, increasing self-reliance, self-intention, and self-direction.

This combination is one of the "Grand Formations" used in Lemurian healing ceremonies and for the retention of the records of the procedures which provide for results.

Pyrite Included Quartz acts as a guide and as a stimulus to the quickening of evolution and to the recognition of those with whom one has been closely associated in other lives. It helps one to attain higher dimensional awareness, expediting the unification with the brothers and sisters of this dimension, with those from the realms of the spiritual and astral spaces, and with those from the stars; during these activities, the consummate energies are synthesized to produce the dazzling golden/white radiance which leads to the understanding of the details of previous associations.

The formation can be used to assist one in the furtherance of the enlightenment of the planet.

It has been used to remove unwanted implants, concurrently healing breaches within the entire chakra system and filling the voids which remain after the removal of the implant, with the healing light of love.

It has been used by the Ayahuasca shamen in South America to bring visions, providing for seeing beyond the physical realm; it has also been used for protection during "journeying" outside of the body, and to remove the cause of dis-ease from within the body.

Pyrite Included Quartz has been used in the treatment of moles and warts, and in the assimilation of Vitamin C, the relief of colds, flus, headaches, backaches, and muscular aches, and in the elimination of infestations of spiders and insects (in houses, and during camping and/or travel to areas where hotels/motels are not at least 3-star). As an elixir it has also acted to bring a glow to the skin.

Vibrates to the number 7.

QUARTZ - TUBED

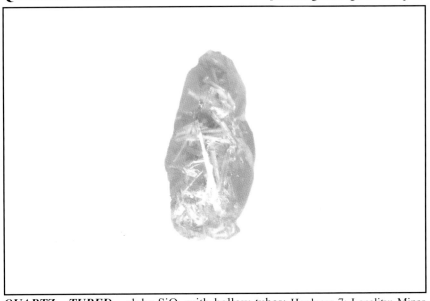

QUARTZ - TUBED - alpha-SiO$_2$ with hollow tubes; Hardness 7; Locality: Minas Gerais, Brasil, South America. The Imaging by HP Scanjet, Assisted by Bob Jackson and ♪ Melody ♫; Collection of ♪ Melody ♫, Applewood, CO, USA.

Tubed Quartz crystallizes as prismatic crystals which are included with hollow tubes. Mineralogical research during 1998 has shown that the hollow tubes once contained Epidote, and that the Epidote was dissolved from the crystal structures during hydrothermal intrusion caused by geological occurrences. Quartz was first described as "Crystallus" (the crystalline formation) by Pliny in 77 A.D. and was further described by U.R. von Kalbe in 1505 to present the history of the name. The name "Quartz", originally spelled "Quertz", represented Quartzite (the compact granular massive configuration); it was named for the Saxon word "cross-vein ore". In the late 1700's, the two configurations (crystalline and massive) were found by T. Bergman to have the same chemical composition and, hence, were consolidated and provided with one name (Quartz). The following properties are in addition to those listed in the QUARTZ section of "Love Is In The Earth - A Kaleidoscope Of Crystals Update". This mineral has been used in remote-viewing of a location and the sending of healing energy via the hollow tubes to that area (the energy of an Epidote crystal has been used to support the healing).

Tubed Quartz has been used to enhance the strength of the "silver cord" connection between the physical and astral bodies, providing protection and assuring that one may always return "home". It assists in astral travel and in the exploration of the parallel dimensions of ones reality, stimulating the opening of the pathway and assisting one in remembering the activities which one experiences and/or views as a non-participant. It can also bring protection during air travel.

The mineral has been used extensively in "The Gateless Gate" exercises as an alternative to the Faden Crystal. It is a mineral of **connection**, uniting the self with that which is chosen as the recipient. It can be used to facilitate the synchronicity between the self and another, and assists in producing/maintaining the ethereal connection of one has with another.

It has been used for past-life ascension, allowing one to maintain a strong-hold on the present reality while observing, without participating in, the events which one accesses; it further provides an understanding of the lessons which were [or could have been] learned, such that one may continue progression beyond the limitations of the lesson.

It has been used to assist one in locating ones complement on the physical plane, serving as a pathway through which ones counterpart may arrive. It promotes the finding of the unknown and/or the hidden.

Tubed Quartz is an excellent stone for centering the self and for gridding disturbed areas of the Earth. It serves to provide a continuous alignment of the physical meridians and the nervous system and can be used to cleanse the aura and to open the chakras.

The mineral serves to stimulate molecular bonding and mending and healing on all levels. It has been used in Jin Shin Jyutsu, to direct disorders to a receptacle filled with white light in order to transmute any concomitant negativity into positivity. It has been used by the Hopi healers to enhance the transfer of specific sounds to locations of the body such that the sounding of these words through the mineral has alleviated dis-ease in those areas. It has also promoted referrals from physicians for laying-on-of-stones.

Vibrates to the number 2.

"YOU ALL SHINE AT YOUR OWN TIME"

River Starr (L.A.M.)
Neosho, Missouri, USA

RADIOLARITE (Sedimentary)

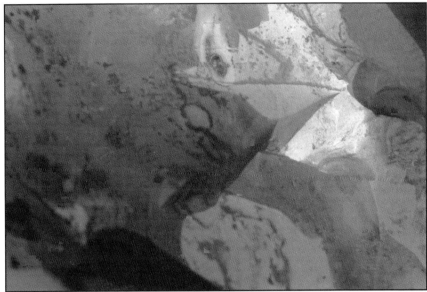

RADIOLARITE (Sedimentary) - SiO_2 with impurities and with the lattice-like skeletal framework of Radiolaria; Hardness 7; Locality: Western Australia, Australia. Imaging by HP Scanjet, Assisted by Bob Jackson and ♪ Melody ♫; In the Collection of ♪ Melody ♫, Applewood, CO, USA. Gift of Glenn Archer, Western Australia, Australia.

Sedimentary Radiolarite crystallizes as dense violet siliceous fine-grained chert-like homogenous consolidated masses; it further exhibits a cream-to-yellow siliceous skeletal framework of actinopoda belonging to the sub-class of Radiolaria. This mineral has been confused with Porcelainite due to the chert-like appearance of same; however, Porcelainite occurs in the white-to-grey colour.

This mineral can be used to eliminate the "fool's errand" and the "borrowing of trouble". It allows one to recognize that futility is never a friend; it enhances ones affectivity and ones knowledge of right-action.

When disbelief gives way to simple astonishment, this mineral can bring a reaction quicker than thought. It tends to crystallize the mental process such that, as the piezoelectricity is ever-present within a crystal, an acuity is ever-present within ones mind. It further provides for the recognition that all actions are prayers, actual invocations of the higher good and requests for blessings that one is in the state of right-action. It promotes quickness in decisions, even if one is stunned by incredulity and even when the detriments of bemusement are attendant.

Sedimentary Radiolarite can be used to dispel confusion within ones life. It dispels the vagueness of the being who stumbles through life, walking into walls and wondering why the impact is painful. It serves one in the creation of opportunities such that one may distinguish between the differing wave and form of situations.

The mineral provides for focus on objectives such that one may become positively obsessed, but never possessed by a goal. It allows one to recognize, to understand, and to celebrate the reasons that others are not identical in "beliefs" and do not share in the joy of the same "things". It promotes the celebration of differences and dispels the theme in which denial (due to martyrdom) works in the guise of self-righteous nobility.

Producing an stony exterior for the emotions, it promotes the knowledge that no matter how "small" one feels, one will never disappear. It, hence, augments ones resistance to embarrassment and has, actually, been used to prevent humiliating situations. It has also been used to allay conditions which are conducive to the frosty silence of disagreement, bringing the prerequisite energy for the stimulation of conversation.

The mineral can bring the action to match the knowledge of "I think I can....I know I can". It brings self-confidence, reliance upon the self, and determination to "do" whatever one wishes and/or needs to "do".

Sedimentary Radiolarite can both cleanse and activate the crown chakra, allowing for energy blockages to be dispersed through same. Placed upon one of the two carotid arteries (at the neck), it has also furthered the determination of the pulse rate during Tibetan pulsing.

It has been used in the treatment of disorders of the colon, to relieve jaw pain caused by temporomandibular disorder (TMD), and to increase adaptability to prostheses. It can also be used to assist one in determining the existence of breath during cardiopulmonary resuscitation.

Vibrates to the number 2.

RHYOLITE - GREEN - A combination of Quartz (SiO_2) and Feldspar (general formula ($K,Na,Ca,Ba,NH_4)(Si,Al)_4O_8$) and Nephelite ($Na,K)AlSiO_4$; Hardness 5 - 7; Locality: Turee Creek Station, Western Australia, Australia. Imaging by HP Scanjet. Assisted by Bob Jackson and ♪ Melody ♫: In the Collection of ♪ Melody ♫, Applewood, CO, USA.

Green Rhyolite is a unique style of spherulitic Rhyolite, the uniqueness due to the colour (Rhyolite does not normally occur in dark green). The mineral crystallizes as finely-grained masses, is an extrusive igneous rock, and is typically porphyritic exhibiting flow texture, with phenocrysts of quartz, nephelite, and alkali feldspar in a glassy-to-cryptocrystalline groundmass. The colour ranges through the green spectrum and contains some brown and tan. It is also known as "Rain Forest Jasper".

The following properties are in addition to those listed in the RHYOLITE, QUARTZ, and FELDSPAR sections of "Love Is In The Earth - A Kaleidoscope Of Crystals Update".

This mineral can assist one to live with intention, to "walk to the edge", to make selections with no regret, and to continue to learn.

It acts to provide the most favourable circumstances for the promotion of wholeness, such that one may share knowledge and expertise joyfully, and use ones skills to the best of ones ability and integrity, suspending all judgments and expectations.

Green Rhyolite has also stimulated the insight to more creative ways of expressing difficult things (problems, solutions, anxieties, etc.).

The mineral assists one to look at ones relationship to change, and to evaluate that relationship, instead of looking at, and evaluating, the change itself. With this insight and energy, one can more easily determine the basis for the change and exactly what that change will bring to ones path.

It brings to one "living proof" of the constructive potential which can allow one to dispense with looking at the more negative expectations, both externally and internally.

Green Rhyolite brings the energy of Chiron which supports a new purpose to ones life. It acts to rid the self of the burdens which no longer serve in ones life, bringing an energy of renewal and original thinking which will lead one to the "new".

It has also been used to assist one in finishing projects, dispelling procrastination and/or deferral of ones responsibilities (or choices which were selected in the past) to another. It further acts to eliminate distractions and to dissipate the illusions of ones reality.

It also has been used to activate contact with loved-ones who have ascended to other planes and can be used in communication with animals.

It also enhances the abilities in pursuits of construction, and architecture.

Green Rhyolite can act to stimulate the optimum levels of well-being within the body, in the treatment of ruptures, diabetes, hypoglycemia, varicose veins, and to calm the animal kingdom.

Vibrates to the number 8 (Green Rhyolite) and the master number 77 (Rain Forest Jasper).

ROSE-CITRINE - A combination of Rose Quartz (SiO_2 with impurities [Mn]) and Citrine (SiO_2 with impurities), occasionally with clear Quartz (SiO_2); Hardness 7; Locality: Minas Gerais, Brasil, South America. Imaging by HP Scanjet, Assisted by Bob Jackson and ♪ Melody ♫; Collection of ♪ Melody ♫, Applewood, CO,

The lovely Rose-Citrine combination displays a chemistry which includes the mass-configuration and, occasionally, the crystal configuration of Rose Quartz, with Citrine (and sometimes clear Quartz) crystals. Rose Quartz was first described by J.D. Dana in 1837; it is named from the colour. Citrine was first described by E.S. Dana in 1892; it is named for the Greek word meaning "citron", referring to the colour. Quartz was first described as "Crystallus" (representing the crystalline formation) by Pliny in 77 A.D. and was further described by U.R. von Kalbe in 1505 to present the history of the name. The name "Quartz" was originally spelled "Quertz" and represented Quartzite (the compact granular massive configuration); it was named for the Saxon word "cross-vein ore". In the late 1700's, the two configurations (crystalline and massive) were found by T. Bergman to have the same chemical composition and, hence, were consolidated and provided with one name (Quartz). The following properties are in addition to those listed in the ROSE QUARTZ,

CITRINE, and QUARTZ sections of "Love Is In The Earth - A Kaleidoscope Of Crystals Update". This mineral has been used to bring intellectual presence to issues of the emotions and heart-felt sentiments, melding the left and right brains in a unification to effect accord.

The Rose-Citrine combination has been used to bring "shelter and warmth" to one such that loneliness is dispelled. It acts as a friend to the user and can bring happiness to those who feel forsaken or abandoned. It has also been used as a focal point for marriage and/or relationships, promoting the members of the union to be true companions, and furthering the knowledge that there is one life to be shared. It brings stability, permanence, and security in these alliances of the heart.

It assists one in realizing that life is full of "if onlys" for everyone, and it further acts to remove any anguish or regret which is associated with ones personal "if onlys" and to assist one in realizing that there are no mistakes - there are only lessons. Placed in ones environment, it has also eliminated the experience of "if only", assisting one in recognizing and in evaluating all options with any situation, prior to executing an action.

The mineral is one which brings the energies of love coupled with the energies of balance. It provides a balance for intellectual activities, emotional issues, relationships, spirituality, and receptivity.

The Rose-Citrine combination promotes the ability to "have ones cake, and eat it, too". It furthers the conveyance of loving situations to the user and instills the energies which promote the enjoyment of same. It also acts to allow one to "have it his/her way", assuring that the "way" is one of love and blessings to all involved.

It has also been used to bring wealth to altruistic pursuits and to pursuits wherein one is performing an action (e.g., business) which is conducted entirely due to humanitarianism and/or love for others.

The mineral has been used to further the practice of "well-ness" and has been used to assist one in dietary changes which will promote same. It has also been used as an elixir to bring clarity to the energy centers.

Vibrates to the number 9.

"IF IT'S NOT FUN, YOU'RE NOT DOING IT RIGHT"

Leif Dragseth
Alaska, USA

SAL AMMONIAC

SAL AMMONIAC - NH$_4$Cl; Hardness Unknown; Locality: Fischbachtal, Germany. Imaging by HP Scanjet, Assisted by Bob Jackson and ♪ Melody ♫; In the Collection of ♪ Melody ♫, Applewood, CO, USA.

Sal Ammoniac crystallizes in the cubic system as a white encrustation, usually about volcanic fumaroles. The colour range includes white, colourless, grey, and yellow. The mineral was first described by G. Agricola in 1546; it was named for the medieval Latin for salt of Ammon, which was found near the Oracle of Ammon in Egypt.

This mineral has been known as a "stone to serve", after "ich dien", the German words for "I serve", and was the motto of Prince of Wales. It has been used extensively in the service industry, as well as, in assisting one in "being of service" to both the self and to others. It has also been used in gridding to bring customers to restaurants, clubs, shops, etc. It has been placed upon business cards, upon advertisements, and within the "sign" structures of independent businesses to increase client base. It has also been used to promote increased "tips" for waiters and waitresses.

It is a mineral which has been used to promote efficiency in money management (e.g., obtaining and spending, saving and investing). It has acted to bring a positive actualization to the application for loans and/or for financial assistance. It has also been used to enhance the understanding of economics.

Sal Ammoniac supports "playing" with abandon, bringing the blessings of overindulgence and self-indulgence in "doing" that which one loves and in living life as if this were the only life that will ever occur. It further assists in the amelioration of lack of tolerance and/or endurance while one is "playing".

The mineral has brought relief to quiet desperation, to fear of the night and to fear of being alone.

It brings the energy to instill the presence of mind so that one may be accustomed to "new" tasks and brings an ease to the learning required for the successful completion of these tasks.

Sal Ammoniac has been used to cleanse the chakras, conveying the energy to facilitate the removal of negative programming and the negative debris which one may gather from circumstances and/or environments in which one may find oneself.

It has also been used to cleanse other minerals (as an elixir), acting to initiate the inherent beneficial energies, and to concentrate the energy of the other mineral for focus to a specific utilization and to promote an enhancement and an endurance of that same energy.

The mineral can be used to impede suicide due to depression; it acts to bring the knowledge that one has not yet learned all that is required during this life, that "this too shall pass", and that life is truly a precious blessing, filled with beauty.

It can be used in the treatment of disorders of the alimentary canal. It has also been used (as an elixir) to ameliorate upset stomach, bladder infections, kidney infections, headaches, dizziness, and fainting.

Do not prepare an elixir via the normal method.

Vibrates to the number 2.

SANIDINE - $(K.Na)(Si.Al)_4O_8$: Hardness 6: Locality: Utah. USA. Imaging by HP Scanjet. Assisted by Bob Jackson and ♪Melody ♫: Collection of ♪ Melody ♫. Applewood. CO. USA.

Sanidine crystallizes tabular crystals often embedded in fine-grained igneous material. The colour ranges from white to grey. The mineral was first described by K.W. Nose in 1808; it is named from the Greek word for "board" or "tablet" due to the flat shape of the crystals.

This mineral can be used to promote the assimilation of multifarious knowledge through the synthesizing power of the mind. It further imparts an energy to free one from conditioning and from acting in a "stimulus/response" manner.

It has acted to assure sufficiency in sustenance of the self (with physical nourishment and a physical abode. It has assisted in bringing plentitude in food and a stable environment in which one may reside.

It can also be used by those who "live by the wits", to assure sufficiency in provisions. equipment. stores. and supplies. which will further the continuance of the preservation of state of life. Hence. it is an excellent energy for back-packing, camping, trekking, etc., assuring one of suitable reserves.

The mineral can bring order to chaos, both within the body and in circumstances of turmoil within ones environment. It can produce a calming, yet energizing, essence which brings composure and eliminates both agitation and aggravation. Placed in ones habitat, it has served to promote the removal of negativity.

Sanidine has also been used to assist one in coping with the qualms of the intensity of ones conscience, providing for an acceptance of that which has already been executed and/or for that which one intends to accomplish; the acceptance has been facilitated via the re-structuring of ones knowledge such that one can "know" that "all is as it needs to be".

It acts to bring cooperative effort and to dispel the aspects of dissension and opposition which occur in ones life. It alleviates fluctuation between states, purposes, and opinions; allowing for the manifestation of wisdom within each situation.

It further acts to provide sanction for actions for which one is uncertain; producing an authoritative "permission" which supports the action one contemplates.

The mineral can be used to further the skill of writing; assisting one in the performance of the actual task, and in remediating that which needs to be corrected. It has been used both for the actual formation of letters and for the preparation of essays, books, etc.

When one desires sanctuary from distressful situations, the energy acts to produce a place of refuge within the environment and within the mind such that the user has protection from detection. It has been used in ashrams and monasteries to promote celibacy.

Sanidine has been used in the treatment of senility, disorders of the sinuses, over-eating, bulimia, addiction, and to abate unbalanced needs for sexual intimacy.

Vibrates to the number 3.

SCHRÖECKINGERITE

SCHRÖECKINGERITE - NaCa$_3$(UO$_2$)(SO$_4$)(CO$_3$)$_3$F♥10H$_2$O; Hardness 2.5; Locity: Wyoming, USA. Imaging by HP Scanjet, Assisted by Bob Jackson and ♪ Melody ♫; Collection of ♪ Melody ♫, Applewood, CO, USA.

Schröeckingerite (also known as Dakeite) crystallizes in the orthorhombic system in colours ranging from grey to greenish-yellow. The mineral was first described by A. Schrauf in 1873; it is named for Baron Schröckinger.

This mineral has been used to promote a holistic sensory integration of the total third-dimensional being via visual, auditory, tactile, olfactory, and kinesthetic regulation of the physiological, emotional, and energetic processes of the physical, emotional, and mental bodies.

It further assists one in recovery from dysfunctional states, serving in the optimization of cognitive ability, motivation, libido, and learning ability. It has also assisted in the creation of statistically significant beneficial changes in brain-wave patterns which can assist one in the access of higher states of consciousness, and in the promotion of the enhancement of ones intellectual life.

Schröeckingerite has also been used to alert one when one has had "enough" - enough food, enough drink, enough time, enough fear, enough depression, enough ..., enough..., enough. It acts to bring a message to the user that the time has come to cease in whatever action has been sufficient for ones experience.

It has also been used to allay pervasive truancy and dereliction and/or negligence in fulfilling ones responsibilities. It dispels the acts of the rebel in riots, bringing the understanding that violence is the unloving method of resolution. It further assists in the elimination of the attributes of the recidivist, acting in the dissipation of the chronic tendency toward repetition of criminal or anti-social behavior patterns.

The mineral can be used to assist one in the development of the character of the eyes which bespeak confidence, bringing the power of the eyes to express ones inner thoughts and to allow others to understand one without communication. It promotes a penetrating gaze which signifies the intensity of ones thoughts, and assists one in building oneself into the person which one desires to be. The mineral serves as a reminder to actualize and to emanate those qualities which one wishes to demonstrate outside of the self.

Schröeckingerite brings a sensitive deep energy which has been used to promote the verbal dialogue to support ones personal process, to provide awareness, and to facilitate a nurturing approach to guide one in ones journey.

It has also assisted in advancing the communication between the self and animals, promoting trust in the guidance of animals and improving the relationship between the self and the animal(s).

The mineral has been used in the treatment of bloating, fibromyalgia, nutritional deficiencies, and in the elimination of the necessity for superfluous prescription drugs and non-legal pharmaceutical drugs.

Do not prepare an elixir via the normal method.

Vibrates to the master number 88 (Schröeckingerite) and the number 1 (Dakeite).

SCORZALITE

SCORZALITE - $(Fe,Mg)Al_2(PO_4)_2(OH)_2$; Hardness 5.5 - 6; Locality: Wermland, Sweden. Imaging by HP Scanjet, Assisted by Bob Jackson and ♪ Melody ♫; Collection of ♪ Melody ♫, Applewood, CO, USA.

Scorzalite crystallizes in the monoclinic system in the form of masses, pyramidal crystals, and grains. The colour range includes blue and blue-green. The mineral was first described by W.T. Pecora and J.J. Fahey in 1947; it is named for E.P. Scorza.

This mineral can be used to eliminate the behavior of philandering and trifling with another. It acts to bring consciousness to the philanderer or the flirt such that he/she will not be able to continue the pretense with a "straight-face". Specifically, when one carries the mineral, the message of non-verity is provided to the user, while the humour of "being caught" is provided to the one who is toying with the user. Hence, it provides a light situation to one which could potentially become painful, and a reciprocation of energy between two independent parties which acts to dispense with conditions of ambiguity and travail; it further produces a mutual exchange of authentic communication between parties such that anamorphic images are dissipated and linear understand is enhanced.

Scorzalite was used by the antediluvian culture as a "worry stone" which provided insight to worries and encouraged the application of intuitive answers.

It assists one in appearing quite calm, glancing neither to the left nor the right in curiosity or apprehension, when one is focussed on a goal. It provides a "global knowing" such that the actions of "looking" are unnecessary and superfluous and assists one in being both in control and certain during ones quest.

It has been used for gridding during gatherings of large numbers of people (e.g., concerts, festivals, etc.), in order to stimulate pacification and composure of the group.

The mineral can also be used to assist in protection from the infiltration of computer viruses; placed upon the hard-drive assembly, it has promoted the non-entry of same when the potential was existent.

Scorzalite brings the ability of bifurcation, promoting the division of ones energies into two avenues of attention, such that one can really "do more than one thing at a time"; it has further assisted one in being in "two places at the same time", acting to further the manifestation of the ethereal form in a location distinct from the area where the physical third-dimensional form is situated.

The mineral can also assist in the promotion of literacy, serving to promote reading capabilities on the remedial level and acting to stimulate the desire to read. It has been used to instill a basic knowledge of the coalescence of letters in the formation of words. It has also been used to enhance skills during the study and retention of other languages.

The mineral has been used by museums to stimulate the appreciation of the quality of that which is on display.

Scorzalite has been used in the treatment of disorders of the pituitary, the cornea of the eye, and the inner canals of the ear, and in the amelioration of dyslexia and parasites.

Vibrates to the number 2.

SELENITE - ENHYDRO

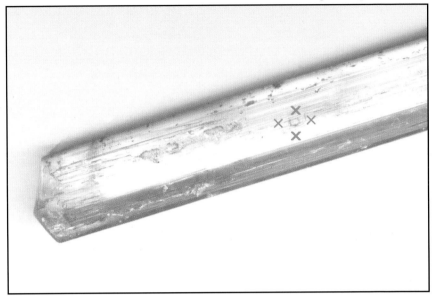

SELENITE - ENHYDRO - $CaSO_4 \heartsuit 2H_2O$ (Selenite) and H_2O (Water); Hardness 1.5 - 2; Locality: Mexico. Imaging by HP Scanjet (Note "X's" surrounding water bubble), Assisted by Bob Jackson and ♪ Melody ♫; Collection of ♪ Melody ♫, Applewood, CO, USA.

The Enhydro Selenite crystallizes as a transparent colourless to white, somewhat flexible form of crystallized gypsum with water inclusions. Selenite was first described by J.G. Wallerius in 1747 and named from the Greek word meaning "the moon", due to the pale reflections inherent within the structure. The Enhydro was first described by T. Egleston in 1887, representing the inclusion of water within geodes. This collective composition of Selenite and Water is included herein due to the additional qualities researched which were due to the combination. The following properties are in addition to those listed in the ENHYDRO and SELENITE sections of "Love Is In The Earth - A Kaleidoscope Of Crystals Update".

This mineral has been used to promote the healing stream that abounds to bring the ethereal healing water to the parched and withering roots of ones life, being like a balm of hope and grace and furthering the actualization of tribulations-small, and triumphs-large.

A stone of both majesty and mystique, it has been likened to the streams of flowing waters which flow forth from rocks to nourish that which they touch (c.f., Psalms 78:16 and Psalms 105:41).

The Enhydro Selenite has been used to facilitate connectiveness with new cycles during the celebration of the new moon. It can be used in gridding during this time and in the promotion of victory and jubilation during the new growth cycle which is approaching.

It has facilitated seeing within the three-dimensional birth sphere to determine the health, sex, position, etc. of the unborn; the results of position can be verified by one looking and by another touching.

When ones faith is as the dew that dries early in the morning sun, this mineral can assist one in eschewing all unnecessary risks, in playing the odds with infinite caution, and bringing gratification in action.

The energy of the mineral acts as an allargando power, increasing in intensity as it receives more attention from the user.

It has been used to promote the Eye-Movement Desensitization and Reprocessing (EMDR) process, furthering the release of abuse and undesired loss, and dissipating emotional distress and negative thinking linked to these specific events.

It has been used by the shamen of Mexico for the transference of the medicinal qualities of herbs to those who would benefit. It has been used as a center structure for medicine circles to stimulate the infiltration of the infinite healing forces of the universe, and to provide for flexibility in ceremonial activities.

The Enhydro Selenite can also be used to assist one in the recognition of the special, sacred "medicine" stones which can be carried, is personal to the user, and is of a protective nature.

The mineral has been used to facilitate ease in the birthing process, and in the treatment of back pain caused by muscular disalignment.

Vibrates to the number 7.

SELENITE - FOSSIL SEEDED   [Astrological Sign of Sagittarius]

SELENITE - FOSSIL SEEDED - $CaSO_4$ ♥ $2H_2O$ (Selenite) and Fossil Seeds; Hardness 1.5 - 2; Locality: Texas/Oklahoma area, USA. Imaging by HP Scanjet, Assisted by Bob Jackson and ♪ Melody ♫; Collection of ♪ Melody ♫, Applewood, CO, USA. Gift of Dan Ryder, Texas, USA.

Fossil-Seeded Selenite crystallizes as a transparent colourless to white to yellow, somewhat flexible form of crystallized gypsum with inclusions of fossilized seeds and hollow seed-holes. Selenite was first described by J.G. Wallerius in 1747 and named from the Greek word meaning "the moon", due to the pale reflections inherent within the structure. The Fossil seed within the structure has been preserved since some past geologic or prehistoric time. The hollow seed-holes indicate the dissolution of a non-fossilized seed during the formation of the Selenite crystals. Occasionally, plant roots are included in the structures.

The following properties are in addition to those listed in the FOSSIL and SELENITE sections of "Love Is In The Earth - A Kaleidoscope Of Crystals Update". This mineral has been used to stimulate cooperative and mutually profitable business associations, bringing a cohesion within same and a solid foundation from which to build.

Fossil-Seeded Selenite can assist to remove the tendency and the actualization of contempt and derision during conversations; it acts to remove the need for sarcasm and further promotes the elimination of the potential for the "tone" of ones voice to contain same.

When one feels that ones weaknesses are "incurable", the mineral acts to stimulate the inner nature toward non-acceptance of the weakness. It actually "nudges" the Inner Self such that information is provided that the inadequacy which is felt is truly unwarranted.

Within relationships, it brings a comfort in silence, such that words unspoken are understood and the necessity for constant talking is eliminated. It acts to place one "at ease" with others such that the nervousness, which precipitates non-stop talking, is eliminated.

Within the field of education and/or scientific pursuits, it assists one in moving with exhilarating rapidity through technical jargon and in understanding the essence of the purpose and the significance of the information.

Fossil-Seeded Selenite has also been used to dispel decay in soils, fruits, and vegetables, and to prevent grain-rot and root-rot.

It has also been used to further syllogistic rationality and deliberation, bringing analytic reasoning. It is a mineral for both the intellect and the crown chakra, stimulating logical knowledge of the events and conditions.

It has been used as a reminder of marriage promises and to assure commitments are maintained.

Fossil-Seeded Selenite has assisted in the "cutting" of the thread - sometimes fragile, sometimes rugged - which holds one to life; it a mineral to assist one in the transition from the physical form. It has also been used to promote nutritional absorption within the body, to stimulate fertility, and to decrease the occurrence of tooth decay. It has also been used in the treatment of gangrene and of wounds and ulcerations which appear difficult to heal.

Vibrates to the number 4.

SEPTARIAN NODULE [Astrological Sign of Taurus]

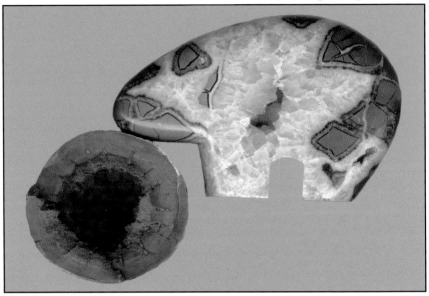

SEPTARIAN NODULE - A spheroidal concretion (of medium-grained to fine-grained sedimentary rock) which contains a cavity lined with, and fissures filled with, calcite ($CaCO_3$) (left top) or with a clay ironstone (right bottom); Hardness 3 - ?; Locality: (Left Image) McKinlay, Queensland, Australia; (Right Image, polished) New York, USA. Imaging by HP Scanjet, Assisted by Bob Jackson and ♪ Melody ♫; Collection of ♪ Melody ♫, Applewood, CO, USA. Left Image Specimen Gift of Kathleen and Andy Mather, Queensland, Australia. Right Image Specimen Gift of Earth-Love Gallery, WheatRidge, CO, USA.

The Septarian Nodule, pictured in both stages of development, is a concretion crossed by networks of fissures in which minerals, commonly Calcite, have been deposited from solution. Prior to the depositing of minerals, the cavity is filled with clay ironstone (see Left Image). It is characterized internally by irregular radiating fissures that become wider toward the center and that intersect a series of fissures which are concentric with the margins. After the clay ironstone stage, the fissures are filled with crystalline calcite, and calcite crystals are, sometimes, formed from the deposition; the crystalline calcite displaces a portion of the clay ironstone and tends to "bond" the calcite together with the clay ironstone. The following properties are in addition to those listed in the CONCRETION section of "Love Is In The Earth - A Kaleidoscope Of Crystals Update".

This mineral has been used to enhance the gift of speaking such that one may speak to an audience in an individualized, personal manner, and facilitating ones presentation such that one displays an aura of being totally interested in each of the members of the audience.

It further promotes the maintenance of a non-captive audience for lengthy periods and with ridiculous ease; it subsequently stimulates a progressively deeper interest, respect, and enthusiasm within and throughout the audience.

Placed in the center of drumming circles which are being used for healing, such that the drumming is focussed and resonating, it assists in the direction of the energy of the mineral to penetrate the area which one desires to be healed.

The Septarian Nodule has been used to facilitate and to enhance neuro-linguistic programming (NLP). It brings the knowledge to the user of the methods and the circumstances for application which will be most productive.

The energy of the power totems for the turtle and the beetle are also activated by the mineral. It assists in instilling patience, endurance, and tolerance.

Bringing an energy which dispels curiosity in others, it has also been used to assist one in maintaining anonymity with respect to ones finances, ones relationships, ones activities, etc.

It has further supported ones survivalist activities, allowing for the motto of "always be prepared" to manifest within ones life, and to transfer to ones outer presentation.

The Septarian Nodule has been used to promote freedom of movement of the body, assisting the body to support its self-healing abilities. It has also been used in the treatment of external tumors and growths; as an elixir, it can be used in the prevention of the degeneration of the bones and teeth and to enhance the muscular structure.

Vibrates to the master number 66.

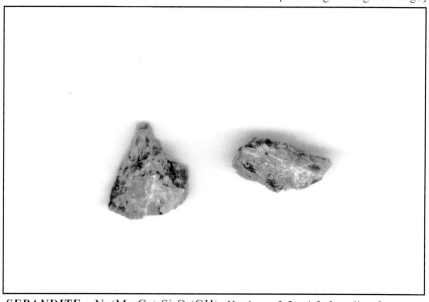

SERANDITE - Na(Mn,Ca)$_2$Si$_3$O$_8$(OH); Hardness 2.5 - 4.5; Locality: Lovozero, Russia. Imaging by HP Scanjet, Assisted by Bob Jackson and ♪ Melody ♫; Collection of ♪ Melody ♫, Applewood, CO, USA.

Serandite crystallizes in the monoclinic system as elongated crystals. The colour range includes orange-brown to rose to red. The mineral was first described by A. Lacroix in 1931; it is named for J.M. Sérand. Serandite occasionally occurs with black Vuonnemite.

This mineral has been used to dispel self-pitying gloom and recrimination, such that when there is a cloud of doubt forming on ones mental horizon, one can maintain confidence in knowing the solution even before the problem had been posed. It also is effective in corroborating ones convictions.

It can assist one in recognizing the shackles which have been self-inflicted, stimulating one to release the restrictions in order to facilitate independence from the servitude of the materialistic world. It assists in correctness and candidness in activities, and stimulates the deeper understanding of living now, in this world.

Serandite further supports one in the admission of guilt, when guilty, and issues an esteem for the user which conveys a sense of accord in candor.

It has been used to bring customers to the salesperson, and clients to a practitioner, generally a variety quite different than the usual, and of the persuasion which will further the activities same.

It is quite helpful in discouraging pugnacity and fervent displays of temperament. It facilitates receptive action for the enquiring minds of youth. It has been used to stimulate the heart, sacral, and base chakras, facilitating inner strength in affairs of the heart. Assisting one to view the self from outside of the realm of personal reality, it acts to inspire and to encourage one toward improvement.

It has also stimulated appreciation during operatic and symphonic performances, and has initiated creativity during music composition.

It brings a working-energy for the elimination of entities from ones environment and from ones corporeal existence. It further acts in gridding operations to bring serenity to an environment and to provide a message of loving energy to those of other worlds.

Placed upon the external portion of ones water supply system (within the structure of ones home), it has provided for a refinement in the purification of water. It has further acted to produce a shielding energy against infiltration of external impurities to the water.

It further assists one in the attainment of the recognition of that component within the self which is ever-watchful, never unaware, and which is always observant and conscious, of that which is in the external world. It helps one to experience direct harmony within this reality and to see no duality or multiplicity.

Serandite has also been used for dimensional work and cellular work. It can be used to treat the cartilaginous portions of the body, to relieve additions to soft drinks, and to assist in bringing one to an emotional balance.

Vibrates to the number 5.

SLATY SHALE - RECORD STONE   [Astrological Sign of Scorpio]

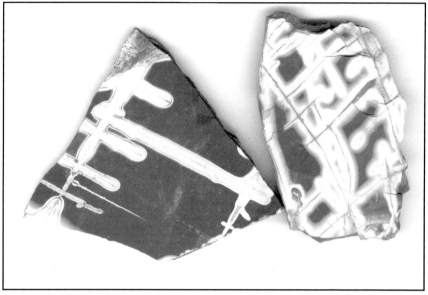

SLATY SHALE - RECORD STONE - A combination of Slaty Shale (fine-grained detrital, sedimentary finely laminated structure), Kaolinite [Al$_2$Si$_2$O$_5$(OH)], and Iron (Fe); Hardness Variable; Locality: The "Melody Green Mine", Arkansas, USA. Imaging by HP Scanjet, Assisted by Bob Jackson and ♪ Melody ♫; In the Collection of ♪ Melody ♫, Applewood, CO, USA.

The Slaty Shale Record Stone crystallizes as laminated masses upon which are glyphic patterns comprised of Kaolinite and Iron. It is thought that the word "shale" was derived from the Teutonic word meaning shell or husk. Kaolinite was first described by S.W. Johnson and J.M. Blake in 1867; it is named for Kauling, a hill in China, which contained Kaolin(ite). The Slaty Shale Record Stone is first described on these pages. The following properties are in addition to those listed in the KAOLINITE section of "Love Is In The Earth - A Kaleidoscope Of Crystals Update".

This composition of the "glyphs" of this mineral has been shown to have originated from a source outside of the original the dispositional location. Translation of the "glyphs" has produced information concerning other-worldly ceremonial techniques and healing techniques based upon the utilization of the mineral kingdom. The "glyphs" are said to have been placed upon the shale via specific action of beings from outside of our dimensional world, specifically to assist us in our progression in healing and in the actualization of our paths.

The Slaty Shale Record Stone has been used in deciphering ancient scripts and codes and has initiated the translation of Etruscan, an ancient language from an ancient civilization; it has been found to contain the energies to assist one in both gaining and maintaining a connection with another area of the world, the spiritual members of another ancient society, and with the Earth - allowing for the transmission of information between the two, and for the conveyance of loving/gentle energy to the defined location.

It can help in the discovery of mineral deposits and in the study of geology and geological forces. It can promote visions, given background information, with respect to locations of that which has not been discovered and/or that which has been "lost" after initial discovery.

The stone has been said to have been an "Escarboucle", a mythical stone used by the Knights of the Round Table to bring insight and solutions to problems.

Although the magic of wishing does not work backward, this mineral has been used to clarify that which one "thought" one wanted and/or did not want, and to subsequently promote the actualization of "wishing" the unwanted to be gone again. It provides for the recognition that although one may have forgotten much, one still has the advantage over those who never knew anything in the beginning.

It has been used in gridding to prevent mindless vandalism and graffiti.

The Slaty Shale Record Stone has been used to take one back to his/her youth (even if it is quite a trip) and to stimulate youthful renewal. It has assisted one to transcend the material essence of the body, bringing about prompt response to healing situations.

Due to possible solubility of the attendant minerals, do not prepare an elixir via the normal method.

Vibrates to the number 6.

STAINIERITE

STAINIERITE - CoO(OH); Hardness 3 - 4; Locality: Clark Co., Nevada, USA. Imaging by HP Scanjet, Assisted by Bob Jackson and ♪ Melody ♫; In the Collection of ♪ Melody ♫, Applewood, CO, USA.

Stainierite crystallizes as colloidal masses. The colour range includes black, reddish, and black-brown. The mineral was first described by V. Cuvelier in 1929; it was named for X. Stainier. However, in 1962, M.H. Hey confirmed the mineral to be Heterogenite, albeit a colloidal form which has not yet been reported. Hence, it is felt that both names can be used with accountability. Heterogenite was first described in 1872 by A. Frenzel; it was named from the Greek word for "of another kind", referring to compositional difference from minerals it otherwise resembles.

This mineral has been used to assist the mind in problem-solving and in the initiation of same. It acts to promote the formation of a "picture" within the mind (rather like the painting-by-numbers exercise, where the colours merge to form a picture of something that, if one had not known, one could not "guess"). It serves one who is "face-to-face" with that which appears to be impossible, such that the mental processes will continue to provide the message that one can begin to undermine that tenable-looking conundrum. It initiates the "painting of several of the colours in the pattern", and although the picture may continue to appear obstinately determined not to reveal itself, promotes the "leap" of the mind into the "dark" to provide the solution (albeit strange or startling).

Stainierite has also been used to enhance "process painting", a mechanism through which one may befriend ones spontaneity to build confidence via a supportive and sportive endeavor. It dispels the curtains through which one hides from the important aspects of the self, promoting the normally resisted inner change and, hence, eliminating emotional crises.

The mineral has been used for the transport of information in all realms - without consummate out-of-body travel (i.e., with "intellectual" travel). The mineral has also been used to stimulate the recognition of details related to Earth-changes, astrological significance, and weather patterns.

It can be used to facilitate the long-term interests of justice concomitant with the short-term benefit of the personal. It initiates "planting the seeds", watching the sprouting of the roots and the unfolding of ones unique needs, and bringing the fruition of that which is planted. It is also an excellent mineral for agricultural growth.

It has been used to promote correct structure, rapid application, and energetic concentration, combined with a slow intensity of practice, the development of internal energy and muscular flexibility, when one becomes involved with the movement discipline of "Tai Ji Quan".

Stainierite can bring the energy for one to discriminate between that which contains disparity, instilling rationality and reason.

Used during muscle-testing and balancing, it assists one in evaluating body function and enables one to correct energy blockages which promote pain and dysfunction. It has been used in the treatment of cancer, chelation therapy, anemia, and can also be used to ameliorate the effects of radiation treatment. It is a mineral to discourage disorderly growth.

Vibrates to the numbers 3 (Stainierite) and 5 (Heterogenite).

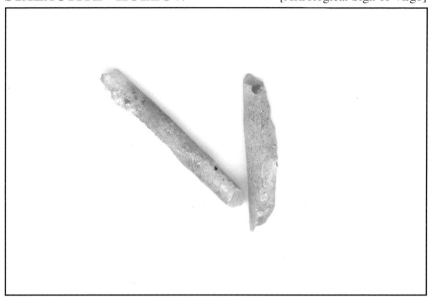

STALACTITE - HOLLOW - Calcium Carbonate; Hardness Unknown; Locality: Mexico. Imaging by HP Scanjet, Assisted by Bob Jackson and ♪ Melody ♫; Collection of ♪ Melody ♫, Applewood, CO, USA.

The Hollow Stalactite crystallizes as pendent columns, cylinders, or elongated cones which are hollow. Stalactites are produced by the percolation of water, holding mineral elements in solution, through the rocky summits of caverns, such that the evaporation of the water produces a deposit of the mineral in the elongated configuration. The hollow aspect is judged to be from one or both of the following scenarios:

1) The stalactite encased a host rock which had like-configuration and due to influx of another mineral, the stalactite became unbound to the host rock and slid off of same;

2) The stalactite encased a host rock which had a very soluble core and there was an influx of liquid which dissolved the core.

The following properties are in addition to those listed in the STALACTITE section of "Love Is In The Earth - Kaleidoscopic Pictorial Supplement A".

The Hollow Stalactite can serve to release repressed emotions and conditions which have produced negative effects upon ones well-being and satisfaction of this life. It has been used to bring tenacity to actions which further the continuance of a situation and can be used to bring the willingness and actions required to release a situation when it is no longer necessary for ones growth. Hence, the energy brings compensating gratification from all situations.

When one experiences self-destructive patterns, the energy facilitates the infusion of humane understanding and brings a compassion such that one can listen carefully to ones inner knowledge and such that one can readily forgive the self and can allow the patterns to disappear. It allows one to experience the final adjudication, and to eliminate any final judgment. It further provides for freedom from conditioning and promoting the natural unfolding of ones path and ones life.

The mineral has been used to facilitate the knowledge and/or insight which will bring cross-cultural solutions, promoting acceptance at each end of the spectrum.

The Hollow Stalactite has been used to provide a tunnel-like passage for the transfer of white light between the third-eye, through the upper portion of the body, and to the Inner Self. The perception of a flow of ethereal liquor throughout the physical form may be discerned and one may intuitively recognizes the clarity or non-clarity of the path. The mineral has also been used to clear the path, when the path is obstructed, via utilization with the "Arkimer Diamond".

The mineral has been used to guide the flow of energy within the body (Chi) and in the home (Feng Shui). It has also been used to stimulate the talents in performance with musical instruments.

It has been used in the treatment of disorders of the throat, the alimentary canal, the nasal and olfactory passages, and to treat acidosis.

Due to the fragility of this stone, do not prepare an elixir via the normal method.

Vibrates to the number 6.

SUNSTONE - COPPER SCHILLER   [Astrological Sign of Leo]

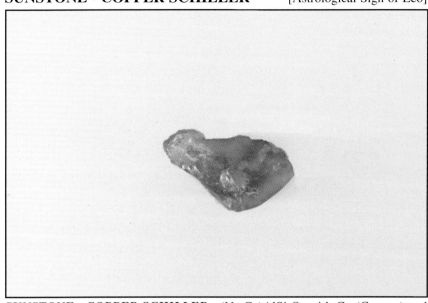

SUNSTONE - COPPER SCHILLER - (Na,Ca)AlSi$_3$O$_8$ with Cu (Copper) and inclusions of sub-microscopic lamellae; Hardness 5-6; Locality: Oregon, USA. Imaging by HP Scanjet, Assisted by Bob Jackson and ♪ Melody ♫; In the Collection of ♪ Melody ♫, Applewood, CO, USA. Gift of Jim Cowan, Oregon, USA.

Sunstone which exhibits a Copper Schiller-effect is dependent upon the play of metallic Copper within the Sunstone. Copper-Schiller Sunstone is a form of oligoclase and crystallizes in the form of masses and, rarely, tabular crystals. Sunstone was originally described by J.D. Dana in 1837 and was named for the brilliant reflections within the stone. The Schiller-effect was named for the German, Schiller. The following properties are in addition to those listed in the SUNSTONE section of "Love Is In The Earth - Kaleidoscopic Pictorial Supplement A".

This mineral has been used to balance the electrical and magnetic energies of the body, assisting in the elimination of energy blockages and elevating the flow of energy and life force throughout the body. It is an excellent mineral for both faith healing and crystal healing. As an elixir it is an excellent energizer and protector of the home environment and for the plant kingdom; it can also be used in the garden or field situation to help to relieve infestations. It has been used in the home environment to protect against insects infiltration, acting with the energy of a "web" to trap the insects prior to entry.

Sunstone which exhibits a Copper Schiller-effect is one of the stones which will be used during the period of the "grand alignment" of the planetary bodies in May, 2000. It brings an energy conducive to the beginning of totally new and enlightening cycles. It brings the message that fear is a negative image of the future, and assists one to modify ones programming such that confidence-based attitudes are prevalent.

It has been used to impart appreciation of beauty. In our world today, there are, sometimes, instances of a person/business wanting to destroy the beauty of our Earth for monetary gain - often stating that the area of the land is being "wasted"; in mind-sets similar to these, the mineral can be used to assist the person/business in realizing that beauty is never "wasted". It has also been used by Earth First members and by other environmental groups for this purpose.

If ones totem is the sudden rainstorm or snowstorm, the mineral can stimulate an ethereal and magnetic connection with the energy of the storm; this provides an additional energy conducive to immediate and intensified energy transfer and healing, to the awakening of the inner forces so that one may actualize that which is desired, and to the facilitation of contact between the self and ones etheric double.

It acts also to arrest leakages of energy from the chakras and to transmute negative energy to the "golden realm of reasoning".

It is said to be the "stone of the Bifrost", the stone in Scandinavian mythology which brings the rainbow bridge of the gods from heaven to Earth. It has been used to bring contact and alliance with the extra-terrestrial realm and to provide for safety and protection during same.

The mineral has been used to assist in treatments where homeopathy or allopathy is the preferred method. It can also be used in the treatment of the radial arteries and to reduce varicose veins.

Vibrates to the number 7.

SURSASSITE

SURSASSITE - $Mn_2Al_3(SiO_4)(Si_2O_7)(OH)_3$; Hardness 4 - 7; Locality: Grisons, Switzerland. Imaging by HP Scanjet, Assisted by Bob Jackson and ♪ Melody ♬; In the Collection of ♪ Melody ♬, Applewood, CO, USA.

Sursassite crystallizes in the monoclinic system in small radial botryoidal masses and elongated needles and crystals. The colour ranges from a deep reddish-brown to copper-red, and exhibits pleochroism. The mineral was first described by J. Jakob in 1926; it is named for Sursass, the name, in the Rhaeto-Romanic dialect, of the locality in Switzerland where it was first discovered.

This mineral has been used to promote understanding of that which is evasive.

It further assists one in dealing with those who are truculent, providing for a pacification of aggression. It can assist one in gazing directly into the thoughts of another, in being alerted immediately to the slightest deviation from the truth; since one will then know the truth prior to asking, one need only to note the inaccuracies and/or distortions which may be forthcoming. The mineral can also be used to assist one in the determination of veracity and validity in emotional issues - i.e., within the self (is it real) and from outside of the self (is it true).

Sursassite has been used to provide an shield of intelligence to facilitate protection from that which is deceitful. It brings strength and courage to confront falsity and provides the perseverance for resolution.

Sursassite has been used to ameliorate adolescent confusion and troubles. It can assist in imparting courtesy and respect within the minds and hearts of the young. It has brought corrective effects to the acts of impertinence, insolence, and arrogance, and has promoted the expedition of substitutions which reflect the charming attitudes of politeness and respectfulness.

It brings an energy to support the continuity of circular breathing, such that the flow of Prana through the body is conducive to both meditation and to healing.

It is a mineral to assist with the alleviation of oppression. It acts to remove the cloak which covers the act, and assists one in viewing the resultant situation with both logic and sensitivity, in order to release it. The energy has been used to transform ones views such that positive thoughts predominate. It is a strong energy for alteration of ones state of being.

It is a mineral from the Earth and for the Earth, stimulating equilibrium and strength; it has provided assistance in the stabilization of those areas of unrest [e.g., areas of volcanic or earthquake potential] which are below the surface. It has also been utilized in Earth rituals and in the cleansing and energizing of minerals.

Sursassite has been used to balance the energies of the yin-yang. It has also been used to assist in acupuncture/acupressure therapy, assisting via dowsing and "pointing" to the correct locations for the therapy.

It has been used to promote the assimilation of manganese, and in the treatment of narcolepsy, myopia, emphysema, and speech disorders.

Vibrates to the master number 33.

SYLVANITE

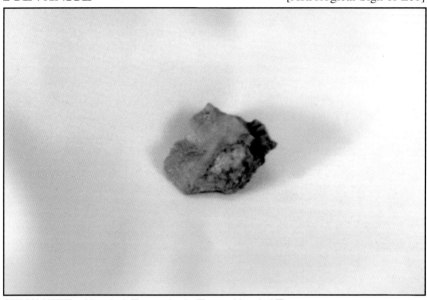

SYLVANITE - $(Au,Ag)_2Te_4$ or $AgAuTe_4$ or $(Au,Ag)Te_2$; Hardness 1.5 - 2; Locality: Cripple Creek, Colorado, USA. Imaging by HP Scanjet, Assisted by Bob Jackson and ♪ Melody ♫; Collection of ♪ Melody ♫, Applewood, CO, USA.

Sylvanite is a Telluride of Silver and Gold which crystallizes in the form of branching arborescent forms resembling written characters, blades, and grains. The colour range includes steel-grey to silver-white, yellow, grey-white, and creamy-white. The mineral was first described by L.A. Necker in 1835; it is named from Sylvanium, one of the names first proposed for the metal Tellurium. The following properties are in addition to those listed in the GOLD and SILVER sections of "Love Is In The Earth - A Kaleidoscope Of Crystals Update".

This mineral brings the energy to allay obsessive behavior and to assist in the centering of the self.

It can also be used to stimulate the intuition toward the recognition of the methodology which can assist in the improvement of monetary affairs, further prompting one to take the immediate action which will be most beneficial.

It further acts to assist one in "burying" that which has departed from ones life; assisting in the realization that that which is "gone" is no longer necessary for ones growth. It serves to help one to remain as a conductive energy during situations of disharmony and/or chaotic confusion.

Sylvanite is being used to promote the healing of the Earth, stabilizing the center and energy vortices, and further assisting in the remediation of the actions of global warming.

It can be used to energize the crown chakra, and has also been used to provide a synthesis between the intellect (third-chakra) and enlightenment (crown chakra), such that one may more easily understand that which is required to attain the enlightened state.

The mineral can facilitate the extension of ones remembrance to the beginning of the Earth phase and assists one in the recall of past-lives relative to the commencement of humanity upon this planet. It has also been used in gridding arrangements to stimulate the restructuring of the ozone layer in ones environment. Used in planetary awareness and global meditations, it can serve in the healing of that stratospheric layer for the Earth. It is also an excellent stone for group work, assisting in the stability of the group.

As a stimulant for the right-brain, Sylvanite has been used to promote the writing and the appreciation of poetry.

It is an excellent stone to promote general vitality.

As an elixir it has been used to relieve fatigue and to provide for an equilibration of body heat. It has been used in the treatment of strep infections, disorders of the skeletal system, the small capillaries, CFS, mononucleosis, and circulation, and in the prevention of RNA/DNA damage. It has also been used to promote growth during the formation of the structures of the young.

Do not prepare an elixir via the normal method.

Vibrates to the number 1.

SYLVINITE
[Astrological Sign of Pisces]

SYLVINITE - A combination of Sylvine (KCl) and Halite (NaCl); the mineral specimens often also contain Kieserite ($MgSo_4$ ♥ H_2O); Hardness 2; Locality: Saxony, Germany. Imaging by HP Scanjet, Assisted by Bob Jackson and ♪ Melody ♫; In the Collection of ♪ Melody ♫, Applewood, CO, USA.

Sylvinite crystallizes as granular and compact masses and cubes. The colour ranges from brown to red-brown. The mineral was first described by A.H. Chester in 1896; it was named by combining portions of the names of the components (i.e., "Sylvin" from Sylvine and "ite" from Halite). The following properties are in addition to those listed in the SYLVITE section "Love Is In The Earth - Kaleidoscopic Pictorial Supplement A" and the HALITE of "Love Is In The Earth - A Kaleidoscope Of Crystals Update".

This mineral has been used to rid oneself of the irrational master, jealousy, serving to dispel feelings of resentment, envy, rivalry, and paranoia. It further serves to allow one to understand that he/she can, truly, have exactly what is desired <u>or</u> that one may release that desire in order to refrain from wanting same - the choice is ours.

It has been used to further the process of adoption (of children, of attitudes, etc.), acting to make the procedures effortless, uncomplicated, and straightforward, <u>and</u> bringing attainment of the object, purpose, and/or action.

Sylvinite can be used to bring success to tantric endeavors, assisting in the act of non-action and in the completion of the exercise.

Assisting one in abstract conceptions, it has been used to further the study of philosophy and psychology.

It assists one in orientation with the body, promoting ones knowledge about ones form and its relationship with others and with time and space.

It has also been used to stimulate "objectified dreaming", such that one may begin a remolding of ones form within the dream state. It further assists one in recognizing the alignment of ones structure/body with the alignment of the magnetic/electrical forces of the biosphere and of the Earth, wind, water, etc.

Sylvinite promotes "asking", and supports one in the process. It has been used to encourage questions on any level, and in any realm, where one desires more information. It has also fostered the dispensing of "answers" to these questions. With the mineral, these processes have occurred with spontaneity, comfort, and rapidity.

Assisting one in remembering courtesies and kindnesses, it acts to bring an energy conducive to "thankfulness" and appreciation without the attending obligation. It helps one to realize that others enjoy the realm of benevolence and that goodwill is a state of being.

It has been used in the treatment of acrotism, heart murmur, and cellular stability with respect to fluidity. It can also be used in the amelioration of the "grating" voice, smoothing and softening same.

Due to the solubility of this mineral do not prepare an elixir via the normal method.

Vibrates to the number 9.

**"IF YOU CAN'T ENJOY YOURSELF,
ENJOY SOMEONE ELSE"**

Hal Jessen
USA

TARNOWITZITE

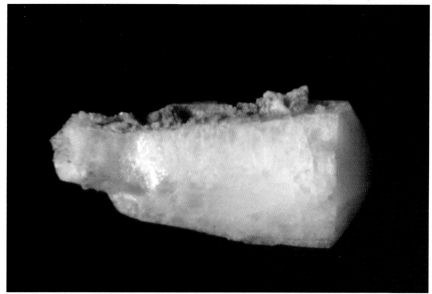

TARNOWITZITE - A combination of Cerussite ($PbCO_3$) and Aragonite ($CaCO_3$); Hardness 3 - 4; Locality: Tsumeb, Namibia, Africa. Imaging by HP Scanjet, Assisted by Bob Jackson and ♪ Melody ♫; Collection of ♪ Melody ♫, Applewood, CO, USA.

Tarnowitzite crystallizes in the orthorhombic system as masses, and aggregates with simple tabular/pyramidal/pseudo-hexagonal crystals, and is, occasionally, a homogeneous mixture of the component minerals. The colour ranges from white to grey. The mineral was first described as Tarnovizit by A. Breithaupt in 1841, and was modified to the current spelling by C.F. Naumann in 1847 to indicate the locality of first discovery (Tarnowitz, Poland). The following properties are in addition to those listed in the CERUSSITE and ARAGONITE sections of "Love Is In The Earth - A Kaleidoscope Of Crystals Update".

This mineral has been used to bring preternatural happiness to the elevated areas one life and to burnish the lower areas with the autumn sun, assisting one in moving toward the door he/she has never opened. It can bring a euphoric state which promotes living "dangerously", loving with abandon, and being with the totality of all and everything; hence, instilling the need to explore the wonderful, eleemosynary unknown.

Tarnowitzite acts to induce expansion of the energy field in the location in which it resides. It can produce a field of attraction for healing, and can stimulate the production of negative ions while clearing the surrounding atmosphere of positive ions; it has further acted to extend the energy of recovery to the totality of ones environment. Hence, it is an extremely useful mineral for sessions of healing.

It has been used for the facilitation of the privatization of business, bringing an energy of unity between one and humanity in order to further the interaction with same. It has promoted the increase of clientele from other countries.

It has served to bring an increase to the bio-magnetic forces in the body, to align the body with the magnetic fields of the Earth, and to promote magnetic healing, providing receptivity to radionic treatment. Wearing or carrying the stone is recommended to facilitate remedial actions and to stabilize alignment.

The mineral can provide one with a magnetic attraction; would that one could attract only those or that which is desired.

Tarnowitzite has assisted in the furtherance of political careers, and in the athletic fields of vaulting, hurdling, and climbing,

It can assist in clearing ones character during situations of slander, libel, and defamation; it tends to bring an energy to remove the results of these actions. It also acts to prevent same.

The mineral has also been used to dispel irrationality.

Tarnowitzite has been used to protect one from over-sensitivity to the sun, and to increase ones tolerance to the sensitivity. It has also been used to reduce the occurrence of flashbacks. Placing the stone on an affected area of the body has stimulated rejuvenation of the organs and the muscle tissue within that area.

Do not prepare an elixir via the normal method.

Vibrates to the number 9.

TETRAHEDRITE

TETRAHEDRITE - $(Cu,Fe)_{12}Sb_4S_{13}$; Hardness 3 - 4.5; Locality: Mexico. Imaging by HP Scanjet, Assisted by Bob Jackson and ♪ Melody ♫; Collection of ♪ Melody ♫, Applewood, CO, USA.

Tetrahedrite crystallizes in the isometric-tetrahedral system as tetrahedral, and granular and compact masses. The colour range includes, flint-grey to iron-black, metallic grey-black, and grey to olive-brown. The mineral was first described by W. Haidinger in 1845; it is named from its tetrahedral crystal form.

This mineral has been used to incite one to recognize and to remember small seemingly insignificant details which will later assume a new-born magnitude. It can enhance ones ratiocinative skills, bringing an ability to measure and to decide, in terms of which elements are conceivable and/or credible, and which are implausible.

It provides for a combination of fortunate coincidences, chances, decisions, and fate (indifference and detachment to situations), such that ones life is filled with adventure and intrigue. One is never in a state of boredom, or without anything to "do" when this mineral is utilized.

Tetrahedrite has been used in study to bring a union, association, and consideration of all, together, such that one not only understands the concept, but also can grasp the basis. It can be used to further orderly thinking and the skills of organization within ones life, ones business, and ones home.

It has been used to advance one in the areas of cooking, chemistry, and alchemy, bringing a melding of the analytical with the intuitive during experimentation.

The mineral can serves to eliminate the potential of severe reprimand and criticism. It further acts to dispels opposition when ones pursuit is not detrimental to another.

It has been used to bring families together in cohesiveness and love. It serves to assist in the conveyance of feelings within the unit and to facilitate bonding and constance.

Tetrahedrite is a mineral to build the foundations for those "castles" one has built "in the sky". It assists one to be both the "weaver of dreams", in appreciating the beauty of same, and in acting to bring reality (via organized thinking and planning) to the dreams. The action bringing the sparkle of the stars to ones wishing.

It has been used to stabilize the infrastructure and substructure of buildings, both during the construction phase and/or after usage and when the building experiences stability. Gridding has proved quite useful during correction of an instability in structures.

The mineral has been used to assist one in the initiation and the sustainment of circular breathing.

Tetrahedrite has been used in the treatment of menopause, the prostate, frigidity, to subdue conditions of inflammation, and to ameliorate disorderly growth within the cellular structure of the body

Do not prepare an elixir via the normal method.

Vibrates to the number 7.

THUNDEREGG - MT. HAY [Astrological Sign of Aquarius]

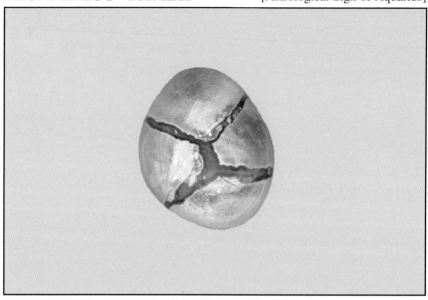

THUNDEREGG - MT. HAY - A fortification [banded in layers] agate, which is enclosed by a hardened compact matrix; the matrix usually contains silica ash; Hardness 3 - 7; Locality: Mt. Hay, Queensland, Australia. Imaging by HP Scanjet, Assisted by Bob Jackson and ♪ Melody ♫; Collection of ♪ Melody ♫, Applewood, CO, USA. Gift of Martin Rosser, New South Wales, Australia.

The Mt. Hay Thunderegg crystallizes in spherical formations and, internally, exhibits a star-like pattern. It is named from its location of occurrence. Although Thundereggs have been found in several parts of the world, the Mt. Hay Thunderegg carries unique physical properties, and is hence, reported here. One of the unique characteristics of this mineral is that when polished on the external surface, the center glows when it is held over a light; in addition, when viewed with short-wave ultraviolet light, the center glows a light, and sometimes shimmering, emerald green. Throughout Europe, the Mt. Hay Thunderegg has been known as "Amulet Stone" and "Star Agate".

The following properties are in addition to those listed in the AGATE and THUNDEREGG sections of "Love Is In The Earth - A Kaleidoscope Of Crystals Update".

The Mt. Hay Thunderegg contains power and energy that was stored from the volcanic action which facilitated the formation; it can further hold power and energy that is stored by the user. It is a lovely exercise to infuse the mineral with healing energy and power and to then present it to one who is in a low energy cycle.

It can assist one in maintaining the rhythmic breathing conducive to entering and to attaining depth in the meditative state. Subsequent to the meditative state, it helps one to maintain the fresh radiance of the conscious reflection of same and to emit the brilliance of the light from within the self, and through ones eyes.

It has been used to enhance electromagnetic waves providing the self-luminous quality and assists one in "seeing" auras and in maintaining the connection between the physical and ethereal planes during the renewal and/or cleansing of auras.

The Mt. Hay Thunderegg serves to initiate those circumstances which are required for attentiveness and totality in that which one pursues; initiating mystery, introducing non-commitment/uncertainty, inspiring intensity (emotional), and, subseequently, imparting just enough risk to activate the intrepid spirit.

Australian legend states that the Mt. Hay Thunderegg is carried for good luck and to protect against negativity.

It has been used to promote the act of subsumation such that a dissimilar idea (which is felt to have great importance) can be included in another idea (which can be totally disparate). The process being one through which incompatible views can be melded.

The mineral has also been used to instill group unity.

It has been used to bring both stamina and wholeness to ones body and has been used in the treatment of disorders of the lungs, stress, and emotional anger.

Vibrates to the numbers 1 (Amulet Stone), 2 (Star Agate), and the master number 77 (Mt. Hay Thunderegg).

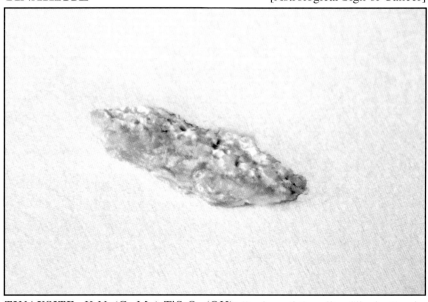

TINAKSITE - $K_2Na(Ca,Mn)_2TiS_7O_{19}(OH)$; Hardness 6; Locality: Siberia, Russia. (Mineral shown with pink Fedorite); Imaging by HP Scanjet, Assisted by Bob Jackson and ♪ Melody ♫; Collection of ♪ Melody ♫, Applewood, CO, USA.

Tinaksite crystallizes in the triclinic system as yellowish acicular radiating crystals. The specimen shown in the image also includes Fedorite (resembling Mica). The mineral was first described by Yu G. Rokov, V.P. Rogova, A.A. Voronkov, and V.A. Moleva in 1965; it is named from the composition (ti-na-k-s [ite]).

This mineral has been used such that "justice will be served". It brings an energy to assure that "wrongs" are "right-ed" and that injustice is corrected. It further serves to induce non-caustic trait and virtues, providing help during mental processing and producing support for the reasoning faculties.

It can be used to assist in the protection of privacy and in the preservation of ones past, such that one may retain anonymity and another cannot access information from ones past. It has also been used by the ancient civilizations of Eurasia in ceremonial healings to provide protection from the past and to dissipate both darkness and to facilitate purification from the rituals during the revering of the Earth.

Tinaksite brings an energy of negative electrification, assisting one in the removal of negative intentions and in the elimination of divergent intellectual thoughts and emotions which could affect the emotional and intellectual bodies.

It tends to promote an abundance of energy, flashes of inspiration, and a stimulation of the application of devotion toward the realization of the path; it has gently assisted in the removal of the obstructions which impede ones progress.

Used in gridding, the mineral has been used to prevent stalking and has eliminated harassment and annoying telephone calls.

The mineral brings precision in strategy with respect to the actualization of the self, and that which one desires during this segment of ones life.

It also brings an energy to banish the fear of failure and the re-living of those same failures such that one is not hostage to those memories.

It has been used to relieve nervousness and to prevent the "nervous laugh".

Tinaksite has assisted in clearing the intellect of "untidy" emotional, physical, or spiritual issues; it further stimulates, cleanses, and activates the third chakra.

The mineral has been used to ameliorate problems associated with Calcium and Potassium deficiencies and Sodium imbalance. It can be used in the treatment of disorders related to infections within the body, in the elimination of fibrous and tissue growths, and has been used in the bath to alleviate painful joints and to reduce swelling.

An elixir has been shown to be of assistance in cases of nutritional deficiency.

Vibrates to the number 9.

TOPAZ - PURPLE

TOPAZ - PURPLE - $Al_2SiO_4(F,OH)_2$; Hardness 8; Locality: Minas Gerais, Brasil, South America. Imaging by HP Scanjet, Assisted by Bob Jackson and ♪ Melody ♬; Collection of ♪ Melody ♬, Applewood, CO, USA.

Purple Topaz crystallizes as prismatic crystals, sometimes vertically striated and sometimes with well-developed terminations. The colour ranges from a pinkish-purple to a light violet-purple. Purple Topaz is a unique colour of Topaz (the colour has not yet been described in mineralogical references) and is, hence, reported here. Topaz was first described by J.G. Wallerius in 1747; the name is derived from the Greek word representing an island in the Red Sea. The following properties are in addition to those listed in the TOPAZ section of "Love Is In The Earth - A Kaleidoscope Of Crystals Update".

This mineral can provide an "inoculation" against attraction to the "wrong"person, a person who will not further ones happiness and/or will bring pain to ones life.

It has also been used to provide a resonance which is audible (or clairaudient) when one is talking with someone as yet "unknown" <u>and</u>

when there is a connection (due to a "holdover" energy from the "old" days) between one and that person. It has been used to relieve complication from liaisons, bringing a protective force to free one from fear and to promote success in the affair and has been used to stimulate the production of rhetorical questions to produce effect.

Purple Topaz is a stone of "Ora pro nobis" bringing the energy of prayer and blessings to ones life. Displaying an energy of spirituality, it promotes a connection between the heart chakra and the crown chakra (moving the Kundalini) and further provides for the transfer of energy between the two; it brings a loving countenance to ones spirituality and a sanctity to the range of ones love. It further acts to assist one in being "content to preach to the choir"; promoting, when necessary, the recognition that no amount of "preaching" and/or moralizing to the general masses will further a cause and providing an alternative paradigm which supports a personal critical self-review of that which one would herald. Hence, a peaceful co-existence between two factions is sustained.

The mineral brings information concerning the weather - acting to stimulate the receipt mechanisms of the ionic energies of the atmosphere so that prediction (and, if necessary, action) is provided. It further acts to bring information with respect to "whether" - acting to stimulate the mechanisms for decision-making by displaying to one any serious flaws in logic, lack of objectivity, misinformation, and/or simple ignorance.

It has been used during scholarship search to ease the pursuit and to bring achievement of the goal.

Bringing an energy to dispel "enemies of truth", it has acted to eliminate false representation, distraction from rational solutions to social problems, corrosion in rationality, and fraud.

Purple Topaz has been used to eliminate pain during the intrusion of needles (and is an excellent mineral for carrying during the receipt of a tattoo). It can also be used in the treatment of autism, and pathological medical conditions (e.g., schizophrenia, personality disorders), and to strengthen the spine.

Vibrates to the number 4.

TOURMALINE - LAVENDER - $(Na,K,Ca)(Mg,Fe,Mn,Li,Al)_3(Al,Fe,Cr,V)_6$ $Si_6O_{18}(BO_3)_3(O,OH,F)_4$; Hardness 7 - 7.5; Locality: Minas Gerais, Brasil, South America. Imaging by HP Scanjet, Assisted by Bob Jackson and ♪ Melody ♫; Collection of ♪ Melody ♫, Applewood, CO, USA. Gift of Eliud Ferres (Salim), Espirito do Santo, Brasil, South America.

Lavender Tourmaline crystallizes as lavender-blue vertically striated prismatic crystals, sometimes slender and sometimes needle-like. Tourmaline was first described as Turmalin (after the locality of Turamali in Cingalese) in 1703 by jewelers of Ceylon who applied the name to Zircon. Later, the name "Turmalin" was "mistakenly" applied to a consignment of tourmaline which was being shipped to Amsterdam. The name evolved over time to the current spelling. Lavender Tourmaline is a unique colour of Tourmaline (the colour has not yet been described in mineralogical references) and is, hence, reported here. The following properties are in addition to those listed in the TOURMALINE section of "Love Is In The Earth - A Kaleidoscope Of Crystals Update".

This mineral has been used to assist one in designing acceptable research protocols and in administering controlled tests in order to supply the analytical and empirical evidence for a process, property, or scientific cause. It further stimulates a philosophy which seeks the knowledge of a broader, more encompassing, reality which includes metaphysics, promoting the melding of both science and pseudo-science.

Lavender Tourmaline can be used to bring order which demonstrates an ultimate goal of connecting with, and supporting, nature; it acts to discourage an ultimate goal of the domination of nature.

The mineral assists one in seeing and in understanding the artificiality of the boundaries between reality and fantasy, between objective science and subjective consciousness, and between nature and the supernatural; it serves to bring the acceptance of the holistic perspective of knowledge and the dissolution of boundaries and greater intellectual freedom. It has further been used to dispel the intrusion of the intellectual-control devotees, such that one may, with ease, maintain ones personal identity.

It assists one in openness and honesty, furthering the openness and honesty of those in proximity.

Bringing the violet ray, coupled with the ability to speak of spirituality, it can be used as the "Electra of Sophocles" to both illuminate the whole and to instill the "all-seeing" qualities of the higher consciousness. It acts to both emancipate and to deliver a fundamental force which emerges to bring a gradual accretion of identity which serves to bring cohesiveness to ones personal world and allows one to realize that one, indeed, is a "human star" upon this planet.

It can bring a peaceful environment to the carrier, acting to dissipate agitation, aggravation, and turmoil.

It can enhance the generation of the life-sustaining negative ions in ones environment, activating the instinct of self-preservation and enhancing the awareness of well-being. It is an energy against self-destruction, and synonymous with preservation of ones physical form/body. It has been used in the treatment of candida, in the soothing the nervous system, and in stabilizing the flow of blood and calming the heart.

Vibrates to the number 2.

TOURMALINE - REVERSED WATERMELON

[Astrological Signs of Libra & Gemini]

TOURMALINE - REVERSED-WATERMELON - (Na,K,Ca)(Mg,Fe,Mn,Li,Al)$_3$ (Al,Fe,Cr,V)$_6$Si$_6$O$_{18}$(BO$_3$)$_3$(O,OH,F)$_4$; Hardness 3 - 4; Locality: Clark Co., Nevada, USA. Imaging by HP Scanjet, Assisted by Bob Jackson and ♪ Melody ♫; Collection of ♪ Melody ♫, Applewood, CO, USA.

Reversed-Watermelon Tourmaline is a configuration of tourmaline which exhibits a pink-to-red rind and a black core. Tourmaline was first described as Turmalin (after the locality of Turamali in Cingalese) in 1703 by jewelers of Ceylon who applied the name to Zircon. Later, the name "Turmalin" was "mistakenly" applied to a consignment of tourmaline which was being shipped to Amsterdam. The name evolved over time to the current spelling. Reversed-Watermelon Tourmaline is a unique configuration of Tourmaline (the colour has not yet been described in mineralogical references) and is, hence, reported here. The following properties are in addition to those listed in the TOURMALINE section of "Love Is In The Earth - A Kaleidoscope Of Crystals Update".

This mineral has been used to promote success during issues of animal-rights, assisting one in direct and correct action which will bring fulfillment to ones cause.

Reversed-Watermelon Tourmaline has provided the "rope" for one who encounters those "sinking feelings", serving to bring an energy to assuage the condition and to provide mitigation for that which provided the cause.

It produces a centering effect which initiates the "Law of the Instrument" and promotes furthers ones gain and ones endeavors in the selected field; acting to assist one in the invasion of new territories with the skills which one possesses, it provides for expansion to adjacent areas of ones proficiency. It, hence, assists one in applying ones expertise to fields which have yet to be traversed.

It has been used to facilitate favorable communications and physical travel which will bring world harmony, assisting in the alleviation of the tension which accompanies an anti-social direction.

The mineral has assisted to bring the opening of the energies required for one to re-center the self in the heart, producing a grounding and centering which also promotes protection during this activity. It serves to provide a catalytic energy for release and change of existing non-heartfelt action.

Used in the prevention of accidents and violence, it serves to stimulate the energy of "forewarning".

It further enhances access to mysticism, bringing same from a source which is ancient and promoting the modern adaptation to the knowledge which is forthcoming.

Bringing empowerment and eliminating the energy of frustration, it provides an alignment with higher purpose, such that opposition is dispelled and one "arrives" at the "right time". The synchronicity and/or fortuitiveness of ones arrival serves to provide that which ones intuitive level of awareness requires.

It has been used to enhance the production of Melatonin, to increase the absorptive functions of the intestines, and to promote the increase in personal reflexes. It can be used in reflexology to provide knowledge of the points to be activated.

Vibrates to the number 8.

"I DON'T SPEAK WITH WORDS, I SPEAK WITH MY HEART"
Jose Luis
Washington, USA

VALLERIITE [Astrological Sign of Sagittarius]

VALLERIITE - 4(Fe,Cu)S ♥ 3(Mg,Al)(OH)$_2$ or 2[(Fe,Cu)S] ♥ 1.53[(Mg,Al)(OH)$_2$]; Hardness 1.5; Locality: Aurora Mine, Nya-Kopparberg, Sweden. Imaging by HP Scanjet, Assisted by Bob Jackson and ♪ Melody ♫; Collection of ♪ Melody ♫, Applewood, CO, USA.

Valleriite crystallizes as a massive brassy metallic mineral resembling Pyrrhotite in colour and Graphite in physical properties, and exhibits pleochroism from golden-white to creamy-bronze along one axis and a dull grey to purple along the other axis. The mineral was first described by C.W. Blomstrand in 1870, with the description corrected by H.T. Evans, Jr., and R. Allmann in 1968. The corrected description reports the configuration to have a layer structure with layers of composition CuFeS$_2$ and (Mg,Al)(OH)$_2$ in a ration of, nearly, 2:3. Valleriite was originally named (Walleriite) for G. Wallerius, and was subsequently changed to replace the "W" with a "V".

This mineral promotes the amassing of ego (in the positive) such that one can determine ones "likes" and "dislikes" <u>and</u> providing for the action of the ego to be similar to our mysterious "gravity" which brings a fundamental force which emerges within the human consciousness and provides one with an individuality unique to all others. It has been used to assist on in meditation upon the face one had prior to birth, to instill ones recognition of ones uniqueness and to promote the understanding of ones value to the self and to our world.

Valleriite produces the energy of courage and physical actualization coupled with the energy of the higher consciousness. Hence, it has assisted in bringing bravery in entering into relationships and furthering spiritual interactions within relationships.

It is an excellent energy for "causes", promoting endurance, tenacity, and stamina to continue in the pursuit of the "cause".

With the attribute of physical properties varying with direction, the mineral has been used to assist one in the transmission of clairsentient sound waves, with different velocities, in two directions different directions. Hence, it can be used to promote telepathic dispatch such that one may enjoy the benefits of "conference calls".

It has been used to promote the study of the Earth plane and the atmosphere, facilitating the understanding of the interactions. It has also been used in the fields of meteorology and geology.

The mineral has also been used to prevent confrontations via acting to prevent the encounter; in addition, it has acted to produce an inner knowledge, when there is an encounter, such that one recognizes that the contention has dissipated.

Valleriite has been used in polarity therapy to balance the horizontal and vertical mass of the body and to initiate energy flow between the two.

It has been used in massage to stimulate the tone of muscles and to relieve tautness.

It can be used to assist the bed-ridden in maintaining muscular awareness and structure, to increase endurance in standing and flexibility in strength of the muscles and tendons. It cal be used influence procreation.

Vibrates to the number 5.

VIOLARITE

VIOLARITE - $FeNi_2S_4$ or $FeNi_2S_4$; Hardness 1.5; Locality: Western Australia, Australia. Imaging by HP Scanjet, Assisted by Bob Jackson and ♪ Melody ♫; Collection of ♪ Melody ♫, Applewood, CO, USA.

Violarite crystallizes twinning lamellae, prismatic crystals, masses, and fibers. The colour ranges from a dull brassy-grey to a metallic violet-grey. The mineral was first described by W. Lindgren and W.M. Davy, and W.F. Buddington in 1924; it is named from its violet-grey colour which occurs in polished sections.

This mineral brings a stream of energy conducive to clearing the aura from impurities and to removing ethereal cords which another has sent to the user.

It has also been used to assist one in "seeing angels", and to report in a clear and concise manner, the sightings, while promoting ones trust in reality and empathetic sensitivity. It further eliminates any potential for attendant panic, and brings a tranquility to the experience. It acts to bring a "break" from physically taxing and mentally arduous work such that one can realize that assistance from other realms is truly available.

Violarite acts to produce an energy which is refreshing and almost romantic; it assists in the transformation of the energies of lesser spiritual ideals to the energies of universal light, hope, and acceptance.

Serving to bring the energy of Shechinah, the divine presence which provides for mercy, it has been used to provide the sanctuary of faith, and to promote the action of assistance when requested. In addition, it has been used to remove the ineffectiveness of the attitude of "zero-tolerance".

It can also be used to assist one in the application of the laws of physics to the metaphysical world. It promotes the gain of knowledge relevant to the similarities and further acts to direct one in the utilization of physics to support metaphysical concepts and principles.

The mineral has been used to provide the recognition that others are actually mirrors of the self, and that when one sees an attribute in another which produces an aversion, then one may identify that attribute within the self and seize the moment to dissipate same.

Further acting as a mirror to the self, it promotes the assuredness that all answers lie within the self, and assists in access of same.

Violarite can be used when ones biorhythms are heterodyning due to fluctuations of the frequencies of energy within the body, in order to return the balance back to same.

It has been used to stimulate tidiness (of mind and environment).

It brings an excellent energy to the plant kingdom, supporting growth (as an elixir) and endurance to a dearth of beneficial circumstances.

The mineral has been used in the treatment of panic attacks, disorders which exhibit symptoms of pasty/grey complexion, and to promote the secretion of enzymes.

Do not prepare an elixir via the normal method.

Vibrates to the number 3.

♪ **IF WE CAN LAUGH AT OURSELVES,**
WE'LL NEVER NEED ENTERTAINMENT ♫

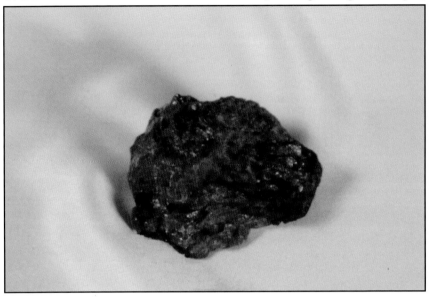

WOLFEITE - $(Fe,Mn)_2PO_4(OH)$; Hardness 4.5-5; Locality: Bavaria, Germany. Imaging by HP Scanjet, Assisted by Bob Jackson and ♪ Melody ♫; In the Collection of ♪ Melody ♫, Applewood, CO, USA.

Wolfeite crystallizes in the form of crystalline aggregates. The colour ranges from yellowish to reddish brown, and from dark brown to black-brown. The mineral was first described by C. Frondel in 1949; it was named for C.W. Wolfe, who first noticed the mineral as Triploidite.

This mineral has been used as a center structure for medicine circles to stimulate the infiltration of the infinite healing forces of ones power animals, and the permeation of the circle with loving guidance and uncomplicated clarity.

It can bring success to the "hunt", on the physical, mental, and spiritual planes.

It is a "stone of blessings", conveying the energy to bring those blessings which one cannot imagine or conceive, but though which one would like to try persist and to manage.

Wolfeite can facilitate ease of movement and acrobatic and gymnastic endeavors. It has assisted in the fine-movements of ballet.

It and can also provide for travel within the astral plane (subsequent to the entry to the astral plane. It promotes the designing of the path through which one can "surf" the astral plane with impunity, bringing information concerning a specific situation - but bringing diversified information which assists one in understanding the situation from a variety of angles.

The mineral has been used to promote two-way communication with animals (on the physical plane). Although unconventional to some, the communication is heard through a vibratory energy which passes between the human and the animal.

It has assisted in the female of a species to bring the agents of the principle of movement of the male (and conversely). It further serves to expose the profane and to banish the veils of allegory.

Wolfeite is an excellent energy to assist one in doing that which is "good". It dispels weariness and indifference, and furthers ones detachment to the outcome/results/returns.

Via gridding into the configuration of the divine triangle, it has provided for insight to, and understanding, of the trinity within each of us. It further acts to bring the "unity of being" and the "unity of the harmonies" to ones life to produce the marvel of equilibrium and the liberation of the soul.

The mineral has assisted in the translation of the symbols used by the ancient alchemists; specifically in the translation of the Hermetic philosophy. When one desires to gain admission to the world of the unknown, Wolfeite can "show the way".

Wolfeite has been as an elixir in the amelioration of body odor and to increase the sensory perceptiveness. It can be used to bring ease to the birthing process, to treat periodontal disorders, and to cleanse the liver.

Vibrates to the number 5.

"NOTHING IS NOTHING"
Tia Maia

YUKSPORITE

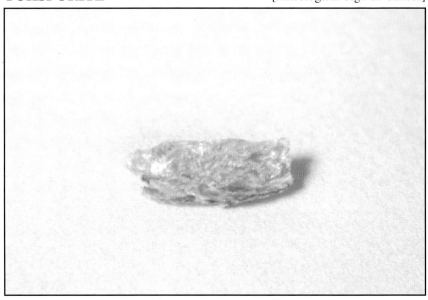

YUKSPORITE - $(K,Ba)NaCa_2(Si,Ti)_4O_{11}(F,OH) \heartsuit H_2O$; Hardness 5; Locality: Yukspor, Kola Peninsula, Russia. Imaging by HP Scanjet, Assisted by Bob Jackson and ♪ Melody ♫; Collection of ♪ Melody ♫, Applewood, CO, USA.

Yuksporite crystallizes in platy or fibrous masses. The colour range includes tannish-pink and yellowish-rose. The mineral was first described by A.E. Fersman in 1922; it is named for the locality where it was originally discovered (Yukspor, Kola Peninsula, Russia).

This mineral has been used to stimulate the actions of one to "try" a variety of things which one has not experienced (e.g., foods, drinks, philosophies, etc.). It has actually assisted in the removal of pre-determined likes and dislikes, such that one is willing to be open to a new and/or novel action.

It can also be used in ending relationships of the heart, such that one does not use the method "of kickin' 'em to the curb", but such that one terminates the affiliation while continuing to maintain a friendship-type relationship after the love-relationship has been completed. It brings an intellectual understanding of "endings" to facilitate loving action.

The mineral has also been used as a sponsion in the intervention of one for another during issues of relationships.

It has been used to enhance pursuits in swimming and has assisted in the increase in the transference of healing energy in hot springs and mineral baths.

Yuksporite can be used to bring knowledge, power, and awareness - without "paying a price". It further assists one in providing form to correspond to the function.

The mineral has provided the Enochian mastery vibration in attunement to all dimensions such that one may access planes which do not presently exist with the structure of ones knowledge (e.g., fourth, fifth, sixth... dimensional access). It promotes a readiness and a willingness to ascend to the other planes or dimensions, and supports the enhancement of skills which are mundane on those levels (e.g., past-life ascension, healing, etc.).

Yuksporite has been used to assist in holistic thought processes, providing a self-reflective awareness, a precision in perception, and an ability to consider, and then to establish, order within a process which culminates in the intuitive expression of the whole system of order. It actually stimulates the capability of multi-dimensional thought-processes.

It has served to provide for attunement with right-brain functions while pragmatically sharpening the left-brain skills.

Due to the production of an increase in vibratory rate, the Kundalini energy is intensified and the concomitant response is dynamic.

It has been used to promote "seeing" a disorder within the body via placement of the mineral upon the affected area. It has been used in the treatment of disorders of the urogenital system and infectious fungal disease which can occur in humans and horses, to ameliorate irregularity in body functions, to assist in the cleansing of the intestines, lymph glands, liver, and pancreas.

Vibrates to the number 6.

"NUNCA PROCURE
O QUE VOCÊ NÃO ESCONDEU"

Orizon de Almeida
Minas Gerais, Brasil

ZEOLITE - PICTURE - $(Na,K,Ca)_{2-3}Al_3(Al,Si)_2Si_{13}O_{36}$ ♥ $12H_2O$ or $(Na,K)_6$ (Al_6Si_{30}) O_{72} ♥ $20H_2O$; Hardness 3.5; Locality: Central Queensland, Australia. Imaging by HP Scanjet, Assisted by Bob Jackson and ♪ Melody ♫; Collection of ♪ Melody ♫, Applewood, CO, USA. Gift of Bruce & Barbara McDougall, Queensland, Australia.

Picture Zeolite, also well-known as CLINOPTILOLITE, crystallizes in the Zeolite group as masses and exhibits a wavey-lined pattern resembling a rose/golden-to-white desert, the wave and form of the universe, and/or other-worldly and/or other-worldly images. The name "Picture Zeolite" was coined by the miner in Australia. Clinoptilolite was first described by W.T. Schaller in 1923; it is named due to the inclination of the optical extinction. The following properties are in addition to those listed in the ZEOLITE section of "Love Is In The Earth - A Kaleidoscope Of Crystals Update".

This mineral has been used to bring the benevolence of other-worldly beings to ones environment during waking hours and/or during dreamtime. One exercise, where the mineral is placed beneath ones pillow, has prompted detailed intellectual knowledge with respect to the ancient colonization of the Earth by other-worldly beings.

Picture Zeolite has also been used to facilitate a clear channel for communication between the physical plane and other planes of existence. It promotes concurrent communication between the self and a multitude of different worlds with centering upon the identical topic.

It can act to dispel severity in ones character and in ones comportment, acting to dissipate anger which has been built upon a conceived or an actual transgression of the past committed by another, toward one.

It has actualized the determination of association one had with another in a past-life. The mineral has exhibited the "magnetic effect", assisting one in gaining.

It has been used, placed within ones environment, to remove pollutants and toxins. It is currently being used in gridding of the Earth to perform the same function and to return an energy of love to each location within the grids. It is truly an environmentally protective mineral.

It has been of great benefit to the Earth, bringing fertility to soils and enhancing balance in acidity; it further stimulates the growth of the plant kingdom and has increased yields in gardens and agricultural crops.

Picture Zeolite can be used to cleanse the aura (eliminating negativity and impurities), to cleanse the chakras, and to provide for the clearing of the pathway so that the physical and ethereal planes have the electrical connection to provide perfection.

The mineral and/or elixir acts to balance the negative and positive electrical charges within ones body and within ones environment, inducing a greater capability for storage of positive energy, nutrients, etc., and has been used extensively in polarity therapy. It can be used for the chelation of chemical toxins, to further the maintenance of body heat, and in the treatment of rheumatism and arthritis due to damp conditions, bacterial infections, ulcers, diabetes, diarrhea, swelling, bloating, dehydration, acidosis, degenerative dis-ease, and disorders of the skeletal system. It has also been used to further the assimilation of Calcium, Potassium, and Magnesium.

Vibrates to the numbers 9 (Clinoptilolite) and 4 (Picture Zeolite).

**"WE WILL EITHER
FIND A WAY
OR
WE WILL MAKE ONE"**

Hannibal (~400, B.C.)

UPDATES OF MINERALS AND CONFIGURATIONS

This section provides information for the following:

Minerals and Configurations which were reported in previous "Love Is In The Earth" books, but for which information from further research has become available.

"FOR THEIR ROCK IS NOT AS OUR ROCK..."

Deuteronomy 32:31 (KJV)

AGATE - Banded White/Brown/Red
[Astrological Sign of Gemini]

In addition to the properties listed in the AGATE section of "Love Is In The Earth - A Kaleidoscope Of Crystals Update", the mineral has been placed in corners to be used to prevent the intrusion of spiders. Any of the banded Agates which exhibit these colours (i.e., Brasilian, Canadian, etc.) are acceptable.

Vibrates to the number 3.

LABRADORITE   [Astrological Signs of Sagittarius, Scorpio, and Leo]

In addition to the properties listed in the LABRADORITE section of "Love Is In The Earth - A Kaleidoscope Of Crystals Update", this mineral has been used to remove warts - taping the mineral to the wart and allowing for emplacement until the wart disappears

Vibrates to the numbers 6 and 7.

MOONSTONE - BLACKENED-ELECTRIC-BLUE
[Astrological Sign of Cancer]

Blackened Electric-Blue Moonstone is comprised such that biotite together with a small amount of pyrite particles form the outer covering of black. Pyrite and biotite are "allowed" to occur together, but the occurrence is very uncommon. The mineral combines the properties reported for MOONSTONE, PYRITE, AND BIOTITE listed in "Love Is In The Earth - A Kaleidoscope Of Crystals Update" and those which reference RAINBOW MOONSTONE in "Love Is In The Earth - Kaleidoscopic Pictorial Supplement A".

In addition, it has been shown to absorb negative energy which it encounters, providing for a removal of negative energy from the self and from ones environment.

Vibrates to the number 5.

MOONSTONE - ELECTRIC-BLUE   [Astrological Sign of Scorpio]

In addition to the properties listed in the MOONSTONE section of "Love Is In The Earth - A Kaleidoscope Of Crystals Update" and the RAINBOW MOONSTONE section in "Love Is In The Earth - Kaleidoscopic Pictorial Supplement A", the mineral has been carried (flash-side out) in the "watch-pocket" and has conveyed an irresistible attractiveness of one to others, while instilling the "non-bartering" of the self to same.

The energy functions most effectively in public areas which are unfamiliar or unknown to the user, and in crowds and group/party situations.

A stone to initiate contact and communication, it also brings the "element of surprise". It has been shown to bring to one both people and gifts/things "out of the blue".

It has acted to bring a pheromonal-type response to others (outside the self), such that a prelude of enchantment is facilitated. It has also provided insight to the "other" who has been attracted such that the user may make an information-based decision with respect to "keeping" the other or allowing the other to "go".

It has been shown to truly emit a patron energy of the Norse Seers which brings a type of "enchantment" to those who one encounters.

Vibrates to the number 2.

NUUMMIT   [Astrological Sign of Sagittarius]

In addition to the properties listed in the NUUMMIT section of "Love Is In The Earth - A Kaleidoscope Of Crystals Update", Nuummit provides an energy which promotes "knowing" when one encounters someone from a past-life and in further determining the past-life association which one experienced with the other.

Vibrates to the number 3.

QUARTZ - "RED PHANTOM"   [Astrological Sign of Scorpio]

In addition to the properties listed in the "RED PHANTOM QUARTZ" section of "Love Is In The Earth - A Kaleidoscope Of Crystals Update", and NOT to be confused with the Chinese Red Phantom Quartz which is reported within the "New Mineral" section of this book, these "Red Phantoms" contain a range from white to yellow to orange to red (and combinations of these colours). The rarity of this mineral for the last several years has prevented additional reporting; however, it is now again available from that great land of Brasil.

The "Red Phantom Quartz" has been used to assist one in planning, thinking, changing, and organizing ones life to be in synchronicity with the goal; it further assists one in the enjoyment of both the mundane and the creative in attaining the end result.

It has facilitated seeing auras and in stimulating the enhancement of same (verified via Kirlian photography).

It further provides for a unification of the three bodies (physical, intellectual, emotional) with the spiritual.

It has been used to remove unwanted "implants", concurrently healing breaches within the chakra system and filling the voids which remain after the removal of the implant, with the healing light of love.

It has been used in the treatment of cancer, tumors, cirrhosis, pancreatic malfunction, and to reduce swelling of the spleen.

Vibrates to the number 1.

SEREFINA   [Astrological Signs of Sagittarius & Taurus]
                   Also Known as Chlorite & Clinochlore

In addition to the properties listed in the CHLORITE and CLINOCHLORE sections of "Love Is In The Earth - A Kaleidoscope Of Crystals Update", the following properties have been verified.

This mineral has also been used in the treatment of lymph glands, body infections, and ear infections.

Vibrates to the numbers 5, 6, and 9.

ZINCITE - POLISH

Several years ago there was a type of semi-natural Zincite which has been named "Polish Zincite"; this formation was said to have been produced in a Zinc mine in Poland, nearly 100 years ago, during a naturally occurring mine fire. Although the fire was naturally-occurring and was not due to the action of man, the mineralogical community did not accept this Zincite as natural.

The "Polish Zincite" which is now available is not from the mine fire. It occurs as a by-product from an industrial zinc-white production kiln in Silesia, Poland. Hence, there is a similarity with the common glass slag, produced in the US and throughout the world, in its formation. This is another case of a change in the vibratory frequencies and is similar to using synthetic stones.

CROSS-REFERENCE INDEX ZODIACAL DESIGNATIONS - MINERALOGICAL ASSOCIATION

"IF YOU'RE NOT HAPPY WITH A SITUATION, CHANGE IT!"

Kelly Ram
Neosho, Missouri, USA

CROSS-REFERENCE INDEX
ZODIACAL DESIGNATIONS - MINERALOGICAL ASSOCIATION

This cross-reference index has been developed from the astrological sign designations which were described for each mineral discussed within this book. Please note that some minerals are related to more than one astrological sign.

ARIES
AGATE - CONDOR
BRUCITE
CRASH-SITE DEBRIS (CSD)
GARNET In SILLIMANITE
HERDERITE - PURPLE
HURÉAULITE
"KEYSTONE"
MURMANITE
PERTHITE
QUARTZ - CHINESE RED
       PHANTOM
SCORZALITE
STAINIERITE
    Heterogenite

TAURUS
CLINOPTILOLITE
CRASH-SITE DEBRIS (CSD)
FERRIMOLYBDITE
FRONDELITE
GEYSERITE
"KEYSTONE"
NUNDERITE
PETRIFIED PALM
"PRINTSTONE"
QUARTZ - ORANGE With STARS
SEPTARIAN NODULE
ZEOLITE - PICTURE

GEMINI
AMETHYST - HONEYCOMB
ANAPAITE
"DALMATIAN STONE"
CRASH-SITE DEBRIS (CSD)
GÖRGEYITE
"KEYSTONE"
MOZARKITE
OLIGONITE
PENWITHITE
    Neotocite
QUARTZ - "ARKIMER DIAMOND"
QUARTZ - With CHERT
ROSE-CITRINE
TOURMALINE - REVERSED
    WATERMELON

CANCER
CAMPBELLITE
CRASH-SITE DEBRIS (CSD)
DELHAYELITE
"KEYSTONE"
KIMZEYITE
LITHARGE
MOONSTONE - Blackened-Electric
    Blue
QUARTZ - DRUSY BOTRYOIDAL
QUARTZ - GINGER
SANIDINE
TINAKSITE
YUKSPORITE

LEO
BRUNCKITE
CALCITE - GOLDEN RAY
CALCITE - SAND
CARPHOLITE
CRASH-SITE DEBRIS (CSD)
EMERALD - CAT'S-EYE
FRIEDELITE
GARNET In SILLIMANITE
GARNIERITE
    Noumeite
GEODE - CHALCOPYRITE
GEYSERITE
"KEYSTONE"
KINGITE
LITHARGE
MICA - YELLOW
    Muscovite - Yellow
OPAL - HYALITE
    Muller's Glass
OTTRELITE
POLYSPHAERITE
QUARTZ - "OURO VERDE"
SUNSTONE - COPPER SCHILLER
SYLVANITE

VIRGO
"COSMIC EGG"
CRASH-SITE DEBRIS (CSD)
ELPIDITE
"FLOWER STONE"
FOSHAGITE
GARNIERITE
    Noumeite
"KEYSTONE"
MENDOZAVILITE
PENWITHITE
    Neotocite
PILSENITE
SERANDITE
STALACTITE - HOLLOW

VIRGO (Continued)
TOURMALINE - LAVENDER
VIOLARITE

LIBRA
CALCITE - Growth Interference
CALCITE - With "SCHMOOS"
CRASH-SITE DEBRIS (CSD)
FOSSIL PINE CONE
JADE - BOTRYOIDAL
"KEYSTONE"
KYANITE - With FUCHSITE
NONTRONITE
OSARIZAWAITE
PYROPHYLLITE
    Pencil-Stone
TARNOWITZITE
TOURMALINE - REVERSED
    WATERMELON

SCORPIO
ALLANITE
BEDIASITE
CARBON - C60
CRASH-SITE DEBRIS (CSD)
DEVILLINE
GEODE - CHALCOPYRITE
"KEYSTONE"
"LINGHAM"
    Shiva Lingham
    Narmadeshvara Lingham
MOONSTONE - Electric-Blue
"NEBULA STONE"
NOVACULITE
    Arkansas Stone
    Washita Stone
OBSIDIAN - MIDNIGHT LACE
QUARTZ - "METAMORPHOSIS"
QUARTZ - PYRITE INCLUDED

SCORPIO (Continued)
QUARTZ - "RED PHANTOM"
QUARTZ - TUBED
SLATY SHALE - RECORD STONE
WOLFEITE

SAGITTARIUS
ATACAMITE
CRASH-SITE DEBRIS (CSD)
DEFERNITE
FOSSIL ALGAE
    Algae Iron
"FRANKLINORE"
"KEYSTONE"
OBSIDIAN - GREEN SHEEN
PIEMONTITE
PLATTNERITE
SELENITE - FOSSIL SEEDED
TOPAZ - PURPLE
VALLERIITE

CAPRICORN
BLIZZARD STONE
BREWSTERITE
CRASH-SITE DEBRIS (CSD)
CREASEYITE
GENEVITE
"KEYSTONE"
KINGITE
NATROJAROSITE
OMPHACITE
PETRIFIED PALM
QUARTZ - LIGHTNING
    "Flashstone"
SAL AMMONIAC
SURSASSITE
TETRAHEDRITE

AQUARIUS
BOWENITE
    "Greenstone"
    Tangawaite
    Tangiwaite
CRASH-SITE DEBRIS (CSD)
EMERALD - CAT'S-EYE
"KEYSTONE"
KURNAKOVITE
LINDGRENITE
MICA - GREEN With QUARTZ
    Clintonite - Green With Quartz
    Margarite - Green With Quartz
QUARTZ - With EPIDOTE
RHYOLITE - GREEN
    Rain Forest Jasper
SCHRÖECKINGERITE
    Dakeite
THUNDEREGG - MT. HAY
    Star Agate
    Amulet Stone

PISCES
AGATE - GRAVEYARD PLUME
BORAX
CHONDRODITE
CRASH-SITE DEBRIS (CSD)
DALLASITE
JASPER - WILLOW CREEK
"KEYSTONE"
MORAESITE
OBSIDIAN - GREEN With PERLITE
OPAL - LIME
QUARTZ - With "LODALITE"
RADIOLARITE (Sedimentary)
SELENITE - ENHYDRO
SYLVINITE

**"SHOOT FOR THE MOON!
BECAUSE, EVEN IF YOU MISS,
YOU'LL ALWAYS BE AMONG THE STARS"**
River Starr (L.A.M.)
Neosho, Missouri, USA

CROSS-REFERENCE INDEX NUMERICAL VIBRATIONS - MINERALOGICAL ASSOCIATION

"Learn to Look - And See What's Before You,
Learn to Listen - And Hear What Is Said,
And Take Obstacles As Stairsteps,
To Climb, But Not Dread.
And Take Them All - One Step At A Time,
With Just A Simple Stride.
Then, Look Back In Awesome Wonder,
And Feel A Little Pride."

Jim Hilton
Neosho, Missouri, USA

CROSS-REFERENCE INDEX
NUMERICAL VIBRATIONS - MINERALOGICAL
ASSOCIATION

This cross-reference index has been developed from the numerical vibration designations which were described for each mineral discussed within this book. Please note that some minerals are assigned more than one numerical vibration due to variation in spelling and/or name designation.

NUMBER 1
Algae Iron
Amulet Stone
Atacamite
Calcite - Golden Ray
Calcite with "Schmoos"
Calcite - Sand
Dakeite
"Lingham"
Margarite - Green with Quartz
Mica - Yellow
Mozarkite
Pilsenite
Pyrophyllite
Quartz - Chinese Red Phantom
Quartz - "Red Phantom"
Quartz - Ginger
Quartz with "Lodalite"
Quartz - "Ouro Verde"
Quartz - Orange
Sylvanite
Tangiwaite
Washita Stone

NUMBER 2
Allanite
Bediasite
Calcite - Growth Interference
Creaseyite
Dallasite
Devilline
"Flashstone"
Mendozavilite

NUMBER 2 (Continued)
Moonstone - Electric-Blue
"Nebula Stone"
Nunderite
Obsidian - Green Sheen
Oliganite
Opal - Lime
Perthite
Quartz - Tubed
Radiolarite (Sedimentary)
Sal Ammoniac
Scorzalite
Star Agate
Tangawaite
Tourmaline - Lavender

NUMBER 3
Agate-Banded - White/ Brown/Red
Bowenite
Clintonite - Green with Quartz
Friedelite
Görgeyite
Huréaulite
Kingite
Kurnakovite
Natrojarosite
Noumeite
Osarizawaite
Penwithite
Sanidine
Stainierite
Violarite

NUMBER 4
Agate - Condor
Agate - Graveyard Plume
Amethyst - Honeycomb
Anapaite
Arkansas Stone
Brunckite
Quartz - "Metamorphosis"
Quartz with Chert
Selenite - Fossil Seeded
Topaz - Purple
Zeolite - Picture

NUMBER 5
Defernite
Geyserite
"Greenstone"
Heterogenite
Kyanite with Fuchsite
Moonstone - Blackened- Electric-Blue
Novaculite
Plattnerite
Quartz - "Arkimer Diamond"
Quartz - "Lightning"
Quartz - Drusy Botryoidal
Serandite
Valleriite
Wolfeite

NUMBER 6

Borax
Crash-Site Debris
"Franklinore"
Genevite
Jade - Botryoidal
Kimzeyite
Moraesite
Murmanite
Pencil Stone
"Printstone"
Quartz - with Epidote
Quartz - Orange with
    Stars
Shiva Lingham
Slaty Shale Record
    Stone
Stalactite - Hollow
Yuksporite

NUMBER 7

Chondrodite
Delhayelite
Fossil Algae
Garnierite
Jasper - Willow Creek
Mica - Green with
    Quartz
Neotocite
Obsidian - Midnight
    Lace
Opal - Hyalite
Ottrelite
Polysphaerite
Quartz - Pyrite
Included
Selenite - Enhydro
Sunstone - Copper
    Schiller
Tetrahedrite

NUMBER 8

Carbon - C60
Carpholite
CSD
Ferrimolybdite
"Flower Stone"

NUMBER 8 (Continued)

Fossil Pine Cone
Garnet In Sillimanite
Narmadeshvara Lingham
Petrified Palm
Rhyolite - Green
Tourmaline - Reversed
    Watermelon

NUMBER 9

"Arkimer Diamond"
Blizzard Stone
Brewsterite
Clinoptilolite
"Cosmic Egg"
"Dalmatian Stone"
Foshagite
Frondelite
Geode - Chalcopyrite
Herderite - Purple
Lindgrenite
Muller's Glass
Nontronite
Obsidian - Green with
    Perlite
Omphacite
Piemontite
Rose-Citrine
Slaty Shale Record
    Stone
Sylvinite
Tarnowitzite
Tinaksite

MASTER # 33

Brucite
"Keystone"
Sursassite

MASTER # 44

Campbellite
Elpidite
Litharge

MASTER # 55

Emerald - Cat's-Eye

MASTER # 66

Muscovite - Yellow
Septarian Nodule

MASTER # 77

Rain Forest Jasper
Thunderegg - Mt. Hay

MASTER # 88

Schröeckingerite

RULING # 1/2

"Keystone"

TABLE OF THE ELEMENTS

"RESOLUTION IS NOT TO BE CONFUSED WITH INTEGRITY"

Bob Jackson
Earth-Love Gallery
Wheat Ridge, Colorado, USA

CHEMICAL ELEMENTS

This section provides a Table of the 105 elements which have been established to date. The table has been prepared with the chemical designation given first, the chemical name given second, and comments (e.g., identifying the accepted category for each element and identifying the "Native Elements", "Rare Earth Elements" and "Transuranic Elements") shown last.

This table is user-friendly to all communities. On occasion, those who are not trained in the Advanced Sciences, have experienced difficulty in locating the name of an element (when given the chemical designation (i.e., abbreviation) in the normal Periodic Table. Hence, if the reader wishes to determine the names of the elements in a chemical composition which is listed within this book (or any of the "Love Is In The Earth" series), he/she may reference the following table with ease (by locating each of the alphabetized chemical abbreviations).

Dmitry Mendeleyev, in 1869, was the first to arrange the chemical elements in the groupings of the "Periodic Table", and the first to predict that there would be new elements to be discovered. The groupings consist of Alkali-Metals, Alkaline Earth Metals, Lanthanide Series, Actinide Series, Other Metals, Non-Metals, Noble Gases, and Transition Metals; these groupings are also shown in the following table.

In addition, due to the growing interest in the 18 "Rare Earths", the "Native Elements" and the "Transuranics", the table defines the elements which reside in each of these categories. Native Elements are those elements which, to date, have been found in an uncombined, non-gaseous state in nature. Rare Earth Elements are those elements which, to date, have been found in the Earth's Crust in very low concentrations. Transuranic Elements are those elements which exhibit a higher atomic number than Uranium (i.e., higher than the atomic number of 92); these are elements are man-made.

"BE OPEN-MINDED,
TRY EVERYTHING"

John Wittman
Colorado, USA

TABLE OF THE ELEMENTS

Element Abbreviation	Element Name	Comments
Ac	Actinium	Actinide Series
Ag	Silver	Transition Metal; Native
Al	Aluminum	Other Metal; Native
Am	Americium	Actinide Series; Transuranic
Ar	Argon	Noble Gas
As	Arsenic	Non-Metal; Native
At	Astatine	Non-Metal
Au	Gold	Transition Metal; Native
B	Boron	Non-Metal
Ba	Barium	Alkaline Earth Metal
Be	Beryllium	Alkaline Earth Metal
Bk	Berkelium	Actinide Series; Transuranic
Bi	Bismuth	Other Metal; Native
Br	Bromine	Non-Metal
C	Carbon	Non-Metal; Native
Ca	Calcium	Alkaline Earth Metal
Cd	Cadmium	Transition Metal; Native
Ce	Cerium	Lanthanide Series; Rare Earth
Cf	Californium	Actinide Series; Transuranic
Cl	Chlorine	Non-Metal
Cm	Curium	Actinide Series; Transuranic
Co	Cobalt	Transition Metal
Cr	Chromium	Transition Metal; Native
Cs	Caesium	Alkali-Metal
Cu	Copper	Transition Metal; Native
Dy	Dysprosium	Lanthanide Series; Rare Earth
Er	Erbium	Lanthanide Series; Rare Earth
Es	Einsteinium	Actinide Series; Transuranic
Eu	Europium	Lanthanide Series; Rare Earth
F	Fluorine	Non-Metal
Fe	Iron	Transition Metal
Fm	Fermium	Actinide Series; Transuranic
Fr	Francium	Alkali-Metal
Ga	Gallium	Other Metal
Gd	Gadolinium	Lanthanide Series; Rare Earth
Ge	Germanium	Other Metal

TABLE OF THE ELEMENTS

Element Abbreviation	Element Name	Comments
Ha	Hahnium	Transition Metal; Transuranic
He	Helium	Noble Gas
Hf	Hafnium	Transition Metal
Hg	Mercury	Transition Metal; Native
Ho	Holmium	Lanthanide Series; Rare Earth
I	Iodine	Non-Metal
In	Indium	Other Metal; Native
Ir	Iridium	Transition Metal; Native
K	Potassium	Alkali-Metal
Kr	Krypton	Noble Gas
La	Lanthanum	Lanthanide Series; Rare Earth
Li	Lithium	Alkali-Metal
Lr	Lawrencium	Actinide Series; Transuranic
Lu	Lutetium	Lanthanide Series; Rare Earth
Md	Mendelevium	Actinide Series; Transuranic
Mg	Magnesium	Alkaline Earth Metal
Mn	Manganese	Transition Metal
Mo	Molybdenum	Transition Metal
N	Nitrogen	Non-Metal
Na	Sodium	Alkali-Metal
Nb	Niobium	Transition Metal
Nd	Neodymium	Lanthanide Series; Rare Earth
Ne	Neon	Noble Gas
Ni	Nickel	Transition Metal; Native
No	Nobelium	Actinide Series; Transuranic
Np	Neptunium	Actinide Series; Transuranic
O	Oxygen	Non-Metal
Os	Osmium	Transition Metal
P	Phosphorus	Non-Metal
Pa	Protactinium	Actinide Series; Rare Earth
Pb	Lead	Other Metal; Native
Pd	Palladium	Transition Metal; Native
Po	Polonium	Other Metal
Pm	Promethium	Lanthanide Series; Rare Earth
Pt	Platinum	Transition Metal; Native
Pr	Praseodymium	Lanthanide Series

TABLE OF THE ELEMENTS

Element Abbreviation	Element Name	Comments
Ra	Radium	Alkaline Earth Metal
Rb	Rubidium	Alkali-Metal
Re	Rhenium	Transition Metal; Native
Rf	Rutherfordium	Transition Metal; Transuranic
Rh	Rhodium	Transition Metal; Native
Rn	Radon	Noble Gas
Ru	Ruthenium	Transition Metal
S	Sulphur	Non-Metal; Native
Sb	Antimony	Other Metal; Native
Sc	Scandium	Transition Metal; Rare Earth
Se	Selenium	Non-Metal; Native
Si	Silicon	Non-Metal; Native
Sm	Samarium	Lanthanide Series; Rare Earth
Sn	Tin	Other Metal; Native
Sr	Strontium	Alkaline Earth Metal
Ta	Tantalum	Transition Metal
Tb	Terbium	Lanthanide Series; Rare Earth
Tc	Technetium	Transition Metal
Te	Tellurium	Non-Metal; Native
Th	Thorium	Actinide Series; Rare Earth
Ti	Titanium	Transition Metal
Tl	Thallium	Other Metal
Tm	Thulium	Lanthanide Series; Rare Earth
U	Uranium	Actinide Series
V	Vanadium	Transition Metal
W	Tungsten	Transition Metal
Xe	Xenon	Noble Gas
Y	Yttrium	Transition Metal; Rare Earth
Yb	Ytterbium	Lanthanide Series; Rare Earth
Zn	Zinc	Transition Metal; Native

"LIFE IS VERY SIMPLE.
WE COMPLICATE IT
BY THINKING TOO MUCH"

Wayne Green
Sedona Crystal Mine
Sedona, Arizona, USA

INDEX

"FOR THOSE WHO CAN "SEE",
EVERY STONE
IS THE PHILOSOPHER'S STONE"
Bob Jackson
Earth-Love Gallery

INDEX

"THE BEGINNING"

**"TALK TO THE UNIVERSE.....
IT'S GOOD TO TALK THINGS OVER
WITH EVERYTHING"**

Paul Ellerman
Colorado, USA

EARTH NOTES

August 30th is the "Day Of The Rock"

EARTH NOTES

EARTH NOTES

EARTH NOTES